The Musician's Guide to Aural Skills

The Musician's Guide to Aural Skills

VOLUME 2

Joel Phillips
Westminster Choir College of Rider University

Jane Piper Clendinning
Florida State University School of Music

Elizabeth West Marvin
Eastman School of Music

W. W. NORTON & COMPANY
NEW YORK · LONDON

Copyright © 2005 by W. W. Norton & Company, Inc.

Manufacturing by Quebecor World, Eusey
Book design by Rubina Yeh
Production manager: JoAnn Simony
Music and page composition: TSI Graphics

Library of Congress Cataloging-in-Publication Data

Phillips, Joel.
   The musician's guide to aural skills / Joel Phillips, Jane Piper Clendinning, Elizabeth
West Marvin.
      p. cm.
   Includes bibliographical references (p.) and index.
   ISBN 0-393-97664-5 (v. 1 : pbk.)—ISBN 0-393-92559-5 (v. 2 : pbk.)
      1. Ear training. 2. Music theory—Elementary works. I. Phillips, Joel. II. Clendinning,
Jane Piper. III. Marvin, Elizabeth West, 1955-IV. Title.

MT35.P49 2004
781.2—dc22

                                                                    2004053190

ISBN 0-393-92559-5 (pbk., volume 2)

W. W. Norton & Company, Inc., 500 Fifth Avenue, New York, N. Y. 10110
        www.wwnorton.com
W. W. Norton & Company Ltd., Castle House, 75/76 Wells Street, London W1T 3QT

2 3 4 5 6 7 8 9 0

Contents

Preface   ix

Part IV   Further Expansion of the Harmonic Vocabulary

Chapter 21   Tonicizing Scale Degrees Other Than V; Asymmetrical Meters   2

    I. Key Concepts 2 • Tonicizing New Scale Degrees 2 • Introduction to Asymmetrical Meters 6

    II. Call and Response 7

    III. Contextual Listening 9

    IV. Melodies for Study 21

    V. Improvisation 24 • Team Improvisation 24 • Consequent Phrases That Include Phrase Expansions 25

    VI. Composition 26 • Single-Line Melody 26 • Keyboard-Style Compositions with Roman Numerals and Figured Bass 26

Chapter 22   Modulation to Closely Related Keys; Mixed Beat Divisions   29

    I. Key Concepts 29 • Modulation 29 • Mixed Beat Divisions: Two Against Three 39

    II. Call and Response 42 • Creating Modulatory Periods 42

    III. Contextual Listening 45

    IV. Melodies for Study 63

    V. Improvisation 66 • Accompanied Melodic Improvisations 66 • Modulatory Periods 68

    VI. Composition 68 • Single-Line Melody 68 • Keyboard-Style Compositions with Roman Numerals and Figured Bass 69

Chapter 23 Binary and Ternary Forms 70

    I. **Key Concepts 70** • The Hierarchy of Form 70 • Binary Forms 71 • Ternary Forms 73 • Composite Form 74

    II. **Call and Response 75**

    III. **Contextual Listening 77**

    IV. **Melodies for Study 93**

    V. **Improvisation 95** • Team Improvisations 95

    VI. **Composition 96** • Single-Line Melody 96 • Keyboard-Style Compositions 97

Chapter 24 Color and Drama in Composition: Modal Mixture and Chromatic Mediants and Submediants 99

    I. **Key Concepts 99** • Modal Mixture 99 • Notating "Borrowed" Chords 100 • Other Types of Altered Chords 101

    II. **Call and Response 103**

    III. **Contextual Listening 105**

    IV. **Melodies for Study 119**

    V. **Improvisation 122** • Team Improvisations 122

    VI. **Composition 123** • Single-Line Melody: Rounded Binary 123 • Keyboard Trio 124

Chapter 25 Chromatic Approaches to V: The Neapolitan Sixth and Augmented Sixths 125

    I. **Key Concepts 125** • The Neapolitan Sixth Chord 125 • Augmented-Sixth Chords 128

    II. **Call and Response 132**

    III. **Contextual Listening 133**

    IV. **Melodies for Study 143**

    V. **Improvisation 146**

    VI. **Composition 148**

Part V Musical Form and Interpretation

Chapter 26 Popular Song and Art Song 150

    I. **Key Concepts 150** • Popular or Art Song? 150 • American Popular Songs 151 • The Blues 151 • Popular-Music Harmonies 152 • Text Painting 153 • Jazz Rhythm 154

    II. **Call and Response 155**

    III. **Contextual Listening 157**

    IV. **Melodies for Study 169**

    V. **Improvisation 171** • Team Improvisations 171 • Solo Improvisation 172

    VI. **Composition 172**

Chapter 27   Variation and Rondo   174

     I. **Key Concepts 174** • Sectional Variations 174 • Continuous Variations 176 • Rondo 177

     II. **Call and Response 178** • Figural Variations 178

     III. **Contextual Listening 179**

     IV. **Melodies for Study 203**

     V. **Improvisation 206** • Continuous Variations 206

     VI. **Composition 207** • Sectional Variations 207

Chapter 28   Sonata-Form Movements   208

     I. **Key Concepts 208**

     II. **Call and Response 211**

     III. **Contextual Listening 213**

     IV. **Melodies for Study 229**

     V. **Improvisation 232**

     VI. **Composition 232** • Sonata-Form Movement for Piano 232

Chapter 29   Chromaticism   234

     I. **Key Concepts 234** • Common-Tone Embellishing Chords 234 • Chromatic Voice Exchanges and the Chromaticized Cadential $^6_4$ 236 • Chromatic Sequences 237

     II. **Call and Response 240**

     III. **Contextual Listening 241**

     IV. **Melodies for Study 261**

     V. **Improvisation 263**

     VI. **Composition 264** • Ragtime Piece 264 • Instrumental Duet 265

Part VI   Into the Twentieth Century

Chapter 30   Modes, Scales, and Sets   268

     I. **Key Concepts 268** • Sounds of the Twentieth and Twenty-first Centuries 268

     II. **Call and Response 274**

     III. **Contextual Listening 275**

     IV. **Melodies for Study 283**

     V. **Improvisation 285**

     VI. **Composition 286**

Chapter 31   Music Analysis with Sets   288

     I. **Key Concepts 288** • Identifying Sets 288 • Transposing Sets 289 • Inverting Sets 291 • Interval-Class Vectors 293

     II. **Call and Response 298**

III. Contextual Listening 299

IV. Melodies for Study 305

V. Improvisation 306 • Duets 306

VI. Composition 307

Chapter 32   Sets and Set Classes   309

I. Key Concepts 309 • Identifying Sets as Members of Set Classes 309

II. Call and Response 315

III. Contextual Listening 319

IV. Melodies for Study 331

V. Improvisation 332 • Duets with Octatonic Scales and Subsets 332

VI. Composition 333

Chapter 33   Ordered Segments, Serialism, and Twelve-Tone Rows   334

I. Key Concepts 334 • Hearing Pitch Relationships Between Ordered Segments 334

II. Call and Response 337

III. Contextual Listening 339

IV. Melodies for Study 359

V. Improvisation 361

VI. Composition 362

Chapter 34   New Ways to Organize Rhythm, Meter, and Duration   364

I. Key Concepts 364 • Changing Meter 364 • Polymeter 365 • More About Asymmetrical Meters 366

II. Call and Response 369

III. Contextual Listening 371

IV. Melodies for Study 385

V. Improvisation 387 • Polymetric Duets 387

VI. Composition 389 • Serial Composition 389 • Percussion Duet 389 • Ametric Composition 390

Appendixes A1

1. Glossary A3

2. Ranges of Orchestral Instruments A21

3. Set-Class Table A25

Credits A29

Index of Music Examples A31

Index of Terms and Concepts A33

Preface

The *Musician's Guide* series is perhaps the most comprehensive set of materials available today for learning music theory. This book, *The Musician's Guide to Aural Skills* (in two volumes), teaches the necessary practical skills—dictation, sight-singing, keyboard, improvisation, composition, and learning to hear theoretical concepts in context—that you will need as a professional musician. Though the book corresponds chapter by chapter to its companion text, *The Musician's Guide to Theory and Analysis*, it can be used by itself or in conjunction with other theory texts. Each volume comes with a CD of music examples for listening and dictation. In addition, you can acquire a special edition of the MacGamut ear-training and dictation software program (www.macgamut.com) organized to correspond with the *Musician's Guide* texts.

The Musician's Guide to Aural Skills is distinctive in two significant ways. First, it emphasizes the integration of skills you need in order to understand and recall common musical patterns. These skills include the ability to imagine and perform the sounds of printed music; to recall music you hear by singing, playing, and writing it; and to demonstrate your grasp of a variety of musical styles in order to invent and perform similar music of your own. Second, the listening examples are from music literature, not contrived. Thus you will gain your understanding from listening to and imitating the music of diverse composers who wrote in a variety of styles, from classical to popular.

Playing the keyboard and singing are two of the most important skills possessed by professional musicians. From the beginning of the text, you are asked to sing and play everything you learn. When you sing, use movable-*do* solfège syllables or scale-degree numbers; these systems reinforce the tonal relationships that are common to all major and minor keys. (If your teacher prefers a different system, the exercises can easily be adapted. Any systematic method will have its advantages and disadvantages, but any system is better than none at all!) The keyboard exercises come in a wide range of difficulty; this deliberate choice provides challenges to students at all levels of keyboard proficiency. While everyone should be able to play the easiest exercises, everyone should *try* to play all of them, because it is important that you learn to play as much as you can as soon as you can. This said, your teacher may assign the most challenging exercises to students whose primary instrument is piano, or simplify tasks in various ways, such as dividing the parts between two or more players.

Since a method that works for one person might not for another, we often provide more than one way to understand concepts. Moreover, if you have multiple ways to recall what you know, you are more likely to understand what you hear. Similarly, by asking you to learn concepts visually, aurally, and kinesthetically, we know that what you learn will be more meaningful and long-lasting.

Using This Book

Each chapter is divided into six parts: (I) "Key Concepts," (II) "Call and Response," (III) "Contextual Listening," (IV) "Melodies for Study," (V) "Improvisation," and (VI) "Composition." Your teacher may sometimes ask you to complete these sections in parallel rather than one after another.

The **Key Concepts** section introduces common aural patterns by asking you to listen to, play, and sing the sounds emphasized in that chapter. Take your book to a keyboard. Read the text, and play and sing the exercises as directed. Even though these exercises may seem time-consuming, they will significantly improve your ability to hear and understand music.

The **Call and Response** section lets you practice hearing small patterns in real time by singing, playing, and notating them in response to your teacher's calls. Be sure to have a pencil and some manuscript paper available. Ideally, the calls should be given in a setting where students have access to a keyboard or their instruments so that instrumental responses are possible. Such kinesthetic reinforcement is critical to learning and remembering common musical sounds.

The **Contextual Listening** section includes several examples from music literature that feature the aural patterns emphasized in the chapter. Each example is accompanied by a series of exercises that help guide your listening. You will find a variety of question types in this section—from multiple-choice questions about form, meter, rhythm, cadence, or sequence types to questions that ask you to take dictation in solfège or scale degrees, or write music notation on a staff. The "Contextual Listening" examples are excellent models for your own improvisation and composition.

This section features an abundance of exercises. You are not expected to answer every single one. Rather, the variety is intended to meet the different needs of all students, providing reinforcement where necessary as well as posing musical challenges. Your teacher might ask the more experienced students to complete the more difficult exercises, while others are asked to complete the more accessible ones. He or she may reserve some examples for extra credit or for quizzes or tests. If you are asked open-ended questions, such as those that relate to the style of a work or some other aesthetic quality, you will be asked to write your answers on a separate sheet.

Performances of all "Contextual Listening" examples are found on the accompanying CDs. To hear an example, choose the track number indicated in the book. Because there are numerous tracks, you might consider cueing the CD in a computer to quickly reach and replay the desired track.

Throughout the book, we emphasize aural relationships between tonal degrees by asking you to think in terms of solfège syllables and/or scale-degree numbers. Your teacher may prefer one system over the other and thus ask you to complete only the questions that refer to solfège syllables, for example.

Most of the time, you will complete the "Contextual Listening" examples by yourself outside of class. Listen to each example as many times as you wish. For some of the more challenging ones, you may want to work with a partner. It's also a good idea to play what you hear on an instrument. Sometimes your teacher might play an example in class, in order to check significant elements such as key and meter before asking you to complete the remaining exercises on your own. If an example is played as a quiz, you will hear it only a limited number of times.

For many, contextual listening will prove the most challenging aspect of your study of music. The main goal of these exercises is to develop and improve your strategies for thinking and listening. Strive for perfection, but don't be discouraged in the least if you don't get everything right. Your teacher is encouraged to evaluate your work in a holistic manner, focusing on whether you have understood the main concepts of an exercise, rather than on every small detail of your answers.

In the **Melodies for Study** section, you will learn melodies that represent the aural concepts introduced in that chapter as well as reinforcing sounds and principles from previous chapters. While these melodies can and should be used for sight-singing, they are *not* intended to be the only source of such material. Throughout this book, you are asked to create original melodies, and these too can be used for sight-singing—as well as for melodic and rhythmic dictation, melody harmonization, error detection, and other related skills.

Most of the "Melodies for Study" serve multiple purposes as well. In particular, they serve as models and source material for improvisation and composition, and as melodies for harmonization. They also provide opportunities for transposition, instrumentation, and the reinforcement of musical rudiments. For more sight-singing practice, your teacher may want to assign additional melodies.

The **Improvisation** section gives you the opportunity to put what you are learning as listeners to work in real-time musical performances. In this section, we hope you will perform ideas covered in the "Key Concepts," "Call and Response," "Contextual Listening," and "Melodies for Study" sections. Many of the improvisations require you to collaborate with classmates, as well as play at the keyboard and on your instrument.

The **Composition** section guides you to integrate the sounds you have learned into musical works you and your peers can perform and critique. Because they embody everything you have studied, your compositions make excellent additional materials for practicing skills such as sight-singing, melody harmonization, rhythmic dictation, harmonic dictation, and error detection. Moreover, you may find that performing and listening to the work of your peers is one of the most rewarding and exciting aspects of your musical studies.

Our Thanks to . . .

A work of this size and scope is helped along the way by many people. We are especially grateful for the support of our families and our students. Our work together as co-authors has been incredibly rewarding, and we are thankful for that collaboration.

For subvention of the compact discs, we thank James Undercofler (director and dean of the Eastman School of Music), as well as Eastman's Professional Development Committee. For CD engineering, we are grateful to recording engineers John Ebert and John Baker. For CD production work, we thank Glenn West, Christina Lenti, and Lance Peeler, who assisted in the recording sessions. We also thank our colleagues at both Westminster Choir College of Rider University and the Eastman School of Music who gave of their talents to help make the recordings. The joy of their music making contributed mightily to this project.

We are indebted to the W. W. Norton staff for their commitment to this project and their painstaking care in producing these volumes. Most notable among these are former music editor Suzanne LaPlante, who originally commissioned the project, and current music editor Maribeth Payne, who saw it through to completion and whose vision has helped launch this project with great enthusiasm. We are especially grateful for the amazingly detailed work of developmental editor Susan Gaustad and copy editors Chris Miragliotta and Mark Stevens. We also wish to thank Allison Benter and Courtney Fitch for their help with numerous aspects of the project, and JoAnn Simony for overseeing the book's production.

Joel Phillips
Jane Piper Clendinning
Elizabeth West Marvin

Further Expansion of the Harmonic Vocabulary

CHAPTER 21

Tonicizing Scale Degrees Other Than V; Asymmetrical Meters

Overview

In this chapter, we will apply what we learned in Chapter 19 to hear tonicizations of scale degrees other than $\hat{5}$ (on which the V chord is built). We will also begin working with asymmetrical meters.

Outline of topics covered

I. KEY CONCEPTS
    Tonicizing New Scale Degrees
    Introduction to Asymmetrical Meters

II. CALL AND RESPONSE

III. CONTEXTUAL LISTENING

IV. MELODIES FOR STUDY

V. IMPROVISATION
    Team Improvisation
    Consequent Phrases That Include Phrase Expansions

VI. COMPOSITION
    Single-Line Melody
    Keyboard-Style Compositions with Roman Numerals and Figured Bass

I. KEY CONCEPTS

Tonicizing New Scale Degrees

In Chapter 19, we learned that we could tonicize any pitch by preceding it with a chord that contains its leading tone (see the "Strategies for Listening," pp. 440–41). Thus, *fi* (♯$\hat{4}$) may be used to tonicize V. We now apply the same thinking here to discover other secondary relationships.

Exercise 21.1: Hearing Tonicizations of New Scale Degrees

Let's apply what we know to the example below.

1. First, perform the example. Play the bass and sing each of the upper parts in turn, then play all four parts while singing a different part on each repetition.

A:

2. Next, recall how to tell whether or not a chromatic pitch indicates a tonicization.

   (a) First, ask: What is the function of the chromatic pitch I hear? Is it simply an *embellishing tone* (i.e., a chromatic passing or neighbor tone)? If so, there is no secondary relationship. If, on the other hand, the chromatic pitch is *functional* (i.e., part of a chord that *leads* to another chord), you probably hear a secondary dominant.

   (b) If you hear a secondary dominant chord, ask the following: Does the chromatic pitch sound *raised*? Could it be a new *leading tone* ($\hat{7}$)? Does the chromatic pitch sound *lowered*? Could it be a new *fa* ($\hat{4}$)?

3. We hear that the example has two secondary tonicizations. On hearing the first chromatic chord, we think: "Bass pitches 2–3 sound like *ti–do* ($\hat{7}$–$\hat{1}$), but pitch 3 is not the tonic pitch."

   (a) In Chapters 12 and 15, we learned that chords with *ti–do* ($\hat{7}$–$\hat{1}$) bass lines begin with V^6, V^6_5, and vii^{o7} and progress to the tonic. Using listening strategies from those chapters, decide which chord harmonizes the first bass pitch. In this example, the chord is V^6_5.

   (b) Write "V^6_5–i" beneath chords 2–3.

   (c) Draw a bracket beneath these chords to show you hear a secondary relationship. (Recall that the bracket means *of*: V^6_5–i *of* the secondary key.)

   (d) If A♯ sounds like *ti* ($\hat{7}$), then B is *do* ($\hat{1}$). In A Major, B is scale-degree $\hat{2}$, so write "ii" beneath the bracket.

4. On hearing the second chromatic chord, we think: "Bass pitches 4–5 sound like *fa–mi* ($\hat{4}$–$\hat{3}$), but chord 5 is not the tonic chord."

   (a) Chords that have *fa–mi* ($\hat{4}$–$\hat{3}$) bass lines begin with V^4_2, vii^{o4}_3, or IV, then progress to I^6. Refer to strategies from Chapters 12, 15, and 16; the chord is V^4_2.

   (b) Write "V^4_2–I^6" beneath chords 4–5.

   (c) Draw a bracket beneath these chords to show you hear a secondary relationship.

   (d) If A is *fa* ($\hat{4}$), then E is *do* ($\hat{1}$). In A Major, E is scale-degree $\hat{5}$, so write "V" beneath the bracket.

Another way: For the second chromatic chord, we think: *"Melodic pitches 4–5 sound like ti-do ($\hat{7}$–$\hat{1}$), but chord 5 is not the tonic chord."*

   (e) The fifth melodic pitch is *sol* ($\hat{5}$). Since *sol* ($\hat{5}$) sounds like a temporary tonic pitch, V is the secondary key.

   (f) Listen to the bass line. If $\hat{5}$ is tonicized, then the bass line sounds like *fa–mi* ($\hat{4}$–$\hat{3}$).

   (g) Follow steps (a)–(d) above.

5. Check your work against the solution below. Look at the way the lower Roman numerals reveal a simple progression in A Major. Now look at the Roman numerals above the brackets. They also reveal simple tonal relationships, but ones that embellish scale degrees other than the tonic.

When we hear simple PD–D–T relationships and apply the steps above, we can understand most passages in tonal music!

6. In Chapter 19, we learned other ways to notate secondary relationships. (See also Chapter 22, p. 30.) Renotate the solution above using the "slash" and "colon" methods.

Exercise 21.2: Hearing Tonicizations in Context

Let's revisit several examples we studied previously and listen for tonicizations of non-dominant as well as dominant scale degrees.

Example 1 (track 1.1):   From a Beethoven piano sonata

(a) Focus on the middle of phrase 2, and listen for the chromatic pitch in the melody.

(b) Beginning with the chord that contains the chromatic pitch, write the D–T progression.

(c) Write a bracket beneath the progression to indicate the secondary relationship.

(d) To which scale degree does the chromatic chord lead? Write the Roman numeral of that scale degree under the bracket.

(e) Renotate the solution above with the slash and colon methods.

Example 2 (track 1.2):   From a piano piece by Mendelssohn

Listen for the three chromatic pitches in this E-Major excerpt. Use the staff below if you wish to sketch the bass pitches.

(a) Beginning with the *first* chord that contains a chromatic pitch, write the D–T progression.

(b) Write a bracket beneath the progression to indicate the secondary relationship.

(c) To which scale degree does the chromatic pitch lead? Write the Roman numeral of that scale degree under the bracket.

(d) Beginning with the *second* chord that contains a chromatic pitch, write the D–T progression.

(e) Write a bracket beneath the progression to indicate the secondary relationship.

(f) To which scale degree does the chromatic pitch lead? Write the Roman numeral of that scale degree under the bracket.

(g) Because (a) and (d) both show a tonicization of the same scale degree, simplify your analysis by combining their notation over a single bracket.

(h) Beginning with the *third* chord that contains a chromatic pitch, write the D–T progression.

(i) Write a bracket beneath the progression to indicate the secondary relationship.

(j) To which scale degree does the chromatic pitch lead? Write the Roman numeral of that scale degree under the bracket.

(k) Renotate the solutions in (g) and (h) with the slash and colon methods.

(l) With which progression does the excerpt conclude?

(m) Write the Roman numerals and figured bass for the last five distinct bass pitches.

Introduction to Asymmetrical Meters

Asymmetrical meters have beat units of unequal duration. Their signatures often show a 5 or 7 as the top number (e.g., $\tilde{5}\atop 4$ or $\tilde{7}\atop 8$). For now, we focus on $\tilde{5}\atop 4$ and $\tilde{5}\atop 8$. Later we will explore other asymmetrical meters.

When conducting asymmetrical meters, we emphasize the beat unit. There are two beat units in meters $\tilde{5}\atop 8$ and $\tilde{5}\atop 4$. In fast tempos, we conduct these meters in two beats, a "short" beat followed by a "long" beat (2 + 3), or vice versa (3 + 2). In slow to moderate tempos, we use the patterns below.

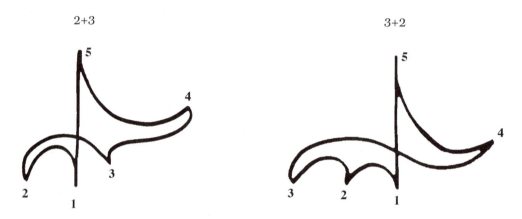

Exercise 21.3: Hearing Asymmetrical Meters

Listen to these excerpts and tap each beat. Accent the first beat of each measure as well as the internal beat units. In which meter(s) might the excerpts be notated? Listen again and conduct, referring to the patterns above.

1. Track 1.3: Gustav Holst, "Mars," from *The Planets*

2. Track 1.4: Paul Desmond, "Take Five"

3. Track 1.5: Walter Piston, Symphony No. 4, second movement

Exercise 21.4: Point and Perform

From the patterns below, your teacher will create rhythms characteristic of asymmetrical meters that divide into 2+3 or 3+2. As soon as he or she points to a pattern, perform the pattern until another is selected. Tap steady subdivisions.

Two-Quarter-Note Patterns

Simple-Meter Patterns

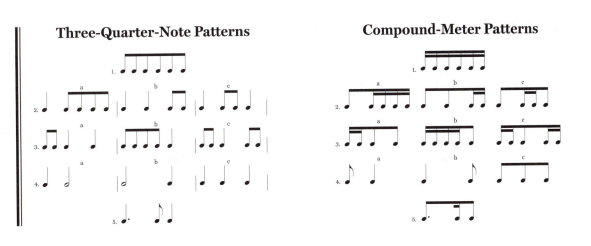

II. CALL AND RESPONSE

Your teacher will perform a pitch pattern, a chord pattern, or a rhythm.

A. If you hear one or two pitches, respond with a harmonization that features a secondary dominant and its resolution.

B. If you hear a chord progression, repeat the progression. Then repeat with an embellished form of the progression—preceding each nontonic chord with a secondary dominant.

C. If you hear a rhythmic pattern, perform, write, or identify what you heard.

Options for performing your response
Maintain the pitch, rhythm, and tempo of the call.

- Sing pitch only (with solfège syllables, scale-degree numbers, note names, or Roman numerals and figures).
- Sing rhythm only.
- Sing pitch and rhythm.
- Sing the progression in arpeggios.
- Conduct (or tap) while singing rhythm only, singing both pitch and rhythm, or singing the progression in arpeggios.
- Play on the keyboard or your instrument.

Options for writing your response

- solfège syllables
- scale-degree numbers
- note names
- note heads only
- rhythmic notation only
- notes and rhythm
- four parts with Roman numerals and figured bass

Part IV Further Expansion of the Harmonic Vocabulary

III. CONTEXTUAL LISTENING

EXAMPLE 1, TRACK 1.6

Listen to an excerpt from a string quartet by Haydn, and complete the exercises below.

1. Which is the meter signature of the excerpt?

   (a) $\frac{2}{4}$

   (b) $\frac{3}{4}$

   (c) $\frac{4}{4}$

   (d) $\frac{9}{8}$

2. Which rhythmic device occurs at the beginning?

   (a) syncopation

   (b) hemiola

   (c) anacrusis

   (d) fermata

3. Write the melody with solfège syllables.

4. Write the melody with scale-degree numbers.

5. On which melodic model is the melody based?

   (a) P pentachord (*do–sol*; $\hat{1}$–$\hat{5}$)

   (b) P+ embellished pentachord (*ti–le*; $\hat{7}$–$\flat\hat{6}$)

   (c) TP tetrachord beneath pentachord (*sol–sol*; $\hat{5}$–$\hat{5}$)

   (d) PT pentachord beneath tetrachord (*do–do*; $\hat{1}$–$\hat{1}$)

6. Write the bass line with solfège syllables.

7. Write the bass line with scale-degree numbers.

8. (a) Notate the pitches and rhythm of the melody and bass line on the staves below. Begin on B3 and B2, respectively. Use the appropriate clefs, key signature (or accidentals), and meter signature. Beam your notes appropriately given your choice of meter signature.

(b) Write Roman numerals and figures beneath the bass pitches in your answer above.

9. The second chord is which type of $^6_4$ chord?

(a) cadential

(b) passing

(c) neighbor

(d) arpeggiating

10. The excerpt concludes with which type of cadence?

(a) half

(b) deceptive

(c) plagal

(d) perfect authentic

11. (a) Conduct the hypermeter as you listen. Is the phrase rhythm regular or irregular?

(1) regular

(2) irregular

(b) If your answer to part (a) was *irregular,* briefly describe the nature of the phrase expansion.

EXAMPLE 3, TRACK 1.8

Listen to an excerpt from a keyboard work by Handel, and answer the questions below.
Draw a phrase diagram to help you remember what you hear.

1. Which is the meter signature of the excerpt?

    (a) $\frac{2}{2}$

    (b) $\frac{3}{2}$

    (c) $\frac{4}{4}$

    (d) $\frac{5}{4}$

The next questions refer to the music of phrase 1 only.

2. Write the melody with solfège syllables.

3. Write the melody with scale-degree numbers.

4. Write the bass line with solfège syllables.

5. Write the bass line with scale-degree numbers.

6. (a) Notate the pitches and rhythm of the melody and bass line on the staves below. Begin on F4 and D3, respectively. Use the appropriate clefs, key signature (or accidentals), and meter signature. Beam your notes appropriately given your choice of meter signature.

(b) Write Roman numerals and figures beneath the bass pitches in your answer above.

(c) Write P or N above each embellishing tone in the melody in your answer above.

7. Phrase 1 concludes with which type of cadence?

(a) Phrygian   (c) plagal

(b) perfect authentic   (d) deceptive

The next questions refer to the music of phrase 2 only.

8. Write the melody with solfège syllables.

9. Write the melody with scale-degree numbers.

10. Write the bass line with solfège syllables.

11. Write the bass line with scale-degree numbers.

12. (a) Notate the pitches and rhythm of the melody and bass line on the staves below. Begin on F4 and D3, respectively. Use the appropriate clefs, key signature (or accidentals), and meter signature. Beam your notes appropriately given your choice of meter signature.

(b) Write Roman numerals and figures beneath the bass pitches in your answer above.

The next questions refer to the entire excerpt.

13. Which is the length of each of the excerpt's subphrases?

(a) one measure

(b) two measures

(c) three measures

(d) four measures

14. (a) Conduct the hypermeter as you listen. Is the phrase rhythm regular or irregular?

(1) regular   (2) irregular

(b) If your answer to part (a) was *irregular*, briefly describe the nature of the phrase expansion.

15. The excerpt concludes with which type of cadence?

(a) Phrygian

(b) perfect authentic

(c) plagal

(d) deceptive

16. Which is the excerpt's phrase structure?

(a) phrase group

(b) contrasting period

(c) parallel period

(d) parallel double period

MUSIC NOTEPAD

Part IV Further Expansion of the Harmonic Vocabulary

EXAMPLE 4, TRACK 1.9

Listen to an excerpt from a work for keyboard by Clara Schumann, and complete the exercises below.

1. Which is the meter signature of the excerpt?

   (a) $\frac{2}{4}$ (b) $\frac{3}{4}$ (c) $\frac{4}{4}$ (d) $\frac{9}{8}$

2. Write the melody with solfège syllables.

3. Write the melody with scale-degree numbers.

4. Write the bass line with solfège syllables.

5. Write the bass line with scale-degree numbers.

6. (a) Notate the pitches and rhythm of the melody and bass line on the staves below. Begin on A4 and A2, respectively. Use the appropriate clefs, key signature (or accidentals), and meter signature. Beam your notes appropriately given your choice of meter signature.

(b) At the beginning, by which means is the tonic chord expanded?

    (1) 5–6 technique

    (2) neighbor $^6_4$ chord

    (3) passing vii^{o6} chord

    (4) passing V$^4_3$ chord

(c) Write Roman numerals and figures beneath the bass pitches in your answer above.

7. The excerpt concludes with which type of cadence?

    (a) half

    (b) perfect authentic in V

    (c) plagal

    (d) deceptive

8. (a) Conduct the hypermeter as you listen. Is the phrase rhythm regular or irregular?

    (1) regular

    (2) irregular

(b) If your answer to part (a) was *irregular*, briefly describe the nature of the phrase expansion.

IV. MELODIES FOR STUDY

For each of the melodies below, prepare to do any of the following:

- Sing on scale-degree numbers or solfège syllables.
- Sing or play the melody in its parallel key.
- Transpose to other keys on your instrument.
- Improvise a variant vocally or on your instrument.
- Identify chords and their inversions implied in the melody.
- Harmonize the melody with chords we have learned since Chapter 12.
- Discuss aspects of phrase rhythm and phrase expansion.

Also be prepared to answer any of the following questions:

- What type of cadence is implied at the end of each phrase?
- What is the key signature for the parallel-key version?
- Which embellishing tones are implied in the melodies?
- From which scale is the melody derived?

Melody 1   Johannes Brahms, String Sextet No. 1 in B♭ Major, Rondo (cello part)

Melody 2   Edvard Grieg, String Quartet in G minor, Op. 27, third movement (violin 1 part)
Model your harmonization on the technique Handel uses in "Contextual Listening"
Example 3.

Melody 3 Piotr Ilyich Tchaikovsky, String Quartet in F Major, Op. 22, Scherzo

Melody 4 Mendelssohn, String Quartet in E♭ Major, Op. 12, fourth movement (violin 1 part)
When you harmonize this melody, tonicize III beginning in measure 6.

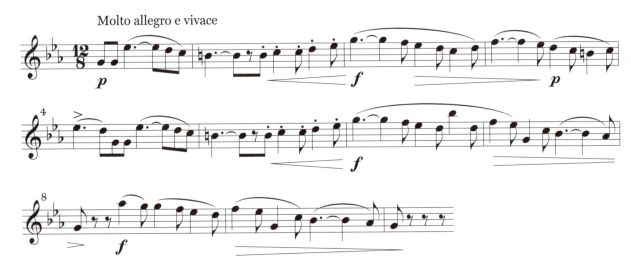

Melody 5   Alexander Scriabin, *Five Preludes,* Op. 15, No. 1

Perform as a trio. Then use solfège syllables and scale-degree numbers to help you write a
setting for these three transposing instruments.

Team Improvisation

Improvise a melody while a partner plays the following lullaby; then switch roles. Add rhythmic interest to your improvisation by choosing from the patterns from Exercise 21.4 in section I. Model your voice-leading on the voice-leading in the accompaniment. Conduct whenever you sing your improvisation.

Strategies

- Accompanists: First perform the rhythm only, tapping the bass part in your left hand and the treble part in your right. Switch hands and perform again.
- Initially, play the chords as block chords; then apply the rhythm.
- Prepare to sing any of the accompanying parts with solfège syllables or scale-degree numbers.

Lullaby

Musical Challenges!

- Transcribe the accompaniment for guitar and perform it on that instrument.
- Transcribe the lullaby to keys ranging from three sharps to three flats.
- Realize Progression 2 on page 27 in $\frac{5}{4}$ meter. Use your realization as the accompaniment for another improvisation.

Consequent Phrases That Include Phrase Expansions

Your teacher will choose a melody from the "Contextual Listening" section that consists of only an antecedent phrase. Improvise a consequent phrase. Include some form of phrase expansion in your consequent phrase, such as (1) an introduction, (2) an internal expansion, or (3) an extension. Perform your improvisations by singing with solfège syllables and scale-degree numbers, or playing them at the keyboard or on your instrument.

Single-Line Melody

Compose a two-phrase melody in the form of a parallel period. Include one or more accidentals that imply the tonicization of a nontonic chord. Use some form of phrase expansion in the second phrase, and some form of motivic development in each phrase. Also:

- Choose a major key signature in the range of three flats to three sharps.
- Choose a simple meter signature.
- Limit yourself to rhythmic values from sixteenth notes to dotted-half notes.
- Group and beam rhythms in patterns characteristic of the meter.
- Make your compositions as musical as possible, marking the score with dynamics, articulations, and phrasing.

Strategies

Please review the strategies for "Single-Line Melody" in Chapter 20, section VI (p. 491).

Variation   Compose in $\frac{5}{8}$ meter, grouping and beaming rhythms in patterns characteristic of the meter.

Keyboard-Style Compositions with Roman Numerals and Figured Bass

Create a two-phrase composition from the following progressions. As you play, sing each part with solfège syllables and scale-degree numbers.

Strategies

- Review the strategies from Chapter 19's Exercise 19.3 (p. 444).
- To create a motive, choose a simple melodic idea and a distinctive rhythm.
- Improve your counterpoint by making the rhythm of each hand distinct.
- Embellish your simple ideas with chordal skips, neighboring tones, and passing tones.
- Prepare to perform in both simple and compound meters.
- Prepare to transpose your compositions to major and minor keys ranging from three flats to three sharps.
- Regarding Progression 1: Base phrase 2 on the motivic idea of phrase 1. Also, since internal repetition is often the way in which phrase expansions occur, consider phrase 2's sequence to be the means of realizing an expansion.

Progression 1

Phrase 1

i–IV$_5^6$–V$_5^6$–i

Phrase 2

i–iv^7–VII–III^7–VI–ii^{ø7}–V–$_2^4$–i^6–ii^{o6}–V$_{4-3}^{6-5}$–i

Sample realization

Realize the chord progression.

c: i   IV$_5^6$ V$_5^6$ i   (i)   iv^7 VII   III^7

Choose a motive and apply the voice-leading from the simple progression.

c: i   IV$_5^6$ V$_5^6$ i   (i)   iv^7 VII   III^7

VI   ii^{ø7} V ——— $_2^4$ i^6 ii^{o6} V$_4^6$ ——— $_3^5$ i

VI   ii^{ø7} V ——— $_2^4$ i^6 ii^{o6} V$_4^6$ ——— $_3^5$ i

Progression 2

Phrase 1

I–V$_5^6$–I–V$_5^6$/ii–ii–$_2^4$–V$_5^6$–V^7–I–V$_5^6$/vi–vi–ii^6–vii^{ø7}/V–V$_{4-3}^{6-5}$

Phrase 2

I–V$_5^6$–I–V$_5^6$/ii–ii–V$_5^6$/iii–iii–iii–$_2^4$–V$_5^6$/ii–ii–V$_5^6$–I–ii$_5^6$–V$^{8-7}$–I

Progression 3 (figured bass)

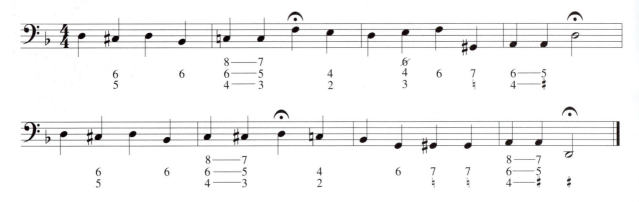

Variations

- Compose according to the melodic characteristics of a particular period, such as Baroque or Classical.
- Replace your motivic rhythm with a new motivic rhythm to create a variation.

Modulation to Closely Related Keys; Mixed Beat Divisions

CHAPTER 22

Overview

In Chapters 19 and 21, we learned to hear and notate tonicizations. Here, we broaden those concepts to include modulation. We also learn to hear and perform common mixed beat divisions.

Outline of topics covered

I. KEY CONCEPTS
Modulation
Closely related keys
Methods for modulation
Notating modulations
Modulatory periods
Mixed Beat Divisions: Two Against Three

II. CALL AND RESPONSE
Creating Modulatory Periods
III. CONTEXTUAL LISTENING
IV. MELODIES FOR STUDY
V. IMPROVISATION
Accompanied Melodic Improvisations

Modulatory Periods
VI. COMPOSITION
Single-Line Melody
Keyboard-Style Compositions with Roman Numerals and Figured Bass

---

I. KEY CONCEPTS

Modulation

Modulation is simply an extended or more substantial tonicization. We feel as though the key has changed temporarily. Thus, in such passages, we analyze chords and pitches as if they *were* in a new key. All the listening strategies we learned for tonicization apply as well to modulation.

CLOSELY RELATED KEYS

The key signatures of closely related keys are identical or differ by one accidental. Thus, in major keys, it is common to modulate to the keys of V, vi, and IV. In minor, it is common to modulate to the keys of III, v, and iv. (Note that in minor keys, the dominant *chord* is typically major, but the dominant *key* is typically minor.)

METHODS FOR MODULATION

Closely related keys have several chords in common. For example, a G-minor chord occurs as vi in B♭ Major and ii in F Major. These **common chords,** also called **pivot chords,** help create smooth shifts from one key to another. Like common chords, **common tones** also make smooth shifts between related keys. Sometimes composers shift to a new key after a rest or at the beginning of a new phrase. Other times, they simply change keys without warning, which can be quite dramatic!

NOTATING MODULATIONS

As we learned earlier, when we hear any tonicization, we indicate the new key, then notate the PD–D–T chords in that key. Look at Example 1, which shows the same progression notated three different ways. Because modulation often involves several chords, the "slash" notation can become difficult to read. The "colon" and "bracket" methods are easier to follow.

Example 1: Three ways to notate modulations

(a) *"Slash" notation* (correct, but sometimes difficult to read)
   ii/V V^7/V V ii^6/V V$^{6-5}_{4-3}$/V V

(b) *"Colon" notation* (easy to read)
   V: ii V^7 I ii^6 V$^{6-5}_{4-3}$ I

(c) *"Bracket" notation* (easy to read)
   $\underline{\text{ii}\ \text{V}^7\ \text{I}\ \text{ii}^6\ \text{V}^{6-5}_{4-3}\ \text{I}}$
   V

   If there is a pivot chord, we can show the modulation in several ways. Perform the progression in Example 2 below in B♭ Major (the key of I). When you reach the deceptive resolution (V–vi), begin thinking in F Major (the key of V). The role of the G-minor chord changes from vi to ii. Finish performing in F Major.

Example 2: Three ways to notate a common-chord modulation

(a) *Box shows pivot chord.*
   I: I   ii^6 V | vi |
   V: | ii | V^7 I   ii^6 V$^{6-5}_{4-3}$ I

(b) *Arrow shows pivot chord.*
   I: I   ii^6 V   vi
                        ↓
   V: ii   V^7 I   ii^6 V$^{6-5}_{4-3}$ I

(c) *Pivot chord simply appears above the chord it becomes.*

I: I ii⁶ V vi

V: ii V⁷ I ii⁶ V$^{6-5}_{4-3}$ I

Strategies for Listening _____

To hear where a pivot chord occurs:

- In both major and minor keys, listen for a chord that contains a chromatic pitch. The pivot chord usually precedes this chord.
- In minor keys, listen for the subtonic pitch. The pivot chord usually precedes the chord that contains the subtonic pitch.
- Listen for cadential or other voice-leading patterns that are outside the tonic. The pivot chord often precedes these patterns.
- Because the pivot chord sounds the same in both the original and new key, we do not notice the modulation until after the pivot chord.

MODULATORY PERIODS

In Chapter 17, we learned how phrases may be grouped into periods. One type of period, called a **modulatory period,** begins in one key and concludes with a perfect authentic cadence in a different key. Perform Example 3, beginning in D Major. Sing the outer voices with solfège syllables and scale-degree numbers. Switch syllables and numbers to the new key (A Major) at the pivot chord.

Example 3: A modulatory period

Phrase 1   *Phrase 2*
I: I V$^6_5$ I V⁶ vi ii⁶ V   I

                                      V: IV V$^4_2$ I⁶ ii⁶ V$^{6-5}_{4-3}$ I

                    HC (I)   PAC (V)

Exercise 22.1: Performing Modulations

We'll use the progressions below to create phrases that modulate to V, III, or vi. Each progression can be the beginning and/or the end of a phrase.

- Perform a progression (1, 2, or 3) to establish the tonic. Each chord in parentheses can be substituted for the chord above it in the original progression.

- Choose a common chord.

    (a) If your tonic is major, choose from the list of I → V or I → vi modulations.

    (b) If your tonic is minor, choose from the list of i → III modulations.

- If the pivot chord becomes a predominant chord in the new key, follow it with a dominant chord.

- Perform the progression again, now in the new key.

Perform these exercises in major and minor keys ranging from three flats to three sharps. Sing the outer voices with solfège syllables and scale-degree numbers. Switch your syllable or number to the new key at the pivot chord.

A sample realization of each progression is given below. Perform these sample realizations and analyze the chords, writing Roman numerals and figures below each bass pitch. Indicate the modulation and pivot chord.

Major-key progressions

1. I   ii⁶   V$^{6-5}_{4-3}$ I
       (IV)   (vi)

2. I   vi   ii$^6_5$ V   I
                  (V$^{8-7}$) (vi)

3. I   V$^6_4$ I⁶   ii⁶   V$^{6-5}_{4-3}$ I
      (vii°⁶)   (IV)   (V$^{8-7}_{6-5}_{4-3}$) (vi)
      (V$^4_3$)

Minor-key progressions

i   ii°⁶   V$^{6-5}_{4-3}$ i
     (iv)   (VI)

i   VI   ii$^{ø6}_5$ V   i
                   (V$^{8-7}$) (VI)

i   V$^6_4$ i⁶   ii°⁶   V$^{6-5}_{4-3}$ i
    (vii°⁶)   (iv) (V$^{8-7}_{6-5}_{4-3}$) (VI)
    (V$^4_3$)

Common chords

• I → V modulations

	(a)	(b)	(c)
I:	I	vi	V
	↓	↓	↓
V:	IV	ii	I

• i → III modulations

	(a)	(b)	(c)	(d)	(e)
i:	i	III	VI	iv	ii°⁶
	↓	↓	↓	↓	↓
III:	vi	I	IV	ii	vii°⁶

• I → vi modulations

	(a)	(b)	(c)	(d)
I:	vi	ii	vii°⁶	IV
	↓	↓	↓	↓
vi:	i	iv	ii°⁶	VI

Sample realization of Progression 1

Sample realization of Progression 2

Sample realization of Progression 3

Variations

- Begin your performance with one progression, but conclude in the new key with another.
- Substitute other key-defining progressions for the three listed above.
- In the sample realization of Progression 3, chromaticize the first cadential $^6_4$ to create vii°⁷/vi. (Hint: Simply raise the second bass pitch one half step.)

Exercise 22.2: Hearing Modulations

Let's listen now to several examples that will help us hear and notate modulations. Each example consists of two phrases.

Example 1 (track 1.11):   From a Haydn piano sonata

(a) Sing the bass pitches of the excerpt on a neutral syllable. By the end of the excerpt, which scale degree do they tonicize?   _____

Strategy ———————————————————————————————————

Sustain this tonicized pitch that you hear at the end, and listen to the beginning of the excerpt again. After you hear the original tonic pitch, sing up or down the scale until you reach the newly tonicized pitch.

———————————————————————————————————

(b) Write the Roman numeral of the tonicized scale degree.   _____   This Roman numeral is the key to which the excerpt modulates.

(c) Listen again, and pay close attention to phrase 2. Since the excerpt is in major, listen for a chromatic pitch—typically *fi* (♯4̂). The pivot chord precedes the chord that contains this chromatic pitch.

(d) Now sing the entire bass line with solfège syllables and scale-degree numbers. Begin in the tonic. At the pivot chord, switch your syllables and numbers to the new key.

(e) Write the solfège syllables of the entire bass line. Begin in the tonic key. At the pivot chord, write the Roman numeral of the new key (your answer to part b) underneath. From that point, write syllables *in the new key*.

(f) Write the scale-degree numbers of the entire bass line. Begin in the tonic key. At the pivot chord, write the Roman numeral of the new key (your answer to part b) underneath. From that point, write numbers *in the new key*.

(g) (1) Notate the pitches and rhythm of the bass line on the staves below. Begin in $\frac{3}{4}$ meter on quarter note D3. Write the appropriate clef, meter signature, bar lines, key signature, and accidentals.

(2) Beneath each bass pitch in your answer above, write the Roman numeral and figure of the chord that harmonizes it. Begin in the tonic and switch to the new key at the pivot chord. (For help, see your answers to the previous questions.)

(h) Which best describes the period formed by these two phrases?

(1) parallel
(2) contrasting
(3) modulatory parallel
(4) modulatory contrasting

Example 2 (track 1.12):   From a Schubert piano sonata

(a) Sing the bass pitches of the excerpt on a neutral syllable. By the end of the excerpt, which scale degree do they tonicize?   _____

Sustain this tonicized pitch and listen to the beginning of the excerpt again. After you hear the original tonic pitch, sing up or down the scale until you reach the newly tonicized pitch.

(b) Write the Roman numeral of the tonicized scale degree. _____ This Roman numeral is the key to which the excerpt modulates.

(c) Briefly describe the method of modulation in this excerpt.

(d) Sing the bass line with solfège syllables and scale-degree numbers. Begin in the tonic. At the new key, switch your syllables and numbers.

(e) Write the solfège syllables of the bass line. Begin in the tonic key. At the location of the change, write the Roman numeral of the new key (your answer to part b) underneath. From that point, write syllables *in the new key.*

(f) Write the scale-degree numbers of the bass line. Begin in the tonic key. At the location of the change, write the Roman numeral of the new key (your answer to part b) underneath. From that point, write numbers *in the new key.*

(g) (1) Notate the pitches and rhythm of the bass line on the staves below. Begin in ¾ meter on eighth note A3. Write the appropriate clef, meter signature, bar lines, key signature, and accidentals.

(2) Beneath each bass pitch in your answer above, write the Roman numeral and figure of the chord that harmonizes it. Begin in the tonic and switch to the new key. (For help, see your answers to the previous questions.)

(h) Which best describes the period formed by these two phrases?

    (1) parallel
    (2) contrasting
    (3) modulatory parallel
    (4) modulatory contrasting

(i) Listen again and conduct the hypermeter. Is the phrase rhythm regular or irregular? If your answer is *irregular*, briefly describe the nature of the phrase expansion(s).

Example 3 (track 1.13):   From a Haydn string quartet

We studied the first phrase of this excerpt earlier. We now focus much of our listening on the second phrase.

(a) Sing the bass pitches of phrase 2 on a neutral syllable. By the end of the phrase, which scale degree do they tonicize?   _____

Strategy _____

Sustain this tonicized pitch and listen to the beginning of the excerpt again. After you hear the original tonic pitch, sing up or down the scale until you reach the newly tonicized pitch.

_____

(b) Write the Roman numeral of the tonicized scale degree.   _____ This Roman numeral is the key to which the excerpt modulates.

(c) Listen to phrase 2 again. Since the excerpt is in minor, listen for the subtonic pitch. The pivot chord precedes the chord that contains this subtonic pitch.

(d) Now sing phrase 2's bass line with solfège syllables and scale-degree numbers. Begin in the tonic. At the pivot chord, switch your syllables and numbers to the new key.

(e) Write the solfège syllables of phrase 2's bass line. Begin in the tonic key. At the pivot chord, write the Roman numeral of the new key (your answer to part b) underneath. From that point, write syllables *in the new key*.

(f) Write the scale-degree numbers of phrase 2's bass line. Begin in the tonic key. At the pivot chord, write the Roman numeral of the new key (your answer to part b) underneath. From that point, write numbers *in the new key*.

(g) (1) Notate the pitches of phrase 2's bass line on the staves below. Begin in $\frac{2}{4}$ meter on eighth note F3. Write the appropriate clef, meter signature, and key signature (or accidentals). Beam notes appropriate to the meter.

(2) Beneath each bass pitch in your answer above, write the Roman numeral and figure of the chord that harmonizes it. Begin in the tonic, and switch to the new key at the pivot chord. (For help, see your answers to the previous questions.)

(h) The excerpt concludes with which type of cadence?

    (1) half cadence in the original key
    (2) perfect authentic cadence in the original key
    (3) half cadence in the new key
    (4) perfect authentic cadence in the new key

(i) Which is the phrase structure of the excerpt's two phrases?

    (1) parallel period
    (2) contrasting period
    (3) parallel double period
    (4) none of the above

Example 4 (track 1.14):   From a keyboard work by Handel

(a) Sing the bass pitches of phrase 2 on a neutral syllable. By the end of the phrase, which scale degree do they tonicize?   _____

Strategy _____

Sustain this tonicized pitch and listen to the beginning of the excerpt again. After you hear the original tonic pitch, sing up or down the scale until you reach the newly tonicized pitch.

_____

(b) Write the Roman numeral of the tonicized scale degree.   _____   This Roman numeral is the key to which the excerpt modulates.

(c) Since the excerpt is in major, listen again for a chromatic pitch. The pivot chord precedes the chord that contains this chromatic pitch. (You may choose an earlier chord as the pivot chord if you think the music there makes more sense in the new key.)

(d) Now sing the bass line with solfège syllables and scale-degree numbers. Begin in the tonic. At the pivot chord, switch your syllables and numbers to the new key.

(e) Write the solfège syllables of the bass line. Begin in the tonic key. At the pivot chord, write the Roman numeral of the new key (your answer to part b) underneath. From that point, write syllables *in the new key.*

(f) Write the scale-degree numbers of the bass line. Begin in the tonic key. At the pivot chord, write the Roman numeral of the new key (your answer to part b) underneath. From that point, write numbers *in the new key.*

(g) The excerpt concludes with which type of cadence?

   (1) half cadence in the original key
   (2) perfect authentic cadence in the original key
   (3) half cadence in the new key
   (4) perfect authentic cadence in the new key

Example 5 (track 1.15)   From a song by Fanny Mendelssohn Hensel

Sometimes composers write progressions or cadences in a secondary key, but never reach the secondary tonic. We can, however, still infer the secondary tonic.

(a) Sing the bass pitches on a neutral syllable. By the end of phrase 1, which scale degree do they tonicize?   _____

Strategies _____

• Sustain this tonicized pitch and listen to the beginning of the excerpt again. After you hear the original tonic pitch, sing up or down the scale until you reach the newly tonicized pitch.
• To find the cadence of phrase 1, listen for the end of a phrase of text.

_____

(b) Write the Roman numeral of the tonicized scale degree.   _____   This Roman numeral is the key to which phrase 1 moves.

(c) Write phrase 1's cadence type and the key in which it occurs (your answer to part b).

(d) Using a neutral syllable, sing the bass pitches again. By the end of phrase 2, which scale degree do they tonicize? (Phrase 2 features a dominant pedal. Sing this pitch, then sing up a P4 to find the implied tonic pitch.) _____

(e) Write the Roman numeral of the tonicized scale degree. _____ This Roman numeral is the key to which phrase 2 moves.

(f) Write phrase 2's cadence type and the key in which it occurs (your answer to part e).

Mixed Beat Divisions: Two Against Three

Some works contain simple and compound beat divisions that sound at the same time. This type of music is challenging, because we must maintain both divisions independently. The most common mixed beat division is two against three. When we hear this during extended passages, it sounds as if we hear two meters simultaneously—a concept called *polymeter*. We'll learn more about polymeter in Chapter 34.

Exercise 22.3: Hearing Two Against Three

Listen to the two examples below, then answer the questions that follow.

Example 1 (track 1.16):   Claude Debussy, Arabesque No. 1

(a) In the higher part, are the beat divisions (1) simple or (2) compound?

(b) In the lower part, are the beat divisions (1) simple or (2) compound?

(c) If we think of each part as being in a different meter, in which meter type(s) might the higher part be notated?

(d) In which meter type(s) might the lower part be notated?

Example 2 (track 1.17):   Debussy, String Quartet in G minor, second movement

(a) In the highest part, are the beat divisions (1) simple or (2) compound?

(b) In the lowest part, are the beat divisions (1) simple or (2) compound?

(c) If we think of the highest and lowest parts as being in different meters, in which meter type(s) might the highest part be notated?

(d) In which meter type(s) might the lowest part be notated?

Exercise 22.4: Performing Two Against Three (Rhythm)

To learn to perform two against three, let's look first at measures that can be divided equally into both two and three—six eighth notes in $\frac{3}{4}$ meter. If we emphasize the first, third, and fifth eighth notes in a $\frac{3}{4}$ measure, we hear "three." If we emphasize the first and fourth eighth notes, we hear "two." As we increase the tempo, measures become the beats of hypermeasures.

1. Start each exercise below (a–g) slowly, then increase your speed. Shift your attention between hands, striving for even, graceful divisions of each measure (a–e) or each beat (f–g). After you master the exercises, perform two or more in succession.

Exercises (a)–(c) feature steady subdivisions, while one hand beats either two or three.

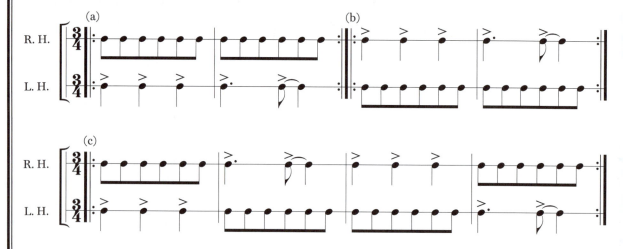

Exercises (d) and (e) are different notations of two against three. As you perform them, imagine the subdivisions we learned in (a)–(c).

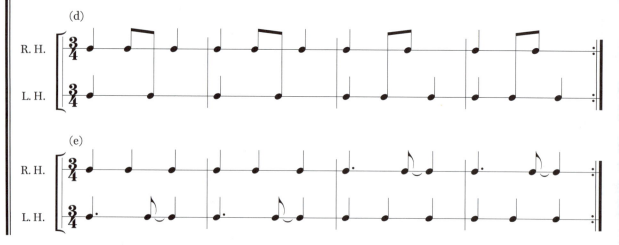

Exercises (f) and (g) are typical of how we find two against three in the music literature.

Variations

- Tap on two different surfaces to create two timbres.
- Tap one part and perform the other with syllables. Switch parts and perform again.
- With permission, tap the rhythms into the palms, knees, or back of a partner.
- Perform the exercises as duets.
- Perform exercises (a) or (b) while a partner performs exercises (d) or (e).
- Create trios; the third person performs only the beat.
- If space permits, perform a part by stepping the rhythm.
- Create duets by adding a second person who steps a different part.
- Create trios by adding a third person who steps the beat.
- On hearing a signal (e.g., a pitch on the piano), switch parts.

Musical Challenges!   Create other mixed divisions, such as four against three. Hint: Find a meter that contains twelve sixteenth notes (twelve equals four times three).

2. Listen to the excerpts of Debussy's music again (tracks 1.16 and 1.17). For each example, tap the rhythm of the melody in one hand and the rhythm of the accompaniment in the other. Switch hands and perform again. Then sing the rhythm of one part while tapping the other. Switch parts and perform again.

Exercise 22.5: Performing Two Against Three (Playing and Singing)

- In the examples below, first perform only the rhythm. Tap each part in separate hands, or tap a part and sing the other with rhythmic syllables.
- Sing each part with solfège syllables and scale-degree numbers.
- Play one part and sing the other with solfège syllables and scale-degree numbers. Switch parts and perform again.
- Perform both parts on the keyboard. Sing either part as you play both parts.

1. Begin with right hand, finger 4, and left hand, finger 5.

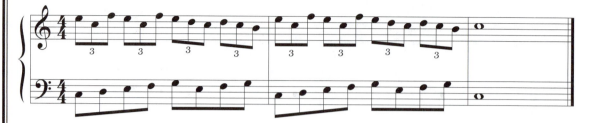

2. Begin with right hand, finger 3, and left hand, finger 5.

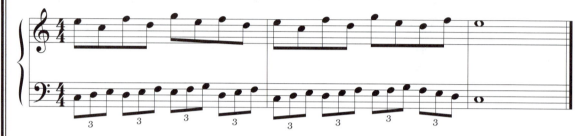

Variations

- Perform measures 1–2 of #1 followed by measures 1–2 of #2. Repeat these four measures, concentrating on the shift between two and three in each hand.
- Perform the triplets *legato* and the eighth notes *staccato*. Switch articulations and perform again.
- Perform the triplets *forte* and the eighth notes *piano*. Switch dynamics and perform again.
- Perform in the parallel minor.
- Transpose the exercises to all major and minor keys ranging from three flats to three sharps.

II. CALL AND RESPONSE

Creating Modulatory Periods

Here, we will learn easy ways to modulate to the dominant, mediant, and submediant keys—by means of two progressions, labeled X and Y. Progression X is a key-defining progression, and Y is a portion of the falling-fifth progression. Perform and write these progressions until you have them memorized.

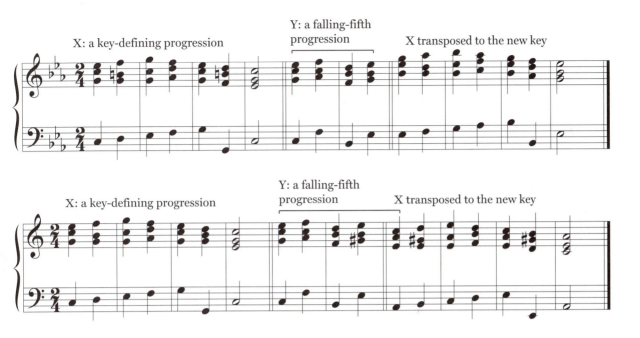

Your teacher will name a starting key and a key to which to modulate—dominant, mediant, or submediant. Respond with progression X, then Y, then X transposed to the new key.

Options for performing your response
Maintain the pitch, rhythm, and tempo of the call.

- Sing pitch only (with solfège syllables, scale-degree numbers, note names, or Roman numerals and figures).
- Sing rhythm only.
- Sing pitch and rhythm.
- Sing the progression in arpeggios.
- Conduct (or tap) while singing the rhythm only, singing both pitch and rhythm, or singing the progression in arpeggios.
- Play on the keyboard or your instrument.

Options for writing your response

- solfège syllables
- scale-degree numbers
- note names
- note heads only
- rhythmic notation only
- notes and rhythm
- four parts (or just outer voices) with Roman numerals and figured bass

Variations

- Substitute a different key-defining progression for progression X.
- Substitute a different linking progression for Y. Can you find ways to link using only one or two chords?
- Perform your response with a three-against-two rhythm, realizing the treble voices as arpeggiated triplets and the bass voice as eighth notes.

III. CONTEXTUAL LISTENING

EXAMPLE 1, TRACK 1.18

Listen to an excerpt from a sonata for violin and piano by Beethoven, and complete the exercises below. Sketch a phrase diagram as you listen.

1. Which is the meter signature of the excerpt?

    (a) $\frac{3}{4}$ (b) $\frac{4}{4}$ (c) $\frac{6}{8}$ (d) $\frac{9}{8}$

2. Using a neutral syllable, sing the bass pitches from the middle of the excerpt to the end. By the end, which scale degree do they tonicize? _____

Strategy

Sustain this tonicized pitch that you hear at the end, and listen to the beginning of the excerpt again. After you hear the original tonic pitch, sing up or down the scale until you reach the newly tonicized pitch.

3. Write the Roman numeral of the tonicized scale degree. _____
    This Roman numeral is the key to which the excerpt modulates.

4. Listen to the second half of the excerpt again. Since it is in major, listen for a chromatic pitch—typically *fi* (♯$\hat{4}$). The pivot chord precedes the chord that contains the chromatic pitch.

5. Now sing the entire bass line with solfège syllables and scale-degree numbers. Begin in the tonic key. At the pivot chord, switch your syllables and numbers to the new key.

For #6–#9, begin in the tonic key. At the pivot chord, write the Roman numeral of the new key, then switch your syllables or numbers to the new key.

6. Write the bass line with solfège syllables.

7. Write the bass line with scale-degree numbers.

8. Write the melody with solfège syllables.

9. Write the melody with scale-degree numbers.

10. The third melodic pitch is which type of embellishing tone?

   (a) suspension

   (b) passing

   (c) neighbor

   (d) anticipation

11. The last embellishing tone in the melody is of which type?

   (a) suspension

   (b) passing

   (c) neighbor

   (d) anticipation

12. (a) Notate the pitches and rhythm of the melody and bass line on the staves below. Begin on C5 and A♭1, respectively. Write the appropriate clef, meter signature, bar lines, key signature, and accidentals. Beam notes appropriately given your choice of meter.

   (b) Beneath each bass pitch in your answer above, write the Roman numeral and figure of the harmony. Notate the key to which the music modulates, and show the pivot chord. Indicate any secondary dominants as well.

13. The first half of the excerpt concludes with which type of cadence?

    (a) half cadence in the original key

    (b) perfect authentic cadence in the original key

    (c) half cadence in the new key

    (d) perfect authentic cadence in the new key

14. The whole excerpt concludes with which type of cadence?

    (a) half cadence in the original key

    (b) perfect authentic cadence in the original key

    (c) half cadence in the new key

    (d) perfect authentic cadence in the new key

15. Which is the phrase structure of the excerpt?

    (a) parallel period

    (b) modulatory parallel double period

    (c) contrasting period

    (d) modulatory contrasting double period

NAME_____

EXAMPLE 3, TRACK 1.20

The following exercises are based on an excerpt from a piano sonata by Haydn.

To help orient your listening:

- The *beginning* of the excerpt lasts until the first perfect authentic cadence.
- The *middle* begins after the first PAC and ends before the return of the original melody.
- The *end* begins with the return of the original melody.
- Trills occur before each of the excerpt's cadences.

1. Which is the meter signature of the excerpt?

   (a) $\frac{3}{4}$ (b) $\frac{4}{4}$ (c) $\frac{6}{8}$ (d) $\frac{9}{8}$

The next exercises refer only to the beginning of the excerpt.

2. Write the melody with solfège syllables. Write *tr* for trills.

3. Write the melody with scale-degree numbers. Write *tr* for trills.

4. Write the bass line with solfège syllables.

5. Write the bass line with scale-degree numbers.

6. (a) Notate the pitches and rhythm of the melody and bass line on the staves below. Begin on C5 and C3, respectively. Write the appropriate clef, meter signature, bar lines, key signature, and accidentals. Beam notes appropriately.

(b) Beneath each bass pitch in your answer above, write the Roman numerals and figures of the harmony.

7. At the beginning, most of the melody's embellishing tones are of which type?

   (a) passing

   (b) neighbor

   (c) chordal skips

   (d) anticipations

8. At the sound of the first trill, which type of $^6_4$ chord occurs?

   (a) passing

   (b) neighbor

   (c) cadential

   (d) arpeggiating

The next exercises are based on the middle of the excerpt.

9. In the middle of the excerpt, which scale degree is tonicized? _____

Strategy

Sing the bass pitches of the middle of the excerpt on a neutral syllable. Then sing the new tonic pitch. Sustain this tonicized pitch and listen to the beginning of the excerpt again. After hearing the original tonic pitch, sing up or down the scale until you reach the newly tonicized pitch.

10. Write the Roman numeral of the tonicized scale degree. _____
    This Roman numeral is the key to which the excerpt modulates.

11. Listen to the middle of the excerpt again. Now sing the bass line with solfège syllables and scale-degree numbers *in the key of your answer above.*

12. Write the Roman numeral of the new key followed by a colon. Then write the solfège syllables of the bass line *in the new key.*

13. Write the Roman numeral of the new key followed by a colon. Then write the scale-degree numbers of the bass line *in the new key.*

14. (a) Notate the bass line of the middle of the excerpt on the staves below in simple-triple meter. Begin on C3. Write the appropriate clef, meter signature, and key signature (or accidentals).

(b) Before the first bass pitch in your answer above, write the Roman numeral of the new key followed by a colon.

(c) Beneath each bass pitch in your answer above, write the Roman numeral and figure of the harmony *in the new key.*

15. The first and last chords of the middle of the excerpt belong to both the original key and the key to which the excerpt modulates. Notate these pivot chords below.

16. The middle of the excerpt concludes with which type of cadence?

(a) HC in the original key

(b) PAC in the original key

(c) HC in the new key

(d) PAC in the new key

The next exercises refer to the end of the excerpt.

17. Now listen to the end of the excerpt, and compare it with the beginning. Conduct the hypermeter. Is the phrase rhythm at the end regular or irregular? If your answer is *irregular*, briefly describe the nature of the phrase expansion.

18. At the end of the excerpt, which type of $^6_4$ chord occurs?

(a) passing   (c) cadential

(b) neighbor   (d) arpeggiating

MUSIC NOTEPAD

EXAMPLE 4, TRACK 1.21

Listen to an excerpt from a trio sonata by Corelli, and complete the following exercises.

1. Which is the excerpt's meter type?

   (a) simple duple

   (b) simple triple

   (c) compound duple

   (d) compound triple

2. Using a neutral syllable, sing the bass pitches. By the end of the excerpt, which scale degree do they tonicize? _____

Strategy _____

Sustain this tonicized pitch and listen to the beginning of the excerpt again. After you hear the original tonic pitch, sing up or down the scale until you reach the newly tonicized pitch.

_____

3. Write the Roman numeral of the tonicized scale degree. _____
   This Roman numeral is the key to which the excerpt modulates.

4. Since the excerpt begins in minor, listen for the subtonic pitch. The pivot chord usually precedes the chord that contains the subtonic pitch.

5. Now sing the entire bass line with solfège syllables and scale-degree numbers. Begin in the tonic key. At the pivot chord, switch your syllables and numbers to the new key.

For #6–#9, begin in the tonic key. At the pivot chord, write the Roman numeral of the new key, then switch your syllables or numbers to the new key.

6. Write the bass line with solfège syllables.

7. Write the bass line with scale-degree numbers.

8. Write the melody with solfège syllables.

9. Write the melody with scale-degree numbers.

10. (a) Notate the pitches and rhythm of the melody and bass line on the staves below. Begin on E5 and A3, respectively. Write the appropriate clef, meter signature, bar lines, key signature, and accidentals. Beam notes appropriately given your choice of meter.

(b) Beneath each bass pitch in your answer above, write the Roman numeral and figure of the harmony. Notate the key to which the music modulates, and show the pivot chord.

11. The first part of the excerpt concludes with which type of cadence?

    (a) Phrygian cadence in the original key

    (b) PAC in the original key

    (c) Phrygian cadence in the new key

    (d) PAC in the new key

12. The excerpt concludes with which type of cadence?

    (a) Phrygian cadence in the original key

    (b) PAC in the original key

    (c) Phrygian cadence in the new key

    (d) PAC in the new key

13. Which is the phrase structure of the excerpt?

    (a) modulatory parallel period

    (b) parallel double period

    (c) modulatory contrasting period

    (d) contrasting double period

EXAMPLE 5, TRACK 1.22

Listen to an excerpt from a string quartet by Haydn, and complete the exercises below. As in Example 3, we will divide the excerpt into three parts—beginning, middle, and end. We studied the beginning in two previous chapters. Now we focus our listening on the middle and end.

To help orient your listening:

- The beginning is repeated.
- The middle begins immediately after the repetition of the beginning.
- The end begins on the highest melodic pitch. The end repeats.

Exercises 1–10 are based on the middle of the excerpt.

1. Using a neutral syllable, sing the bass pitches of the middle of the excerpt. By the end of this middle portion, which scale degree do they tonicize? _____

Strategy

Sustain this tonicized pitch and listen to the beginning of the excerpt again. After you hear the original tonic pitch, sing up or down the scale until you reach the newly tonicized pitch.

2. Write the Roman numeral of the tonicized scale degree. _____
   This Roman numeral is the key the excerpt tonicizes.

3. Listen to the middle of the excerpt again. Since it is in major, listen for a chromatic pitch—typically *fi* (♯$\hat{4}$). The pivot chord usually precedes the chord that contains the chromatic pitch.

4. Now sing the bass line of the middle of the excerpt with solfège syllables and scale-degree numbers. Begin in the tonic key. At the pivot chord, switch your syllables and numbers to the new key.

For #5–#9, begin in the tonic key. At the pivot chord, write the Roman numeral of the new key, then switch your syllables or numbers to the new key. (These exercises still pertain to the middle of the excerpt.)

5. Write the bass line with solfège syllables.

6. Write the bass line with scale-degree numbers.

7. Write the melody with solfège syllables.

8. Write the melody with scale-degree numbers.

9. (a) Notate the pitches and rhythm of the melody and bass line on the staves below. Begin on A4 and D3, respectively. Write the appropriate clef, meter signature, bar lines, key signature, and accidentals. Beam notes appropriately given your choice of meter.

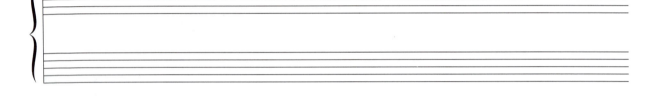

(b) Beneath each bass pitch in your answer above, write the Roman numeral and figure of the harmony. Notate the newly tonicized key, and show the pivot chord.

10. The middle of the excerpt concludes with which type of cadence?

   (a) HC in the original key

   (b) PAC in the original key

   (c) HC in the new key

   (d) PAC in the new key

Exercises 11–17 refer to the end of the excerpt. Write only once; do not include the repetition.

11. Write the melody with solfège syllables.

12. Write the melody with scale-degree numbers.

13. Write the bass line with solfège syllables.

14. Write the bass line with scale-degree numbers.

Part IV Further Expansion of the Harmonic Vocabulary

15. (a) Notate the pitches and rhythm of the melody and bass line on the staves below. Begin on G5 and B3, respectively. Write the appropriate clef, meter signature, bar lines, key signature, and accidentals. Beam notes appropriately given your choice of meter.

(b) Beneath each bass pitch in your answer above, write the Roman numeral and figure of the harmony.

16. The last melodic embellishing tone is of which type?

(a) passing   (b) neighbor   (c) chordal skip   (d) anticipation

17. The excerpt concludes with which type of cadence?

(a) HC in the original key

(b) PAC in the original key

(c) HC in the new key

(d) PAC in the new key

Musical Challenge! Draw a diagram of the phrases of the entire excerpt. Use repeat signs to indicate internal repetitions.

MUSIC NOTEPAD

Part IV Further Expansion of the Harmonic Vocabulary

EXAMPLE 6, TRACK 1.23

Listen to an excerpt from a song by Brahms, and complete the following exercises.

1. Which is the meter signature of the excerpt?

   (a) $\frac{3}{4}$ (b) $\frac{4}{4}$ (c) $\frac{6}{8}$ (d) $\frac{9}{8}$

2. Using a neutral syllable, sing the bass pitches. By the end of the excerpt, which scale degree do they tonicize? _____

Strategies _____

- Because the last chord sounds dominant, sing up a P4 from its bass pitch to find the implied tonic.
- Sustain this tonicized pitch and listen to the beginning of the excerpt again. After you hear the original tonic pitch, sing up or down the scale until you reach the newly tonicized pitch.

_____

3. Write the Roman numeral of the tonicized scale degree. _____
   This Roman numeral is the key to which the excerpt moves.

4. Listen to the excerpt again and search for a chromatic pitch. The pivot chord usually precedes the chord that contains the chromatic pitch.

5. Now sing the entire bass line with solfège syllables and scale-degree numbers. Begin in the tonic key. At the pivot chord, switch your syllables and numbers to the new key.

For #6–#9, begin in the tonic key. At the pivot chord, write the Roman numeral of the new key, then switch your syllables or numbers to the new key.

6. Write the bass line with solfège syllables.

7. Write the bass line with scale-degree numbers.

8. Write the melody with solfège syllables.

9. Write the melody with scale-degree numbers.

10. (a) Notate the pitches and rhythm of the melody and bass lines on the staves below. Begin on A4 and F4, respectively. Write the appropriate clef, meter signature, bar lines, key signature, and accidentals. Beam notes appropriately given your choice of meter.

(b) Beneath each bass pitch in your answer above, write the Roman numeral and figure of the harmony. Notate the key to which the music modulates, and show the pivot chord.

11. The first half of the excerpt concludes with which type of cadence?

(a) HC in the original key

(b) authentic cadence in the original key

(c) HC in the new key

(d) authentic cadence in the new key

12. The excerpt concludes with which type of cadence?

(a) HC in the original key

(b) PAC in the original key

(c) HC in the new key

(d) PAC in the new key

13. **Musical Challenge!** Briefly describe the means by which the final cadence is extended.

IV. MELODIES FOR STUDY

For each of the melodies below, prepare to do any of the following:

- Sing on scale degrees or solfège syllables.
- Sing or play in its parallel key.
- Transpose to other keys on your instrument.
- Improvise a variant vocally or on your instrument.
- Identify chords and their inversions implied in the melody.
- Harmonize with chords we have learned since Chapter 12.
- Discuss aspects of phrase rhythm and phrase expansion.

Also be prepared to answer any of the following questions:

- What type of cadence is implied at the end of each phrase?
- What is the key signature for the parallel-key version?
- Which embellishing tones are implied in the melody?
- From which scale is the melody derived?
- Is there a tonicization or modulation implied in the melody?

Melody 1   Brahms, String Sextet No. 1 in B♭ Major, Rondo (violin 1 part)

Melody 2   Handel, Suite in D minor, Gigue

Melody 3   Brahms, String Quartet No. 3 in B♭ Major, second movement (viola part)

Melody 4   Bach, Courante, from Cello Suite No. 1 in G Major
Transpose the melody to a different octave when you harmonize it. Recall how we deal
with compound melodies; see if you can give a different character or timbre to the different strands of the melodic line.

Melody 5   Haydn, String Quartet in C Major, Op. 20, No. 2, first movement
Perform as a quartet. As is usual with melodies that exceed your range, transpose them
into a comfortable octave.

Melody 6   Johann Sebastian Bach, "Et in Spiritum Sanctum Dominum," from *Mass in B minor*
Perform this excerpt as a trio.

V. IMPROVISATION

Accompanied Melodic Improvisations

Let one person play the accompaniment below at the keyboard, while another improvises
a melody. Before beginning, decide on the order in which you will perform segments 1–4
and on the number of repetitions of each segment. Conclude with segment 3.

During each performance, the rest of the class should conduct in four-beat hypermeasures, expressing the accent of each hyperbeat division by tapping or using rhythmic
syllables.

Variations

- Perform only the rhythm of the accompaniment. Tap each part in different hands, or tap one part and sing the other with syllables. Perform in pairs, tapping on your partner's palms, knees, or back (with permission!).
- Instead of deciding on the segment order in advance, decide *during* the performance. For example, a third person might hold up one to four fingers to indicate the next segment to be performed.
- The class continues to conduct four-beat hypermeasures, but this time they perform hyperbeat divisions opposite those that occur in the duet. For example, measure 1 of each segment divides into three, so the class would perform division into two.
- If space permits, the class *steps* and conducts each hyperbeat while performing the hyperbeat divisions.
- If space permits, the class conducts each hyperbeat while *stepping* and performing the hyperbeat divisions.

Modulatory Periods

Use the progressions we learned in Exercise 22.1 to improvise modulatory periods at the keyboard. (1) Omit the second tonic chord in the first progression to create an antecedent phrase that concludes with a half cadence. (2) Begin the first progression again, include a pivot chord, and modulate to the related key.

Variations

- Animate the texture, playing arpeggios, "boom-chick," and so on.
- Embellish your improvisation with passing tones, neighbor tones, suspensions, and chordal skips.
- Play a simple accompaniment while improvising a melody.
- One person plays an accompaniment while another improvises a melody.
- Begin phrase 2 with a different progression.
- Choose your own tonicization progression, and follow the same procedure.

VI. COMPOSITION

Single-Line Melody

Compose a three-phrase melody. Begin with a two-phrase modulatory period. Make phrase 3 a variation of phrase 1 that features some form of phrase expansion. Conclude with a PAC in the tonic.

Complete this assignment twice—once in a major key and once in minor. In major, modulate to V; use one or more accidentals in your melody that imply the modulation. In minor, modulate to III; "cancel" the leading tone, using the subtonic pitch as the dominant of III. Include some form of motive development in each phrase. Also:

- Choose a key signature in the range of three flats to three sharps.
- Choose a simple-meter signature for one melody, a compound-meter signature for the other.
- Use alto clef for one melody and your choice for the other.
- Limit yourself to rhythmic values from sixteenth notes to dotted-half notes.
- Group and beam rhythms in patterns characteristic of the meter.
- Make your compositions as musical as possible, marking the score with dynamics, articulations, and phrasing.

Strategies

- Review the strategies from section VI in Chapter 20, "Single-Line Melody" (p. 491).
- Model your modulatory period on "Contextual Listening" Example 2 (track 1.19).
- Model the return of phrase 1 on the return in "Contextual Listening" Example 3 (track 1.20).
- Model the range and character of your alto-clef melody on Brahms's String Quartet in B♭ Major ("Melodies for Study," Melody 3).

Keyboard-Style Compositions with Roman Numerals and Figured Bass

Create a three-phrase composition from one or more of the following progressions. Roman numerals for the first two phrases are given. Make phrase 3 a variation of phrase 1 that features some form of phrase expansion. Conclude with a PAC in the tonic. Use motive-development techniques in each phrase as well as embellishing tones.

Perform your composition, singing the melody with solfège syllables and scale-degree numbers. At the pivot chord, switch your syllables or numbers to the new key. Switch back when you return to the tonic key.

Review the strategies from Chapter 19, Exercise 19.3 (p. 444), and Chapter 21, section VI, "Keyboard-Style Compositions with Roman Numerals and Figured Bass" (p. 26).

Progression 1:   Bach, "Cum Sancto Spiritu," from *Mass in B minor*

Phrase 1	*Phrase 2*	*Phrase 3*
I–V$_5^6$–V^7–I	vi–I^6	Variation of phrase 1 that includes some form of
	V: IV^6–V$_5^6$–I	phrase expansion. Conclude with a PAC in the tonic.

Progression 2:   Corelli, *Sonata da Camera*, Op. 4, No. 8, Allegro (adapted)

Phrase 1	*Phrase 2*	*Phrase 3*
I–V$_3^4$–I^6–IV–V–V^7–I	I–V^6–vi^7	Variation of phrase 1 that includes some form of
	V: ii^7–V$_{4-3}^7$–I	phrase expansion. Conclude with a PAC in the tonic.

Progression 3 (figured bass):   Corelli, *Sonata da Camera*, Op. 4, No. 1, Corrente

Again, create a variation of phrase 1 that includes some form of phrase expansion and that concludes with a PAC in the tonic.

Progression 4 (figured bass):

Again, create a variation of phrase 1 that includes some form of phrase expansion and that concludes with a PAC in the tonic. To add more embellishments, augment the rhythm of the progression.

CHAPTER 23 Binary and Ternary Forms

Overview

In Chapters 12, 17, and 20, we mastered four elements of musical structure—motive, subphrase, phrase, and period. Here, we will learn how to craft phrases and periods into sections and sections into movements. In addition, we will continue to practice hearing modulations to closely related keys.

Outline of topics covered

I. KEY CONCEPTS
The Hierarchy of Form
Binary Forms
Ternary Forms
Composite Form

II. CALL AND RESPONSE
III. CONTEXTUAL LISTENING
IV. MELODIES FOR STUDY
V. IMPROVISATION
Team Improvisations

VI. COMPOSITION
Single-Line Melody
Keyboard-Style Compositions

I. KEY CONCEPTS

The Hierarchy of Form

The structure of a piece or movement is called its **form**. Like other elements of music, form is hierarchical. Look at the diagram below, which lists formal structures from the smallest (at the bottom) to the largest.

Entire composition (symphony, sonata, suite, etc.)

Movement

Section

Period (or other phrase structure, such as phrase group)

Phrase

Subphrase

Motive

Understanding the relationship of the parts to the whole and the whole to its parts helps us shape our performance of a piece of music, and helps us find aural guideposts as we listen to music.

Many compositions divide into movements; these movements in turn divide into sections. **Sections** are composed of one or more phrases or periods associated by their thematic design and harmonic structure. Earlier we learned that motives, subphrases, and phrases are represented by lowercase letters. Sections are represented by uppercase letters.

Sections may conclude (1) with either an authentic cadence in the tonic, or (2) any other cadence. In the first case, we call the music **sectional**. In the second, because nontonic conclusions imply continuation, we call the music **continuous**.

Binary Forms

Binary forms have two sections. In **simple binary** forms, like early Baroque dances, the two sections are roughly equal in length, and each is repeated. Their designs are ||: **A** :||: **A′** :|| or ||: **A** :||: **B** :||. More common are **rounded binary** pieces, whose second section often includes a return of music from the beginning, creating an ||: **A** :||: **B A** :|| or ||: **A** :||: **B A′** :|| design. In some binary forms, each section may conclude with similar music, like the rhyme in a couplet. When we hear this repetition, we say the sections are **balanced.**

One kind of rounded binary form is familiar to us through such songs as "Satin Doll," "I Got Rhythm," and "Yesterday." Such songs, called **quaternary forms**, or **quatrains**, actually have a distinctive four-part design. The most common design is **a a b a**. We hear this particular quaternary design as a rounded binary in which only section 1 is repeated (||: **a** :|| **b a** ||).

Strategies for Listening _____

- In all binary pieces: Listen for two sections, each of which is usually repeated.
- Simple binary: Listen for two roughly equal sections.
- Rounded binary: Listen for section 2 to include a return of music from the beginning. Section 2 is often longer than section 1.
- Sectional: At the end of section 1, listen for an authentic cadence in the tonic.
- Continuous: At the end of section 1, listen for any nontonic cadence.
- Balanced: Listen for the conclusion of each section to sound similar.
- Quaternary: Listen for rounded binary in which only the first part is repeated.

Exercise 23.1: Hearing Binary Forms

We now apply these listening strategies to works we've heard before. The strategic questions we ask each time we hear a binary work are in italic. The other questions will help answer these strategic questions.

Example 1: Track 1.24

As you listen to this piece, sketch a formal diagram.

What is the design of each section?

(a) Does section 2 begin with melodic material that is (1) the same (**A**), (2) similar (**A′**), or (3) different (**B**)?

(b) Write the design letters for the beginning of each section. _____ and _____

Is the binary form simple or rounded?

(c) (1) Are the sections roughly equal, or (2) is the second section significantly longer than the first?

(d) Does section 2 feature a return of music from the beginning? If so, what is the third design letter? _____

(e) Is the form (1) simple or (2) rounded binary?

Is the form sectional or continuous?

(f) At the end of section 1, is there an authentic cadence in the tonic?

(g) Is the form (1) sectional or (2) continuous?

Are the sections balanced?

(h) Does the end of section 2 sound similar to the end of section 1?

(i) Are the sections balanced?

Example 2: Track 1.25

As you listen, sketch a formal diagram.

What is the design of each section?

(a) Does section 2 begin with melodic material that is (1) the same (**A**), (2) similar (**A′**), or (3) different (**B**)?

(b) Write the design letters for the beginning of each section. _____ and _____

Is the binary form simple or rounded?

(c) (1) Are the sections roughly equal, or (2) is the second section significantly longer than the first?

(d) Does section 2 feature a return of music from the beginning? If so, what is the third design letter? _____

(e) Is the form (1) simple or (2) rounded binary?

Is the form sectional or continuous?

(f) At the end of section 1, is there an authentic cadence in the tonic?

(g) Is the form (1) sectional or (2) continuous?

Are the sections balanced?

(h) Does the end of section 2 sound similar to the end of section 1?

(i) Are the sections balanced?

Example 3: Track 1.26

As you listen, sketch a formal diagram.

What is the design of each section?

(a) Does section 2 begin with melodic material that is (1) the same (**A**), (2) similar (**A′**), or (3) different (**B**)?

(b) Write the design letters for the beginning of each section. _____ and _____

Is the binary form simple or rounded?

(c) (1) Are the sections roughly equal, or (2) is the second section significantly longer than the first?

(d) Does section 2 feature a return of music from the beginning?
    If so, what is the third design letter? _____

(e) Is the form (1) simple or (2) rounded binary?

Is the form sectional or continuous?

(f) At the end of section 1, is there an authentic cadence in the tonic?

(g) Is the form (1) sectional or (2) continuous?

Are the sections balanced?

(h) Does the end of section 2 sound similar to the end of section 1?

(i) Are the sections balanced?

Ternary Forms

Ternary forms consist of three sections, both by design *and* by harmonic structure: || **A** || **B** || **A** || or || **A** || **B** || **A′** ||. Though the designs of ternary and rounded-binary forms look similar, the **B** section of ternary form is generally more tonally stable and independent than the **B** section of rounded binary. Like binary forms, ternary forms may be sectional or continuous, depending on the type of cadence at the end of the **B** section.

Strategies for Listening _____

- Compared with rounded binary, the middle (**B**) section of a ternary form often is more independent, contrasts in key, and features different melodic material.
- In a composite ternary (see below), the middle section often sounds in the key of the subdominant.
- Changes in character, dynamics, orchestration, register, and texture enhance the contrast between sections.
- Arias are frequently in ternary form. Listen for the return of the beginning, either exact or embellished.

Composite Form

Composite form refers to a large form made up of smaller forms.

Composite ternary is the most common composite form, typically occurring as a movement in sonatas, symphonies, and concertos. Such a movement consists of a pair of binary dances (e.g., minuet and trio, scherzo and trio, allegretto and trio). We hear the first dance (**A**—the minuet, say), then the second dance (**B**—the trio), then a repetition of the first dance (**A**). The large **A B A** is a ternary form, each section of which is a binary form. (If a ternary form is *not* a composite, we can refer to it as a **simple ternary**.)

The diagram below shows the composite form of a typical minuet and trio.

Ternary:	**A**	**B**	**A**
	Minuet—tonic key	Trio—subdominant key	Minuet repeated—tonic key
Sections:	binary	binary	binary
	(‖: **A** :‖: **B A′** :‖)	(‖: **A** :‖: **B A′** :‖)	(‖: **A** :‖: **B A′** :‖)

Another type of composite form, **composite binary**, occurs in marches and rags. Compare the diagram below with the one above. It is basically the same plan, minus the return of the first large section (march or rag).

Binary:	**A** (march or rag—tonic key)	**B** (trio—subdominant key)
Sections:	ternary (‖: **A** :‖: **B** :‖ **A** ‖)	binary (‖: **A** :‖: **B** :‖)

Exercise 23.2: Hearing Ternary and Rounded Binary Forms

Listen to each example, and then write a brief paragraph that summarizes the bulleted questions below. Illustrate your paragraph with a diagram of the form; write design letters that represent all sections.

- Is the form ternary or rounded binary? List substantive musical reasons for your decision.
- Is the form a composite form? If so, what is the form of each individual section?
- Is the example sectional or continuous?
- If the form is binary, are its sections balanced?

Example 1: Track 1.27

Example 2: Track 1.28

Example 3: Track 1.29

Example 4: Track 1.30

II. CALL AND RESPONSE

Your teacher will perform a chord progression and tell you which key you should modulate to.

1. Repeat the call.
2. Listen for the instruction about which key to modulate to.
3. Repeat the original call, and add or choose a pivot chord.
4. If your pivot chord is a predominant chord, follow it with a dominant chord in the new key.
5. Now add the original call, transposed to the new key.

Options for performing your response
Maintain the pitch, rhythm, and tempo of the call.

- Sing pitch only (with solfège syllables, scale-degree numbers, note names, or Roman numerals and figures).
- Sing rhythm only.
- Sing pitch and rhythm.
- Sing the progression in arpeggios.
- Conduct (or tap) while singing rhythm only, singing both pitch and rhythm, or singing the progression in arpeggios.
- Play on the keyboard or your instrument.

Options for writing your response

- solfège syllables
- scale-degree numbers
- note names
- note heads only
- rhythmic notation only
- notes and rhythm
- four parts (or just outer voices) with Roman numerals and figured bass

Variations

- Instead of repeating the call in the new key, tonicize the new key with a different progression.
- Perform your response, realizing the treble voices as arpeggiated triplets and the bass voice as eighth notes.

III. CONTEXTUAL LISTENING

EXAMPLE 1, TRACK 1.31

Listen to an excerpt from a ballet by Copland, and complete the exercises below.

1. Which is the section design of the excerpt?

   (a) **A A**

   (b) **A A′**

   (c) ||: **A** :||: **B** :||

   (d) ||: **A** :||: **B A′** :||

2. Section 2 concludes in which key?

   (a) I

   (b) IV

   (c) V

   (d) vi

3. Which is the form of the excerpt?

   (a) simple binary

   (b) rounded binary

   (c) simple ternary

   (d) composite ternary

Before proceeding . . .

   • If your answer to #3 was (a) or (b), complete #4 and #5. (Do not complete #6.).
   • If your answer to #3 was (c), you have finished this example. (Do not complete #4–#6.)
   • If your answer to #3 was (d), skip to #6. (Do not complete #4–#5.)

4. Is the binary (a) sectional or (b) continuous?

5. (a) Which is the form of section 1?

   (1) parallel period

   (2) contrasting period

   (3) simple binary

   (4) rounded binary

If your answer was (3) or (4), complete parts (b) and (c).

(b) Is the binary (1) sectional or (2) continuous?

(c) Are the sections balanced?

6. (a) Which is the form of section 2?

    (1) parallel period

    (2) contrasting period

    (3) simple binary

    (4) rounded binary

If your answer was (3) or (4), complete parts (b) and (c).

(b) Is the binary (1) sectional or (2) continuous?

(c) Are the sections balanced?

EXAMPLE 2, TRACK 1.32

Listen to an excerpt from a piano work by Schubert, and complete the exercises below. Questions 1–3 refer to the entire movement. To help you remember what you hear, sketch structural diagrams as you listen.

1. Which is the section design of the entire movement?

    (a) **A A**

    (b) **A A′**

    (c) **A B**

    (d) **A B A′**

2. Section 2 is in which key?

    (a) I

    (b) IV

    (c) V

    (d) vi

3. Which is the form of the entire movement?

    (a) simple binary

    (b) rounded binary

    (c) simple ternary

    (d) composite ternary

Before proceeding . . .

   • If your answer to #3 was (a) or (b), complete #4–#6, then skip to #8. (Do not answer #7.)
   • If your answer to #3 was (c), skip to #8. (Do not complete #4–#7.)
   • If your answer to #3 was (d), skip to #6. (Do not complete #4–#5.)

4. Is the binary (a) sectional or (b) continuous?

5. Are the sections balanced?

6. (a) Which is the form of section 1?

    (1) parallel period

    (2) contrasting period

    (3) simple binary

    (4) rounded binary

   If your answer was (3) or (4), complete parts (b) and (c).

    (b) Is the binary (1) sectional or (2) continuous?

    (c) Are the sections balanced?

7. (a) Which is the form of section 2?

   (1) parallel period

   (2) contrasting period

   (3) simple binary

   (4) rounded binary

   If your answer was (3) or (4), complete parts (b) and (c).

   (b) Is the binary (1) sectional or (2) continuous?

   (c) Are the sections balanced?

8. Which is the meter signature of the excerpt?

   (a) $\frac{2}{4}$

   (b) $\frac{3}{4}$

   (c) $\frac{6}{8}$

   (d) $\frac{9}{8}$

9. Using a neutral syllable, sing the bass pitches. In the middle of the excerpt, sing the newly tonicized pitch. Sustain this pitch. Which scale degree is tonicized here? _____

Strategy

Sustain this tonicized pitch and listen to the beginning of the excerpt again. After you hear the original tonic pitch, sing up or down the scale until you reach the newly tonicized pitch.

10. Write the Roman numeral of the tonicized scale degree. _____
    This Roman numeral is the key to which the excerpt modulates.

For #11–#14, begin writing syllables or numbers in the tonic key. At the appropriate time, write the Roman numeral of the new key, then switch syllables or numbers to the new key.

11. Write the solfège syllables of the bass notes that occur on each beat.

12. Write the scale-degree numbers of the bass notes that occur on each beat.

13. Write the melody with solfège syllables. Write ~ for the turn.

14. Write the melody with scale-degree numbers. Write ~ for the turn.

15. The second melodic pitch is which type of embellishing tone?

    (a) suspension

    (b) passing

    (c) neighbor

    (d) anticipation

16. The fourth melodic pitch is which type of embellishing tone?

    (a) suspension

    (b) passing

    (c) neighbor

    (d) anticipation

17. Notate the pitches and rhythm of the melody and bass lines on the staves below. Begin on G♯4 and E2, respectively. Write the appropriate clef, meter signature, bar lines, key signature, and accidentals. Beam notes appropriately given your choice of meter.

EXAMPLE 3, TRACK 1.33

Listen to an excerpt from a piano sonata by Mozart, and complete the exercises below.

1. Which is the meter signature of the excerpt?

   (a) $\frac{3}{4}$

   (b) $\frac{4}{4}$

   (c) $\frac{6}{8}$

   (d) $\frac{9}{8}$

2. Using a neutral syllable, sing the bass pitches. By the end of the excerpt, which scale degree do they tonicize? _____

Strategy _____

Sustain this tonicized pitch and listen to the beginning of the excerpt again. After you hear the original tonic pitch, sing up or down the scale until you reach the newly tonicized pitch.

_____

3. Write the Roman numeral of the tonicized scale degree. _____
   This Roman numeral is the key to which the excerpt modulates.

For #4–#6, begin in the tonic key. At the appropriate moment, write the Roman numeral of the new key, then switch your syllables, numbers, and Roman numerals to the new key.

4. Staff 1 is a rhythmic reduction of the bass line.

   (a) Using staff 1's rhythm as a guide, write the bass line with solfège syllables and scale-degree numbers. (At the beginning, assume the first bass note is prolonged by means of embellishments for three beats.)

   (b) Transcribe staff 1's syllables and numbers to pitches in staff 2. Keep the same rhythm as in staff 1.

   (c) Taking these pitches as the bass notes, write the Roman numerals and figures in the spaces below staff 2. From measure 9 on, choose the lower bass pitch in each measure to decide which chord inversion to write. Indicate any secondary dominants, notate the key to which the music modulates, and notate the remaining chords in the new key.

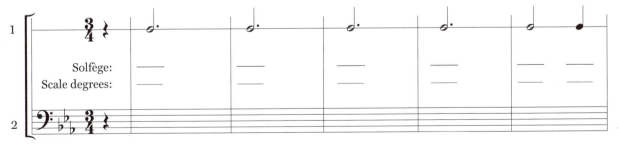

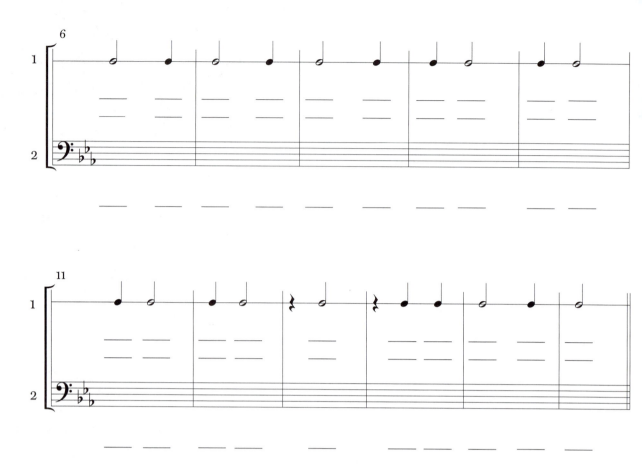

5. Write phrase 1's melody with solfège syllables.

6. Write phrase 1's melody with scale-degree numbers.

7. Notate the pitches and rhythm of the melody and bass lines on the staves below. Use the reduction of the bass line (your answer to #4). Begin on B♭4 and E♭4, respectively. Write the appropriate clef, meter signature, bar lines, key signature, and accidentals. Beam notes appropriately given your choice of meter.

8. The second and fourth melodic pitches are which type of embellishing tone?

(a) suspension

(b) passing

(c) neighbor

(d) anticipation

9. The excerpt concludes with which type of cadence?

(a) HC in the original key

(b) PAC in the original key

(c) HC in the new key

(d) PAC in the new key

10. Which is the phrase structure of the excerpt?

(a) parallel period

(b) modulatory parallel period

(c) contrasting period

(d) modulatory contrasting period

11. Briefly discuss the internal organization of the excerpt's phrases.

Part IV Further Expansion of the Harmonic Vocabulary

EXAMPLE 4, TRACK 1.34

Listen to a movement from a piano sonata by Mozart, and answer the questions below. Questions 1–4 refer to the entire movement. To help you remember what you hear, sketch structural diagrams as you listen.

1. Which is the section design of the entire movement?

    (a) **A A**

    (b) **A A′**

    (c) **A B**

    (d) **A B A**

2. Section 2 is in which key?

    (a) I

    (b) IV

    (c) V

    (d) vi

3. Is the form of the entire movement (a) sectional or (b) continuous?

4. Which is the form of the entire movement?

    (a) simple binary

    (b) rounded binary

    (c) simple ternary

    (d) composite ternary

Before proceeding . . .

   • If your answer to #4 was (a) or (b), complete #5 and #6. (Do not complete #7–#8.)
   • If your answer to #4 was (c), you have finished this example. (Do not complete #5–#8.)
   • If your answer to #4 was (d), skip to #7. (Do not complete #5–#6.)

5. Is the binary (a) sectional or (b) continuous?

6. Are the sections balanced?

7. (a) Which is the form of section 1?

    (1) parallel period

    (2) contrasting period

    (3) simple binary

    (4) rounded binary

If your answer was (3) or (4), complete parts (b) and (c).

(b) Is the binary (1) sectional or (2) continuous?

(c) Are the sections balanced?

8. (a) Which is the form of section 2?

    (1) parallel period

    (2) contrasting period

    (3) simple binary

    (4) rounded binary

If your answer was (3) or (4), complete parts (b) and (c).

(b) Is the binary (1) sectional or (2) continuous?

(c) Are the sections balanced?

EXAMPLE 5, TRACK 1.35

Listen to an art song by Bach, and complete the exercises below. Questions 1–4 refer to the entire piece. To help you remember what you hear, sketch structural diagrams as you listen.

1. Which is the section design of the entire piece?

   (a) **A A**

   (b) **A A′**

   (c) **A B**

   (d) **A B A**

2. Section 2 concludes in which key?

   (a) I

   (b) IV

   (c) V

   (d) vi

3. Is the form of the entire movement (a) sectional or (b) continuous?

4. Which is the form of the entire piece?

   (a) simple binary

   (b) rounded binary

   (c) simple ternary

   (d) composite ternary

Before proceeding . . .

   • If your answer to #4 was (a) or (b), complete #5 and #6 and skip to #9. (Do not complete #7–#8.)
   • If your answer to #4 was (c), skip to #9. (Do not complete #5–#8.)
   • If your answer to #4 was (d), skip to #7. (Do not complete #5–#6.)

5. Is the binary (a) sectional or (b) continuous?

6. Are the sections balanced?

7. (a) Which is the form of section 1?

   (1) parallel period

   (2) contrasting period

   (3) simple binary

   (4) rounded binary

If your answer was (3) or (4), complete parts (b) and (c).

(b) Is the binary (1) sectional or (2) continuous?

(c) Are the sections balanced?

8. (a) Which is the form of section 2?

    (1) parallel period

    (2) contrasting period

    (3) simple binary

    (4) rounded binary

If your answer was (3) or (4), complete parts (b) and (c).

(b) Is the binary (1) sectional or (2) continuous?

(c) Are the sections balanced?

9. At the beginning, at which generic interval are the flutes doubled?

    (a) third

    (b) fifth

    (c) sixth

    (d) octave

10. At the end of the introduction, at which generic interval are the flutes doubled?

    (a) third

    (b) fifth

    (c) sixth

    (d) octave

Exercises 11–16 refer only to the music of section 1.

11. Write the vocal melody with solfège syllables. Write *tr* for the trill.

12. Write the vocal melody with scale-degree numbers. Write *tr* for the trill.

13. Notate the pitches and rhythm of the melody on the staves below. Begin on B♭4. Use the appropriate clef, meter signature, bar lines, key signature, and accidentals. Beam notes appropriately given your choice of meter.

14. At the beginning of the vocal melody, which is the harmonic progression?

   (a) I–I–vii°⁷–I

   (b) I–ii⁶–V–I

   (c) I–ii$^4_2$–V$^6_3$–I

   (d) I–IV–V$^4_2$–I⁶

15. After the singer cadences, section 1 concludes with an instrumental postlude. Which best describes the final instrumental cadence of section 1?

   (a) IAC in I

   (b) PAC in V

   (c) deceptive resolution followed by a PAC in I

   (d) PAC in vi followed by a HC in IV

16. Which is the form of section 1?

   (a) introduction + parallel period + codetta

   (b) introduction + contrasting period + codetta

   (c) introduction + parallel double period

   (d) introduction + contrasting double period

17. From the beginning of section 2, which are the first two keys tonicized?

   (a) ii then IV

   (b) IV then V

   (c) V then I

   (d) vi then ii

Part IV Further Expansion of the Harmonic Vocabulary

IV. MELODIES FOR STUDY

For each of the melodies below, prepare to do any of the following:

- Sing on scale-degree numbers or solfège syllables.
- Sing or play the melody in its parallel key.
- Transpose to other keys on your instrument.
- Improvise a variant vocally or on your instrument.
- Identify chords and their inversions implied in the melody.
- Harmonize with chords we have learned since Chapter 12.
- Discuss aspects of phrase rhythm and phrase expansion.

Also be prepared to answer any of the following questions:

- What type of cadence is implied at the end of each phrase?
- What is the key signature for the parallel-key versions?
- Which embellishing tones are implied in the melodies?
- From which scale is the melody derived?
- Is there a tonicization or modulation implied in the excerpt?

Melody 1 "On the Erie Canal" (traditional)

Melody 2 John Hill Hewitt, "All Quiet Along the Potomac To-night"

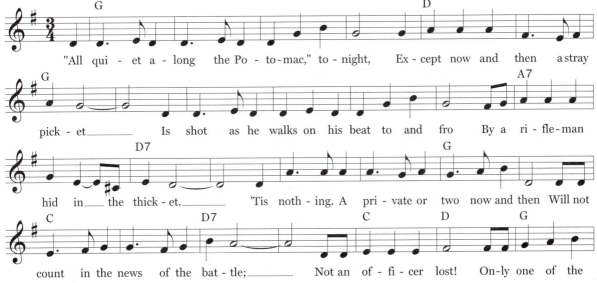

men Moan-ing out   all a - lone   the death rat - tle._____

Melody 3 Beethoven, Écossaise, WoO 23

Melody 4 Mozart, String Quartet in B♭ Major, K. 458, Menuetto (violin 1 part)

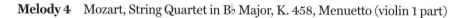

Melody 5 Beethoven, "Lustig, traurig," WoO 54

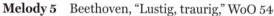
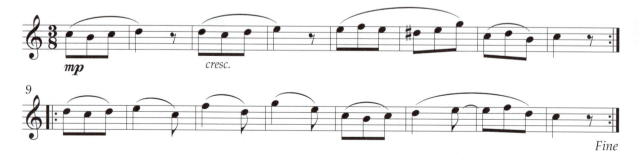

Fine

D. C. al Fine

V. IMPROVISATION

Team Improvisations

Improvise a rounded binary form following the harmonic outline of Mozart's Menuetto below. While one person realizes the figured bass at the keyboard, another improvises a melody. If the soloist sings, use solfège syllables and/or scale-degree numbers; switch the syllables or numbers at the modulation.

Mozart creates phrase expansions at the end of the **B** section and leading into the recapitulation of **A**. Improvise musical gestures appropriate to those passages. For example, the accompanist might thin the texture at the lead-in while the soloist creates a link to the original register of **A**.

Mozart, String Quintet in B♭ Major, K. 174, Menuetto (cello part)

Musical Challenge!   Use the Menuetto to create a composite ternary form.

A   Perform the Menuetto in its parallel minor, B♭ minor.

B   Make a **B** section by transposing the Menuetto to B♭ minor's relative major, D♭ Major.

A   Perform the Menuetto again in its parallel minor, B♭ minor.

VI. COMPOSITION

Single-Line Melody

ROUNDED BINARY

Compose a four-phrase melody. Begin with a two-phrase modulatory period, and conclude with a contrasting period. Make phrase 4 a variation of phrase 1 that features some form of phrase expansion. End with a PAC in the tonic.

Complete this assignment twice, once in a major key and once in minor. In major, modulate to V; include one or more accidentals in your melody that imply the modulation. In minor, modulate to III; "cancel" the leading tone, using the subtonic pitch as the dominant of III. Feature some form of motive development in each phrase. Also:

- Choose a key signature in the range of three flats to three sharps.
- Choose a simple-meter signature for one melody, a compound-meter signature for the other.
- Use alto clef for one melody and your choice of clef for the other.
- Limit yourself to rhythmic values from sixteenth notes to dotted-half notes.
- Group and beam rhythms in patterns characteristic of the meter.
- Make your compositions as musical as possible, marking the score with dynamics, articulations, and phrasing.

Strategy _____

- Review the strategies from Chapter 20, section VI, "Single-Line Melody" (p. 491).

_____

SIMPLE TERNARY

Now compose two simple-ternary pieces, one in major and one in minor, following the bulleted criteria for the "Rounded Binary" assignment. Begin each with a parallel period in the tonic. Then compose a parallel period in a related key. Conclude the piece with a repetition of period 1 (*D. C. al Fine*, if you like). Enhance the contrast of your **B** section by varying several musical elements (dynamics, register, character, articulation, rhythm, etc.).

Keyboard-Style Compositions

Create four-phrase binary compositions from the four progressions you realized in Chapter 22, section VI, "Keyboard-Style Compositions with Roman Numerals and Figured Bass" (p. 69). For each progression, keep the three phrases you wrote. Now compose a new, contrasting phrase that follows phrase 2 and creates a contrasting period with your old phrase 3.

Follow the guidelines and strategies from Chapter 19, Exercise 19.3 (p. 444); from Chapter 21, section VI, p. 26; and from the "Rounded Binary" assignment above.

Color and Drama in Composition:
Modal Mixture and Chromatic Mediants and Submediants

CHAPTER 24

Overview

In Chapter 24, we will hear how composers use chords from parallel keys and other altered chords to add color and drama to their music.

Outline of topics covered

I. KEY CONCEPTS
Modal Mixture
Notating "Borrowed" Chords
Other Types of Altered Chords

II. CALL AND RESPONSE
III. CONTEXTUAL LISTENING
IV. MELODIES FOR STUDY

V. IMPROVISATION
Team Improvisations
VI. COMPOSITION
Single-Line Melody: Rounded Binary
Keyboard Trio

I. KEY CONCEPTS

Modal Mixture

When composers want to expand a piece's harmonic palette, they might "borrow" chords from the piece's parallel key. This technique is called **modal mixture**, or simply **mixture**, because chords of the major and minor modes are "mixed." Mixture is more common in major keys, where elements from the parallel minor are introduced.

Notating "Borrowed" Chords

When we hear mixture, we change our analysis to the Roman numerals of the parallel key to represent the chord root and chord quality we hear. Some of these chords are built on scale degrees that are altered from the major scale. In these cases, we place an accidental *before* the Roman numeral to show how it was altered: ♭ means *lowered* and ♯ means *raised*.

Strategies for Listening

Assume you are listening to a major-key composition. (Look carefully at the notation of the "borrowed" chords below.)

1. In general, listen for *me* (♭$\hat{3}$), *le* (♭$\hat{6}$), or *te* (♭$\hat{7}$). These "modal" scale degrees are from the natural (descending melodic) minor scale.
2. Listen for unexpected chord quality in predominant chords.
   - ii or ii⁶ → ii° or ii°⁶
   - ii⁷ → ii⌀⁷
   - IV → iv
   - vi → ♭VI
   - iii → ♭III
3. Listen for a quality change in the leading-tone seventh chord: vii⌀⁷ → vii°⁷.
4. Listen for *me* (♭$\hat{3}$) in the cadential $^6_4$ chord.

Exercise 24.1: Performing Progressions with Modal Mixture

Go back to section I of Chapter 16 (p. 354), where we first learned about predominant chords. Perform every major-key example in Exercises 16.1, 16.4, 16.5, 16.7, and 16.9, substituting predominant chords from the parallel minor. Refer to the list of chords in the strategies above.

Exercise 24.2: Performing Phrases from Roman-Numeral Progressions

The following progressions are based on those in Chapter 16's Exercise 16.10. Play them in keyboard style (three voices in the right hand, one in the left). Substitute *me* (♭$\hat{3}$) in the cadential $^6_4$ chords.

Phrase 1

1. I–iv–I–ii°⁶–V
2. I$^{5-6-5}_{3-4-3}$–♭VI–ii°⁶–V$^{6-5}_{4-3}$
3. I–vii°⁶–I⁶–ii°⁶–V–I–V
4. I–V$^6_4$–I⁶–iv–V$^{6-5}_{4-3}$
5. I–vii°⁷–I–iv–I⁶–ii°⁶–V

Phrase 2

I–iv–I⁶–ii°⁶–V$^{6-5}_{4-3}$–I

I$^{5-6-5}_{3-4-3}$–♭VI–ii°$^6_5$–V$^{4-3}$–i

I–V$^4_3$–I⁶–ii°⁶–V$^{8-7}$–I

I–V$^6_4$–I⁶–iv–V$^{6-5}_{4-3}$–I$^{5-6-5}_{3-4-3}$

I⁶–vii°$^6_5$–I–V–I–ii°⁶–V⁷–I

Exercise 24.3: Performing Phrases from Figured-Bass Notation

Realize the following figured-bass lines in four parts, in keyboard style. (They are based on those in Chapter 16's Exercise 16.11.) As you play, sing each of the parts with solfège syllables, scale-degree numbers, and letter names.

Variations

- Once you learn the progression, add melodic embellishing tones. With modal mixture, you need to make sure the embellishing tones do not create augmented or diminished melodic intervals.
- For ii⁷–V⁷, perform an incomplete seventh chord followed by a complete seventh chord (or vice versa).
- Perform each progression again, inserting the figures ♮–3 beneath each dominant pitch. (The third in this figure will always be the leading tone!)

Other Types of Altered Chords

We can also borrow a chord from a parallel key, then change its quality. This type of alteration is most common in mediant and submediant harmonies. We call such chords **chromatic mediants** and **submediants**.

Exercise 24.4: Performing Chromatic Mediants and Submediants Derived from the Parallel Minor

Tonicize each major key below (a–e) by performing a key-establishing progression such as I–ii⁶–V♮–3–I. Then follow these three steps:

1. Perform and spell the given chord in that key.

2. Now perform and spell that same given chord in the parallel minor key.

3. Change the quality of chord 2 from major to minor. Perform and spell this chord.

Finally, perform the original key-establishing progression again followed by the chord from step 3. Listen for the "exotic" quality produced by the chromatic mediant or submediant!

Example

	Step 1 Diatonic chord		Step 2 Borrow from the parallel key.		Step 3 Change its quality.
C Major:	iii: E-G-B	→	♭III: E♭-G-B♭	→	♭iii: E♭-G♭-B♭

(a) C Major: vi

(b) A Major: iii

(c) F Major: vi

(d) B Major: iii

(e) E Major: vi

If you think you hear a chromatic mediant in musical context, make sure you listen for its function and resolution. Don't confuse chromatic mediants with secondary dominants, such as III for V/vi.

Exercise 24.5: Performing Other Chromatic Mediants and Submediants

Tonicize each major key below (a–e) by performing a key-establishing progression such as I–vi–ii⁶—V⁸⁻⁷–I. Then follow these two steps:

1. Perform and spell the given chord in that key.

2. Now change the quality of that chord from minor to major. Perform and spell this new chord.

Finally, perform the original key-establishing progression again followed by the chord from step 2. These chords can sound startling.

Examples

	Step 1 Diatonic chord		Step 2 Borrow from the parallel key.
G Major:	iii: B-D-F♯	→	III: B-D♯-F♯
E♭ Major:	vi: C-E♭-G	→	VI: C-E-G

(a) D Major: iii

(b) B♭ Major: vi

(c) F Major: iii

(d) G♭ Major: vi

(e) A♭ Major: iii

II. CALL AND RESPONSE

Your teacher will perform a chord progression. After you respond with the call, respond with a variation of the call: alter any predominant chord by means of modal mixture.

Options for performing your response

Maintain the pitch, rhythm, and tempo of the call.

- Sing pitch only (with solfège syllables, scale-degree numbers, note names, or Roman numerals and figures).
- Sing rhythm only.
- Sing pitch and rhythm.
- Sing the progression in arpeggios.
- Conduct (or tap) with any of the above.
- Play on the keyboard or your instrument.

Options for writing your response

- solfège syllables
- scale-degree numbers
- note names
- note heads only
- rhythmic notation only
- notes and rhythm
- four parts (or just outer voices) with Roman numerals and figured bass

Part IV Further Expansion of the Harmonic Vocabulary

III. CONTEXTUAL LISTENING

EXAMPLE 1, TRACK 1.36

1. Which is the meter signature of the excerpt?

    (a) $\frac{2}{4}$

    (b) $\frac{3}{4}$

    (c) $\frac{9}{8}$

    (d) $\frac{12}{8}$

2. Write the bass line with solfège syllables.

3. Write the bass line with scale-degree numbers.

4. Write the melody with solfège syllables.

5. Write the melody with scale-degree numbers.

6. (a) Notate the pitches and rhythm of the melody and bass line on the staves below. Begin on C4 and F2, respectively. Include the meter signature, bar lines, key signature, and accidentals. Beam notes appropriately given your choice of meter.

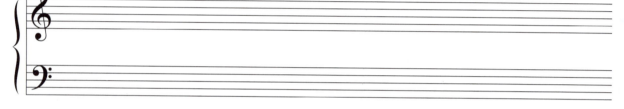

   (b) Beneath each bass pitch in your answer above, write the Roman numerals and figures of the harmony, or P if the pitch represents a passing tone.

   (c) Circle the symbol of each chord that is an example of modal mixture.

   (d) Write popular-music chord symbols above the melody in your answer above.

7. In chords 3–6, which is the linear intervallic pattern?

   (a) 6–6

   (b) 8–5

   (c) 10–7

   (d) 10–10

EXAMPLE 2, TRACK 1.37

Listen to an excerpt from a piano sonata by Mozart, and complete the exercises below.

1. Which is the excerpt's meter type?

    (a) simple triple

    (b) simple quadruple

    (c) compound triple

    (d) compound quadruple

2. Which best describes the excerpt's bass line?

    (a) basso continuo

    (b) pedal point

    (c) Alberti bass

    (d) walking bass

3. The highest melodic pitch is which type of embellishing tone?

    (a) anticipation

    (b) suspension

    (c) passing tone

    (d) incomplete neighbor *appogiatura*

4. The scale that descends from the highest melodic pitch is of which type?

    (a) major

    (b) natural (descending melodic) minor

    (c) harmonic minor

    (d) ascending melodic minor

5. Just after the highest melodic pitch, which of the following resolutions occurs?

    (a) deceptive

    (b) Phrygian

    (c) plagal

    (d) Picardy

6. Compared with the first chord, on which chord does the excerpt end?

   (a) I

   (b) ♭III

   (c) V

   (d) ♭VI

7. Which is the excerpt's phrase structure?

   (a) parallel period

   (b) modulatory parallel period

   (c) contrasting period

   (d) modulatory contrasting period

8. Beginning with the first bass pitch, write the strong-beat pitches of the bass line with solfège syllables (i. e., every fourth bass pitch).

9. Beginning with the first bass pitch, write the strong-beat pitches of the bass line with scale-degree numbers (i. e., every fourth bass pitch).

10. Write the melody with solfège syllables.

11. Write the melody with scale-degree numbers.

12. (a) Notate the pitches and rhythm of the melody and bass line on the staves below. Begin on B♭4 and B♭3, respectively. Write the appropriate clef, meter signature, bar lines, key signature, and accidentals. Beam notes appropriately given your choice of meter.

(b) Beneath each change of harmony in your answer above, write the Roman numerals and figures.

(c) Circle the symbol of each chord that is an example of modal mixture.

(d) Identify each dissonant embellishing tone in the melody in your answer above with P or N.

EXAMPLE 3, TRACK 1.38

Listen to an excerpt from a piano trio by Arensky, and complete the exercises below.

1. Which is the meter signature of the excerpt?

   (a) $\frac{3}{4}$ (b) $\frac{4}{4}$ (c) $\frac{6}{8}$ (d) $\frac{9}{8}$

2. Write the bass line with solfège syllables.

3. Write the bass line with scale-degree numbers.

4. Write the melody with solfège syllables.

5. Write the melody with scale-degree numbers.

6. (a) Notate the pitches and rhythm of the melody and bass line on the staves below. Begin on B♭3 and G1, respectively. Include the meter signature, bar lines, key signature, and accidentals. Beam notes appropriately given your choice of meter.

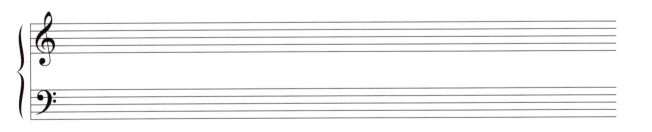

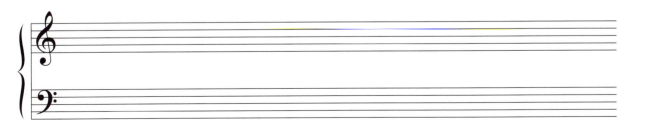

(b) Beneath each bass pitch in your answer above, write the Roman numerals and figures of the harmony.

(c) Circle the symbol of each chord that is an example of modal mixture.

(d) Identify each dissonant embellishing tone in the melody in your answer above with P or N.

7. Briefly discuss the internal structure of this phrase.

8. The excerpt employs which type of $^6_4$ chord?

(a) passing

(b) neighbor

(c) cadential

(d) arpeggiating

9. The cadential extension includes which type of resolution?

(a) deceptive

(b) plagal

(c) Phrygian

(d) Lydian

EXAMPLE 4, TRACK 1.39

Listen to an excerpt from an art song by Brahms, and complete the following exercises.

1. Which is the meter signature of the excerpt?

   (a) $\frac{2}{4}$ (b) $\frac{3}{4}$ (c) $\frac{4}{4}$ (d) $\frac{5}{4}$

2. In the piano introduction, which is the rhythmic relationship between the higher and lower parts?

Higher part		*Lower part*
(a) two pitches	against	three
(b) three pitches	against	two
(c) three pitches	against	four
(d) four pitches	against	three

3. In the piano introduction, the higher parts move in which generic harmonic intervals?

   (a) thirds

   (b) fourths

   (c) fifths

   (d) sixths

4. At the beginning of the first vocal phrase, which describes the motion between the vocal and bass lines?

   (a) voice exchange

   (b) contrary, then parallel

   (c) parallel, then contrary

   (d) entirely parallel

5. The first vocal phrase concludes with which type of $\frac{6}{4}$ chord?

   (a) neighbor (pedal)

   (b) passing

   (c) cadential

   (d) arpeggiated

6. During the first half of the vocal melody, the piano's higher part relates to the vocal line in which way?

   (a) It is an exact doubling.

   (b) It is a simplified doubling.

   (c) It moves in parallel sixths.

   (d) It is the same rhythmically, but uses different pitches.

Chapter 24 Color and Drama in Composition: Modal Mixture and Chromatic Mediants and Submediants

7. The entire vocal melody is based on which scale?

   (a) ascending melodic minor

   (b) natural (descending melodic) minor

   (c) harmonic minor

   (d) Dorian mode

8. Beginning on *fa*, write the solfège syllables of the vocal melody.

9. Beginning on $\hat{4}$, write the scale-degree numbers of the vocal melody.

10. Beginning on *re*, write the solfège syllables of the bass line that accompanies the vocal melody.

11. Beginning on $\hat{2}$, write the scale-degree numbers of the bass line that accompanies the vocal melody.

12. Notate the pitches and rhythm of the vocal melody and its accompanying bass line on the staves below. Begin on D5 and B2, respectively. Write the appropriate key signature and accidentals, meter signature, and bar lines. Beam notes to show their proper rhythmic grouping.

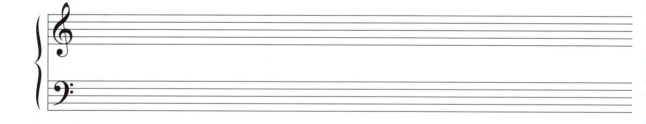

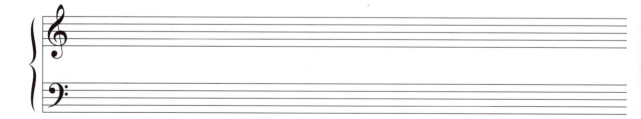

13. The cadences of the four vocal phrases occur in which order?

    (a) HC in III   PAC in i   HC in i   PAC in III

    (b) HC in III   PAC in VII   HC in i   PAC in i

    (c) HC in i   PAC in VII   HC in III   PAC in i

    (d) HC in i   PAC in i   HC in III   PAC in III

14. (a) In vocal phrase 3, the penultimate chord is of which quality?

       (1) Mm^7

       (2) mm^7

       (3) $\varnothing7$

       (4) $o7$

    (b) That chord quality is the result of

       (1) modal mixture;

       (2) cross relations;

       (3) chromatic descent in the bass;

       (4) the melodic minor scale.

15. The four vocal phrases form which larger structure(s)?

    (a) a phrase group

    (b) two simple periods

    (c) a parallel double period

    (d) a contrasting double period

16. Listen to the piano music that follows the vocal melody. How does it compare with the piano introduction?

    (a) The music is contrasting.

    (b) The music is the same.

    (c) The higher part is the same, but the lower part is varied.

    (d) The higher part is varied, but the lower part is the same.

MUSIC NOTEPAD

Part IV Further Expansion of the Harmonic Vocabulary

EXAMPLE 5, TRACK 1.40

This example is a folk song arranged for chorus by Bartók. The setting is deeply rooted in traditional music, but as you will hear, many of the sounds stretch the boundaries of functional tonality. Listen first to the entire excerpt, then as directed in the exercises below.

1. Which is the meter signature of the excerpt?

    (a) $\frac{2}{4}$ (b) $\frac{3}{4}$ (c) $\frac{9}{8}$ (d) $\frac{12}{8}$

2. Listen from the beginning until the voices enter. The chord that accompanies the first vocal pitch is the tonic. Is the tonic (a) major or (b) minor?

3. Listen to the piano introduction again. Write the first five pitches of the bass line with solfège syllables.

4. Write the first five pitches of the bass line with scale-degree numbers.

5. (a) Notate the first five pitches of the bass line on the staff below. Begin with B♭3.

    (b) Over each pitch in your answer above, write the quality of the triad that harmonizes it.

    (c) Write Roman numerals beneath each pitch. Use the quality of each triad to help you decide whether that Roman numeral should be upper- or lowercase. Circle any chord whose quality is the result of mixture or other chromatic alteration.

6. At the end of the piano introduction and overlapping the entrance of the voices, listen for a two-chord progression that is heard three times. This two-chord progression employs which type of resolution?

    (a) plagal

    (b) deceptive

    (c) Phrygian

    (d) Aeolian

Chapter 24 Color and Drama in Composition: Modal Mixture and Chromatic Mediants and Submediants   117

Listen to the excerpt again, concentrating on the vocal melody.

7. Beginning on *do,* write the melody with solfège syllables.

8. Beginning on $\hat{1}$, write the melody with scale-degree numbers.

9. Notate the pitches and rhythm of the vocal melody on the staves below. Begin on Bb4. Notate the pitches as the composer did, using accidentals without a key signature. Write the appropriate clef, meter signature, and bar lines.

10. Briefly describe the internal structure of each vocal phrase.

11. At the beginning of vocal phrase 2, which are the qualities of the piano's first two triads?

    (a) M–M

    (b) M–m

    (c) m–M

    (d) m–m

12. Which are the qualities of the piano's last two chords?

    (a) $\mathrm{Mm^7\text{–}M\substack{5\\3}}$

    (b) $\mathrm{mm^7\text{–}M\substack{5\\3}}$

    (c) $\mathrm{{}^{\varnothing7}\text{–}m\substack{5\\3}}$

    (d) $\mathrm{{}^{\circ7}\text{–}m\substack{5\\3}}$

For each of the melodies below, prepare to do any of the following:

- Sing on scale-degree numbers or solfège syllables.
- Sing or play the melody in its parallel key.
- Transpose to other keys on your instrument.
- Improvise a variant vocally or on your instrument.
- Identify chords and their inversions implied in the melody.
- Harmonize with chords we have learned since Chapter 12.
- Discuss aspects of phrase rhythm and phrase expansion.

Also be prepared to answer any of the following questions:

- What type of cadence is implied at the end of each phrase?
- What is the key signature for the parallel-key version?
- Which embellishing tones are implied in the melody?
- From which scale is the melody derived?
- Is there an implied tonicization or modulation?
- Which melodic pitches or implied chords are a product of modal mixture?

Melody 1   Brahms, Intermezzo, Op. 117, No. 1
Conduct this excerpt in a slow duple meter.

Earlier, we learned to conduct a quick "six" tempo in duple meter. In a slow duple meter, like Melody 1, follow the pattern below.

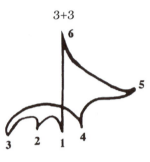

Melody 2 Ludwig van Beethoven, Piano Sonata in C Major, Op. 53 (*Waldstein*), first movement

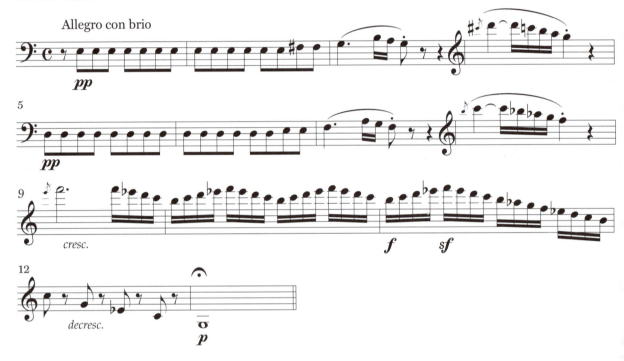

Melody 3 Brahms, Piano Sonata No. 1 in C Major, first movement (adapted)

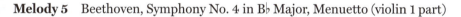

Melody 4 Brahms, String Sextet No. 2 in G Major first movement (violin 1 part)

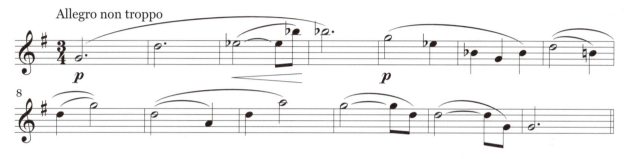

Melody 5 Beethoven, Symphony No. 4 in B♭ Major, Menuetto (violin 1 part)

Melody 6   Richard Strauss, from *Don Juan* (viola part)

Team Improvisations

Improvise a waltz from the melodic and harmonic outline below. While one person realizes the figured bass at the keyboard, another improvises a melody. If the soloist sings, use solfège syllables and scale-degree numbers that reflect the modal mixture.

At the end, there is a codetta; improvise musical gestures appropriate to that passage. For example, the performers might repeat the motive in increasingly embellished forms. Which chords are the product of modal mixture? How is the final cadence delayed? By what means is the last phrase extended?

Waltz

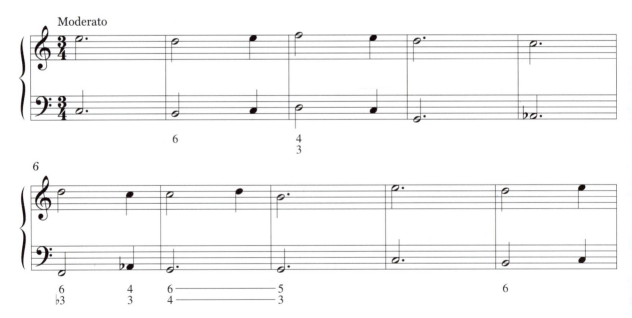

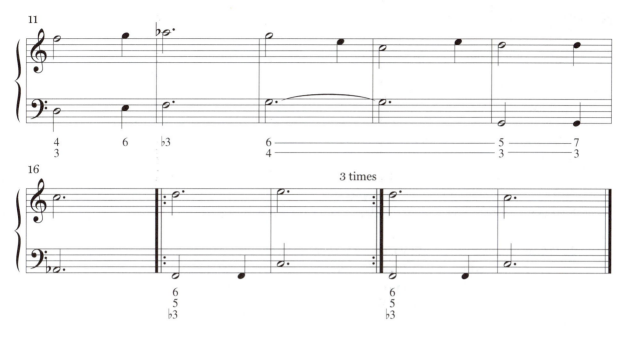

Variations

- A member of the class supplies a motive to the performing team, who must base their improvisation on it.
- Perform as a trio. A third performer plays a repeated accompaniment figure based on the first performer's motive.

Musical Challenge!   Transpose the **A** section of the Menuetto from Mozart's String Quintet (Chapter 23, p. 95) to the key of ♭VI. Use it as the **B** section of a sectional ternary form. To enhance the degree of contrast, change several aspects of the music, such as the register, texture, figuration, dynamics, and articulation.

- **A** Perform the Waltz (above).
- **B** Transpose the **A** section of Mozart's Menuetto to the key of ♭VI.
- **A** Perform the Waltz (above).

VI. COMPOSITION

Single-Line Melody: Rounded Binary

Compose a four-phrase, major-key melody that includes a tonicization of ♭III or ♭VI. Also include one or more predominant mixture chords (e.g., ii°⁶, ii°⁶₅, or iv). Follow the formal scheme outlined in the instructions in Chapter 22, section VI, "Single-Line Melody" (p. 68).

Use the "Contextual Listening" examples and "Melodies for Study" as models for your work, as well as ideas you learned in your improvisations.

Keyboard Trio

We realized the progression of the Allegro from Corelli's *Sonata da Camera*, Op. 4, No. 8, as a figured bass in Chapter 19 and as a composition in Chapter 22. Now we will combine those ideas with that of modal mixture to create a new work for keyboard and two instruments. Perform your compositions in class.

(a) Compose two parallel periods based on the progression of the Corelli movement (below).

(b) Choose a different meter from the one you previously realized.

(c) Add a codetta to the end of your composition.

(d) Notate the keyboard part as a figured bass and realize it in four parts, in keyboard style.

(e) To that accompaniment, add two instruments from those available in your class.

- Choose a concert key that will be "friendly" to your instrumentalists.
- One instrument should assume the primary role in phrases 1 and 3.
- The other instrument should be prominent in phrase 3.
- Feature both equally in phrase 4.

Adapted from Corelli, *Sonata da Camera*, Op. 4, No. 8, Allegro

Phrase 1   *Phrase 2* (We'll learn more about the sound of $\flat$II in Chapter 25.)

$\text{I}-\text{V}^4_3-\text{I}^6-\text{IV}-\text{V}-\text{V}^7-\text{I}$ $\text{i}-\text{v}^6-\flat\text{VI}^7$

                        V: $\flat\text{II}^7-\text{V}^7_{4-3}-\text{I}$

Phrase 3: Make a variation of phrase 1. Conclude with a PAC in the tonic.

Phrase 4: Start with the beginning of phrase 2, but return to a PAC in the tonic. Include a borrowed predominant chord in the final cadence.

Codetta: Extend the final cadence with a plagal resolution that includes a borrowed predominant. Model your conclusion on ideas from your improvisations above and in Chapter 23.

Chromatic Approaches to V:

The Neapolitan Sixth and Augmented Sixths

CHAPTER 25

Overview

In Chapter 25, we will learn to perform and identify two types of chromatic predominant chords that are native to minor keys: the Neapolitan sixth and the family of augmented-sixth chords.

Outline of topics covered

I. KEY CONCEPTS
  The Neapolitan Sixth Chord
  Augmented-Sixth Chords

II. CALL AND RESPONSE
III. CONTEXTUAL LISTENING
IV. MELODIES FOR STUDY

V. IMPROVISATION
VI. COMPOSITION

I. KEY CONCEPTS

The Neapolitan Sixth Chord

In a minor-key piece, when we hear *fa* (4̂) in the bass line move up to *sol* (5̂), we can ask: Is the chord over *fa* (4̂) *diatonic* or *chromatic*? If the chord is diatonic, we are hearing iv or ii°⁶. If it is chromatic, we are hearing a **Neapolitan sixth chord** (**N⁶**).

    To help us learn to perform and hear Neapolitan sixth chords, we first need to review the resolution of diatonic predominant chords. Each of the following numbered steps is illustrated in the music below. Play each step at the keyboard, and sing the outer voices with solfège syllables and scale-degree numbers.

1. Perform iv → V in the key of D minor.
2. Perform again, this time changing iv into ii°⁶ with a 5–6 technique.
3. Perform step 2 again, but lower *re* (2̂) one half step to *ra* (♭2̂), the Neapolitan pitch.
4. Finally, perform the progression Neapolitan sixth → V.

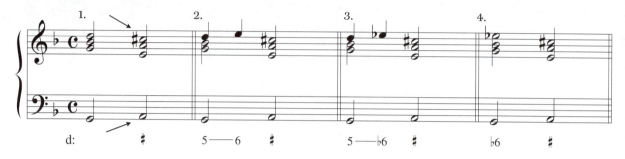

This method gives us the characteristic voice-leading and doubling for the Neapolitan sixth chord. The soprano falls from *ra* to *ti* (♭2̂–7̂) over a bass line that rises from *fa* to *sol* (4̂–5̂). *Fa* (4̂) is doubled, and the upper voices move contrary to the bass. Perform steps 1–4 again, in A minor, G minor, and B minor.

Because the Neapolitan sixth features ♭2̂ (indeed, if we stack the chord in thirds, ♭2̂ becomes the root), some textbooks label this harmony ♭II⁶. But because the origin of this chord is best explained by the voice-leading of the upper lines rather than by an altered root, the label N⁶ is preferable.

Like other predominant chords, the N⁶ may resolve to the cadential $^6_4$ (see example 5 below). It is also characteristic to hear the N⁶ move through vii°⁷/V to either V (example 6) or the cadential $^6_4$ (example 7). Perform examples 5–7 in C minor, E minor, and F minor. As you play and sing, listen for the chromatic melodies in the outer voices.

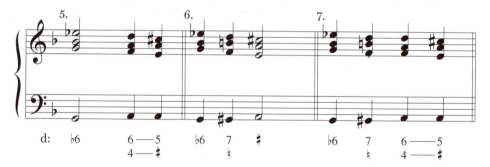

Exercise 25.1: Performing Neapolitan Sixth Chords from Figured Bass

Realize (i.e., play and/or notate) each figured-bass progression below, in keyboard style.

- Sing the outer voices with solfège syllables, scale-degree numbers, and pitch names.
- Analyze each progression, writing the correct Roman numerals beneath the staff. (The figures are already present, so there is no need to repeat them.)

Strategies for Listening and Performing

- Move the upper voices contrary to the bass.
- Double *fa* ($\hat{4}$) in the Neapolitan chord.
- Begin your soprano voice on *do* ($\hat{4}$) and let it fall toward *ti* ($\hat{7}$).
- Listen to make sure the quality of both the N⁶ and V chord is major.
- Use examples 1–7 above as models for your realizations.

Exercise 25.2: Performing Neapolitan Sixth Chords from Roman Numeral Progressions

1. Realize the following progressions in four voices, in keyboard style. Use keys that range from four flats to four sharps. Follow the strategies from Exercise 25.1. However, for (e) and (f), begin your soprano line on *me* ($\flat\hat{3}$).

   (a) i–N⁶–V–i

   (b) i–N⁶–V$^{6-5}_{4-3}$–i

   (c) i–N⁶–vii°⁷/V–V

   (d) i–N⁶–vii°⁷/V–V$^{6-5}_{4-3}$

   (e) i–i⁶–N⁶–V$^4_2$–i⁶

   (f) i–V$^4_3$–i⁶–N⁶–V$^{6-5}_{4-3}$–i

2. Give yourself the tonic pitch and sing these progressions as arpeggios in the keys of A minor, D minor, C minor, F minor, and B minor. Use solfège syllables, scale-degree numbers, or pitch names, and maintain good voice-leading.

(a) i–N⁶–V–i

(b) i–N⁶–V$^{6-5}_{4-3}$–i

(c) i–N⁶–vii°⁷/V–V$^{6-5}_{4-3}$–i

Sample realization of (c): The notes with the stems down are the implied bass line.

Augmented-Sixth Chords

When *le* (♭6̂) in the bass line falls to *sol* (5̂) in a minor-key piece, we usually hear one of two things. If the chord over *le* (♭6̂) is diatonic, the harmonization is typically iv⁶–V: a Phrygian cadence. If the chord over *le* (♭6̂) is chromatic, the harmonization is typically an **augmented-sixth chord** (A⁶) resolving to the dominant. We can use the Phrygian cadence to help us perform A⁶ chords and to help us hear the difference between these *le–sol* (♭6̂–5̂) bass resolutions. In each step below, sing the outer voices with solfège syllables and scale-degree numbers.

1. Begin on the tonic. Perform a Phrygian cadence in F minor. Tip: When we add a passing tone, the bass line descends by step from *do* (1̂) to *sol* (5̂) by means of the Phrygian tetrachord.

2. Perform step 1 again, but now create a chromatic passing tone between melody pitches *fa* (4̂) and *sol* (5̂). This chromatic tone, *fi* (♯4̂), and the bass pitch create the A⁶ interval that gives the chord its name and distinctive sound.

3. Like other predominant chords, A⁶ chords may also resolve to the cadential $^6_4$.

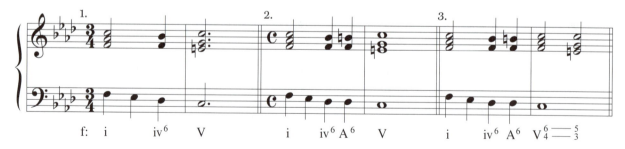

Another way to perform and resolve an A⁶ chord:

1. Play *sol* (5̂) in the outer voices (since the destination of an A⁶ chord is the dominant).

2. Play the chromatic lower and upper neighbors to the dominant—*fi* (♯4̂) and *le* (♭6̂). This creates the A⁶ interval. Resolve these chromatic tones outward by half step to *sol* (5̂).

3. Play the outer voices again, but add *do* (1̂) falling to *ti* (7̂) in an inner voice. This creates parallel tenths with the bass line. This A⁶ chord, with only three distinct pitch classes, is called the **Italian sixth chord (It⁶)**.

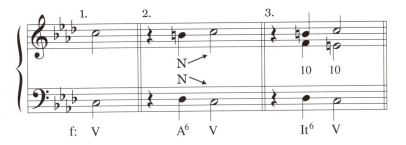

Besides the It⁶, there are two other common A⁶ chords: the **French (Fr⁶)** and the **German (Gr⁶)**. Perform the example below to hear all three types.

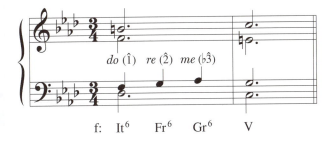

All types of A⁶ chords share the pitches of the It⁶ (the dotted-half notes in the example above). The pitches in the tenor voice above give each type of A⁶ chord its distinct sound and name: the fourth pitch of an It⁶ is another *do* (1̂), that of a Fr⁶ is *re* (2̂), and that of a Gr⁶ is *me* (♭3̂). To recall the sound of these chords easily, try to associate the melody *do–re–me* (1̂–2̂–♭3̂) with It⁶, Fr⁶, and Gr⁶.

This listening strategy can also help us recall the complete figured-bass notation for A⁶ chords. The figures for the It⁶ (⁶ and ³) appear as the top and bottom figures beneath each A⁶ chord. Between these figures is *do*, *re*, or *me* (1̂, 2̂, or 3̂), a third, fourth, or fifth above the A⁶ bass note. These are the pitches that distinguish one type of A⁶ from another. The figures are often abbreviated, as shown below.

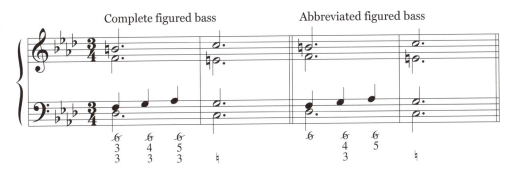

Although we could label A⁶ chords with Roman numerals, the labels make little functional sense, since the A⁶ chords are just voice-leading chords leading to V. If we are listening to the broader outlines of a work and hear an A⁶ chord, we simply write A⁶. If we are listening carefully to the tendency tones and inner voices, we write It⁶, Fr⁶, and Gr⁶ instead of Roman numerals.

- Compare the sound of the V^7/V chord with that of the Fr^6 chord. They both contain the same upper voices and lead to V chromatically, but their bass pitches sound a tritone apart. Thus, many jazz musicians hear A^6 chords as tritone substitutions for V^7/V.

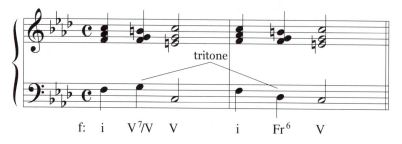

- The Gr^6 chord sounds like a dominant seventh chord (Mm^7), but one that resolves a tritone away from its usual chord of resolution—the Neapolitan.

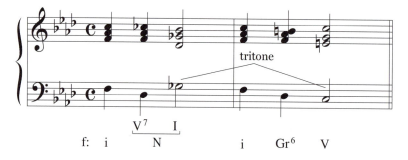

- The Fr^6 often features a M2 that resolves like the children's piece "Chopsticks" (but over a chromatic bass line).

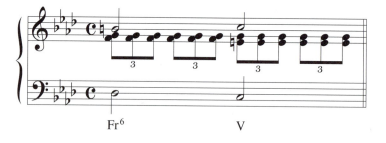

Exercise 25.3: Performing Augmented-Sixth Chords from Figured Bass

Realize (i.e., play and/or notate) each figured-bass progression below, in keyboard style.

- Sing each part with solfège syllables, scale-degree numbers, and pitch names.
- Analyze each progression, writing the correct Roman numerals or symbols (It^6, Fr^6, or Gr^6) beneath the staff. (The figures are already present, so there is no need to repeat them.)

- Move the soprano *fi–sol* (♯$\hat{4}$–$\hat{5}$), contrary to the *le–sol* (♭$\hat{6}$–$\hat{5}$) descent in the bass.
- Each A⁶ chord contains *do* ($\hat{1}$). Let this *do* ($\hat{1}$) fall to *ti* ($\hat{7}$).
- Double *do* ($\hat{1}$) in the It⁶ chord. Move this second *do* ($\hat{1}$) up to *re* ($\hat{2}$).
- Keep the *re* ($\hat{2}$) of the Fr⁶ as a common tone in V.
- Let *me* (♭$\hat{3}$) in the Gr⁶ fall toward *re* ($\hat{2}$) in V or the cadential $^6_4$.
- Perform with and without the A⁶ chord to hear the difference between the diatonic and chromatic approaches to *sol* ($\hat{5}$) over a *le–sol* (♭$\hat{6}$–$\hat{5}$) bass.
- Use the examples in this section ("Augmented-Sixth Chords," pp. 126–28) as models for your realizations.

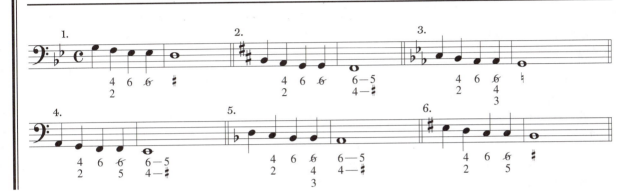

Exercise 25.4: Performing Augmented-Sixth Chords from Roman Numeral Progressions

1. Realize the following progressions in four voices, in keyboard style. Use keys that range from four flats to four sharps. Follow the strategies from Exercise 25.3. Where A⁶ is indicated, prepare to perform It⁶, Fr⁶, and Gr⁶.

    (a) i–iv⁶–A⁶–V or V⁴⁻³

    (b) i–iv⁶–A⁶–V$^{6-5}_{4-3}$–i

    (c) i–V$^4_2$–i⁶–A⁶–V

    (d) i–V$^4_3$–i⁶–iv–iv⁶–A⁶–V

    (e) i–i⁶–iv–i$^6_4$ –iv⁶–A⁶–V

    (f) i–V$^6_5$–i–A⁶–V$^{6-5}_{4-3}$–i

2. Give yourself the tonic pitch and sing these progressions as arpeggios in the keys of B minor, G minor, E minor, F♯ minor, and D minor. Use solfège syllables, scale-degree numbers, or pitch names, and maintain good voice-leading.

    (a) i–iv⁶–A⁶–V

    (b) i–iv⁶–A⁶–V$^{6-5}_{4-3}$

    (c) i–V–i–iv⁶–A⁶–V

Sample realization of (c): The notes with the stems down are the implied bass line.

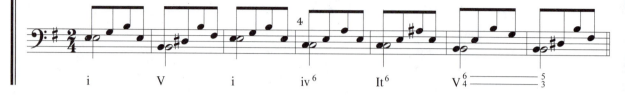

i   V   i   iv⁶   It⁶   V⁶₄ ——— ⁵₃

II. CALL AND RESPONSE

Your teacher will establish a key and then perform either a short or a long call. Your response will include either a N^6 or an A^6 chord.

A. An example of a short call is a chord followed by a rest. During the silence, determine which chord (N^6 or A^6) was played. Respond by repeating the chord of the call followed by one of its typical resolutions.

B. One type of long call will consist of a two-to-six-pitch melody. Respond first with the melody and then again with a harmonization of the melody.

C. A second type of long call will consist of a two-to-six-pitch bass line that includes figures. Respond by repeating the bass line with the harmonization indicated by the figures.

Options for performing your response
Maintain the pitch, rhythm, and tempo of the call.

- Sing pitch only (with solfège syllables, scale-degree numbers, or note names).
- Sing rhythm only.
- Sing pitch and rhythm.
- Conduct (or tap) while singing the rhythm only or singing both pitch and rhythm.
- Play on your instrument.

Options for writing your response

- solfège syllables
- scale-degree numbers
- note names
- note heads only
- rhythmic notation only
- notes and rhythm

Variations

- Listen for calls in compound meter(s) as well as simple meter(s).
- Listen for rhythmic patterns we learned in Chapters 2 and 5.
- Listen for calls from previous chapters.

III. CONTEXTUAL LISTENING

EXAMPLE 1, TRACK 1.41

Listen to an excerpt from an art song by Schubert, and complete the following exercises.

1. What is the meter type of the excerpt?

    (a) simple duple

    (b) simple triple

    (c) compound triple

    (d) compound quadruple

2. The beginning of the excerpt features all of the following *except*

    (a) tonic pedal point;

    (b) slow harmonic rhythm;

    (c) rhythmic ostinato in the accompaniment;

    (d) Alberti figure.

3. The third melodic pitch is which type of dissonant embellishing tone?

    (a) passing tone

    (b) neighbor tone

    (c) appoggiatura

    (d) anticipation

4. The first skip in the melody is which pitch interval?

    (a) M3   (c) P5

    (b) P4   (d) m6

5. The highest pitch in the melody occurs on which pitch?

    (a) *do* ($\hat{1}$)   (c) *le* ($\flat\hat{6}$)

    (b) *fa* ($\hat{4}$)   (d) *ti* ($\hat{7}$)

6. Compared with the beginning of the excerpt, the end is

    (a) transposed to the relative key;

    (b) an almost literal repetition;

    (c) rhythmically diminished;

    (d) in a different meter.

7. (a) Notate the pitches and rhythm of the melody and bass lines in the staves below. Begin on D5 and G2, respectively. Write an appropriate meter signature and key signature (or accidentals). Use shortcuts to help you recall repetitions in the music (for example, "⁄.," which means "repeat previous measure," or "c. 1," which means "copy m. 1").

(b) Listen again to hear the harmonies, then write the correct Roman numerals and figures beneath each bass note in your answer above.

Musical Challenge!

8. Listen again and transcribe the other pitches of the accompaniment. Use your answers to previous questions to help you.

EXAMPLE 2, TRACK 1.42

Listen to this excerpt from a work for piano by Clara Schumann, and complete the exercises below.

1. Which is the meter of the excerpt?

    (a) $\frac{2}{4}$

    (b) $\frac{3}{4}$

    (c) $\frac{6}{8}$

    (d) $\frac{9}{8}$

2. Which is the first pitch interval in the melody?

    (a) M2

    (b) m3

    (c) M3

    (d) P4

3. How does the rhythm of phrase 2 compare with that of phrase 1?

    (a) The rhythm is the same throughout.

    (b) The rhythm is the same at the beginning, but different at the end.

    (c) The rhythm is different at the beginning, but the same at the end.

    (d) The rhythm is different throughout.

4. Notate the pitches and rhythm of the melody of the staves below. Begin on G♯4. Use the appropriate clef and key signature (or accidentals).

5. Phrase 1 concludes with which harmonic progression?

    (a) IV–Fr⁶–V

    (b) ii⁶–vii°⁷/V–V

    (c) IV⁶–V⁶–I

    (d) V$^{6-5}_{4-3}$–I

6. Phrase 2 concludes *in the key of vi* with which harmonic progression?

    (a) V^7–i

    (b) $vii^{\circ 7}$–I

    (c) iv^6–It^6–V

    (d) iv–N^6–V

7. Which are the last two generic harmonic intervals between the melody and bass line?

    (a) 4–6

    (b) 5–8

    (c) 10–8

    (d) 10–10

EXAMPLE 3, TRACK 1.43

The questions below are based on an excerpt from a work for piano by Chopin.

1. The melody is based on which of the following scales?

   (a) ascending melodic minor

   (b) harmonic minor

   (c) major

   (d) chromatic

2. The beginning of each phrase features which type of $^6_4$ chord?

   (a) passing   (b) neighbor (pedal)   (c) cadential

3. At the end of phrase 1, which chord embellishes the cadence?

   (a) N^6 (c) Fr^6

   (b) It^6 (d) Gr^6

4. The excerpt concludes with which harmonic progression?

   (a) $ii^{o6}-V^{6-5}_{4-3}-i-V-i$

   (b) $iv-V^{6-5}_{4-3}-i-V-i$

   (c) $N^6-V^{6-5\ 8-7}_{4-3}-i-V-i$

   (d) $Fr^6-V^{6-5\ 8-7}_{4-3}-i-V-i$

5. The last phrase is expanded by which means?

   (a) There is a longer introduction.

   (b) The phrase beginning repeats.

   (c) There is a harmonic sequence.

   (d) A deceptive resolution delays the final cadence.

6. Which best represents the meter and duration of this excerpt?

   (a) $\frac{2}{4}$, 24 measures

   (b) $\frac{3}{4}$, 20 measures

   (c) $\frac{4}{4}$, 18 measures

   (d) $\frac{6}{8}$, 16 measures

7. What is the form of the excerpt?

   (a) parallel period

   (b) contrasting period

   (c) parallel double period

   (d) contrasting double period

MUSIC NOTEPAD

Part IV Further Expansion of the Harmonic Vocabulary

EXAMPLE 4, TRACK 1.44

Listen to an excerpt from a symphony by Brahms, and complete the following exercises.

1. Which is the meter type of the excerpt?

    (a) simple duple

    (b) simple triple

    (c) compound duple

    (d) compound triple

2. Which instrument doubles the violins' melody?

    (a) clarinet

    (b) bassoon

    (c) horn

    (d) trombone

3. (a) Notate the pitches and rhythm of the melody and the bass line on the grand staff below. Begin on G♯4 and E3, respectively (but be aware that the bass line is doubled an octave lower). Write the appropriate meter signature and key signature (or accidentals).

    (b) Listen again. Write the correct Roman numerals and figures beneath each bass pitch in your answer above.

4. Which pitch interval occurs between bass pitches 3 and 4?

    (a) P4

    (b) A4

    (c) d5

    (d) TT (tritone)

5. Label the generic harmonic intervals between the staves in your answer to #3.

6. The excerpt concludes with which type of cadence?

   (a) half

   (b) imperfect authentic

   (c) perfect authentic

   (d) plagal

7. At the cadence, the chromaticism is due to which of the following?

   (a) modulation to the relative minor

   (b) modulation to the dominant

   (c) Neapolitan sixth

   (d) modal mixture

EXAMPLE 5, TRACK 1.45

Listen to an excerpt from a work for piano by Bartók, and complete the following exercises.

1. Which is the meter signature of the excerpt?

    (a) $\frac{2}{4}$ (b) $\frac{3}{4}$ (c) $\frac{6}{8}$ (d) $\frac{9}{8}$

2. Write the melody with solfège syllables.

3. Write the melody with scale-degree numbers.

4. Write the bass line with solfège syllables.

5. Write the bass line with scale-degree numbers.

6. (a) Notate the pitches and rhythm of the melody and bass line on the staves below. Begin on E4 and E2, respectively. Write the appropriate clef, meter signature, bar lines, key signature, and accidentals. Beam notes appropriately given your choice of meter.

   (b) Beneath each bass pitch in your answer above, write the Roman numerals and figures of the harmony.

7. The fourth melodic pitch is which type of embellishing tone?

    (a) neighbor

    (b) passing

    (c) suspension

    (d) anticipation

8. During the last four pitches, the inner voice outlines which tetrachord?

    (a) major

    (b) minor

    (c) harmonic

    (d) Phrygian

9. The excerpt concludes with which type of cadence?

    (a) half

    (b) imperfect authentic

    (c) perfect authentic

    (d) deceptive

10. Briefly describe the internal organization of the phrase.

For each of the melodies below, prepare to do any of the following:

- Sing on scale-degree numbers or solfège syllables.
- Sing or play the melody in its parallel key.
- Transpose to other keys on your instrument.
- Improvise a variant vocally or on your instrument.
- Identify chords and their inversions implied in the melody.
- Harmonize with chords we have learned since Chapter 12.
- Discuss aspects of phrase rhythm and phrase expansion.

Also be prepared to answer any of the following questions:

- What type of cadence is implied at the end of each phrase?
- What is the key signature for the parallel-key versions?
- Which embellishing tones are implied in the melody?
- From which scale is the melody derived?
- Is there an implied tonicization or modulation?

Melody 1 Schubert, "Die Liebe hat gelogen" ("Love Has Proved False")

Translation: Love has proved false, sorrow weighs heavily.

Melody 2 Johann Sebastian Bach, Gigue, from Partita No. 3 in C minor (adapted)

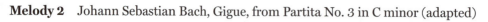

Melody 3 Mozart, Piano Sonata in F Major, K. 280, second movement (adapted)

Melody 4   Bach, Agnus Dei, from *Mass in B minor*

Melody 5   Mozart, Piano Sonata in F Major, K. 332, first movement
If singing, transpose the notes on the treble staff down one octave.

Melody 6 Bach, Kyrie, from *Mass in B minor*
Perform as a duet while a third person realizes the figured bass.

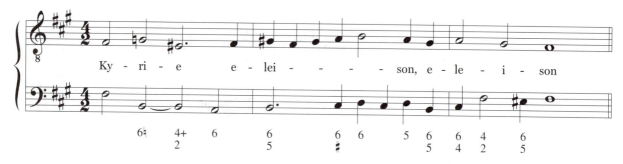

Ky - ri - e   e - lei - - - - son, e - le - i - son

V. IMPROVISATION

Improvise a melody to each of the accompaniments below. Prepare to perform as a soloist, singing the improvisation while you accompany yourself at the keyboard. You may also perform the progressions as duets. In that case, one person may sing or play an instrument while the other accompanies at the keyboard.

Strategies

- Practice each progression until you can play it in tempo.
- Begin by tracing a voice-leading line throughout the texture as you play.
- Fall to $\hat{2}$ at the conclusion of the first phrase and $\hat{1}$ at the final cadence.
- When you feel secure performing your melodic outline, gradually add consonant skips and passing and neighbor tones.

Improvisation progression 1

Write the correct Roman numerals and figures in the blanks below the bass pitches.

bb: _____ _____ _____ _____ _____ _____ _____ _____

Improvisation progression 2

Realize the progression below in four voices, in keyboard style.

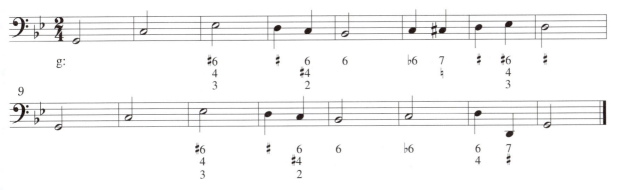

Variations

- Use solfège syllables or scale-degree numbers to help transpose these progressions to the keys of A minor, B minor, and C minor.
- Animate the texture of the accompaniment. For example, arpeggiate the chords instead of playing them as block harmonies.
- Once you have analyzed the chords in progression 1, perform using only the Roman numerals.
- Perform progression 1 in compound-duple meter and progression 2 in simple-triple meter.
- Establish a characteristic motivic rhythm with one of the patterns from Chapters 2 and 5.

VI. COMPOSITION

Composition 1

Compose a parallel period for piano and an instrumental soloist selected from members of your class. Include the following elements:

1. Two Neapolitan sixth chords. Resolve one directly to V; resolve the other with vii°⁷/V.
2. A cadential $\frac{6}{4}$ chord.
3. A passing $\frac{6}{4}$ chord.
4. Simple-quadruple meter.
5. Rhythmic values from sixteenth notes to dotted half notes.

Notate both solo and accompaniment, and prepare to perform your accompaniment.

Composition 2

Compose a parallel period for piano with yourself as soloist. Include the following elements:

1. An augmented-sixth chord in each phrase (you may choose which type).
2. Criteria 2 through 5 in Composition 1 above.

Notate your accompaniment as a figured bass. While you perform the solo, ask a classmate to perform from your figured bass.

PART V

Musical Form
and Interpretation

CHAPTER 26

Popular Song and Art Song

Overview

In Chapter 26, we will continue our aural analysis of art songs and learn to recognize the parts of classic American popular songs, contemporary popular songs, and the blues.

Outline of topics covered

I. KEY CONCEPTS
  Popular or Art Song?
  American Popular Songs
  The Blues
  Popular-Music Harmonies
  Extensions to major or minor triads

  Extensions to seventh chords
  Extensions to major-minor seventh chords
  Text Painting
  Jazz Rhythm
II. CALL AND RESPONSE

III. CONTEXTUAL LISTENING
IV. MELODIES FOR STUDY
V. IMPROVISATION
  Team Improvisations
  Solo Improvisation
VI. COMPOSITION

I. KEY CONCEPTS

Popular or Art Song?

There is a joke among musicians: What is the difference between an art song and a popular song? Answer: The number of copies sold.

The best of *both* art and popular songs feature a level of artistry and sophistication that the vast majority of their counterparts lack. Judged on their own terms, the "popular" songs of Duke Ellington, George Gershwin, Cole Porter, the Beatles, and Billy Joel are every bit as artful as the "art" songs of Schubert, Brahms, and Debussy. Thus, when we listen to *any* music with a critical ear, we should recognize those works that demonstrate exceptional creativity, sensitivity, and invention as "art" music.

In previous chapters, we have learned many techniques for the analysis of art songs. We use essentially the same strategies for popular songs. In this chapter, we will look at how composers interpret text through form, harmony, rhythm, melodic tessitura and shape, motivic structure, and other musical means.

American Popular Songs

Classic American popular songs originated in Broadway musicals and the music of Tin Pan Alley. Contemporary songs are more likely to be heard on the radio and in music videos. In terms of their form, both types of song share many features.

Classic popular songs may include three parts—**verse**, **chorus** (or **refrain**), and **bridge**. The verse is like a recitative, and the chorus-bridge is like an aria. Outside musicals, popular-song performances consist of only the chorus-bridge portion of the song. As we learned in Chapter 23, this portion usually follows a quaternary phrase design (**a a b a**, **a b a c**, etc.).

Contemporary popular songs typically alternate between one or more verses and a chorus. Verses convey the "story" of the song and create the energy that leads to the contrast, which is the chorus. While verses may be varied, the chorus is almost always identical each time. The "hook," the most memorable part of a song, often occurs at the end of the verse or during the chorus and frequently includes the lyrics of the song's title. Sometimes pop songs include a bridge, a segment that provides a moment of reflection, transition, or contrast. The bridge might be an instrumental interlude, for example.

The structure of contemporary popular songs can be traced back hundreds of years to the bar form. Often heard in the music of French trouvères, German Minnesingers, and early chorales, **bar forms** are a type of binary in which only the first part repeats (||: **a** :|| **b** ||)—much like the verse-verse-chorus plan of many contemporary songs.

The Blues

Originating in the music of Africa and transformed by African Americans in the United States, the blues may be the single most important influence in popular music throughout the world today. The blues style draws on the pitches of its own scale—the blues scale. Its structure is a recurring twelve-measure harmonic progression that is divided into three four-measure subphrases.

Perform the blues scale below with solfège syllables or scale-degree numbers. The spelling of the "flatted fifth" (e.g., the F♯ or G♭) changes to indicate that the intonation is higher when ascending and lower when descending. The accidentals in the scale are a form of modal mixture called **blue notes.** Despite the accidentals, we use the major key signature of the starting pitch.

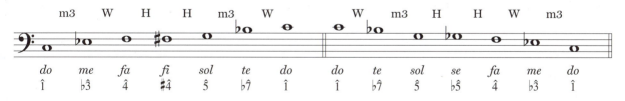

The blues progression typically features major triads or Mm^7 chords on $\hat{1}$, $\hat{4}$, and $\hat{5}$ in a twelve-measure form. The slashes in the notation mean that you should keep time as you prolong and embellish each chord. Play the progression without the parenthetical chords, then play with them to create a common variant.

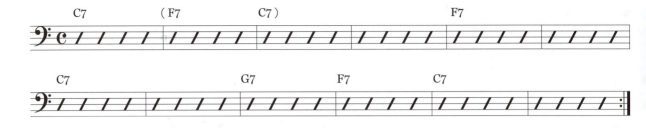

Exercise 26.1: Performing Blues Scales

Perform ascending and descending blues scales from each of the given pitches. If singing, use solfège syllables, scale-degree numbers, and letter names.

(a) B♭

(e) F

(b) E♭

(f) D

(c) A

(g) D♭

(d) G

(h) F♯

Popular-Music Harmonies

In Chapter 7, we learned popular-music symbols for triads and seventh chords. To these we can add additional pitches called **extensions.** From the perspective of traditional music, extensions are unresolved dissonances. However, in popular music, extensions can be *chord members,* equal in importance to the traditional root, third, fifth, and seventh.

EXTENSIONS TO MAJOR OR MINOR TRIADS

Common notations	*What to play*
Cmaj.^{6}, Cma^6, CM^6, C^{add6}, C$^{\Delta6}$, C^6	C-Major triad + M6
Cmin.^{6}; Cmi^6, Cm^6, C^{-6}, c^{add6}	C-Minor triad + M6
Cmaj.$^9_6$, Cma$^9_6$, CM$^9_6$, CY$^{\Delta9}_6$, C$^9_6$	C-Major triad + M6 + M9
Cmin.$^9_6$, Cmi$^9_6$, Cm$^9_6$, C$^{-9}_6$, c$^9_6$	C-Minor triad + M6 + M9
C^{sus4}, C^{sus}	C, F, and G (the fourth displaces the third)

EXTENSIONS TO SEVENTH CHORDS

Common notations	*What to play*
Cmaj.^{9}, Cma^9, CM^9, C$^{\Delta9}$	Cma^7 + M9 (MM^7 + M9)
Dmin.^{9}, Dmi^9, Dm^9, d^9, d^{-9}	Dmi^7 + M9 (mm^7 + M9)
Dmin.^{11}, Dmi^{11}, Dm^{11}, d^{11}, d^{-11}	Dmi^7 + M9 + P11 (mm^7 + M9 + P11)

EXTENSIONS TO MAJOR-MINOR SEVENTH CHORDS

Extensions occur most frequently with the Mm^7 chord, notated in parentheses. More than one extension may be played at a time. Depending on which extension is used, the Mm^7 chord may be complete or incomplete. Incomplete Mm^7 chords leave out the fifth.

Common notations	*What to play:* Mm^7 plus	$\rightarrow$	*additional pitch(es)*
G^9	complete		G^7 + M9 (Mm^7 + M9)
G$^{7\,(\flat 9)}$	complete		G^7 + m9
G$^{7\,(\sharp 9)}$	complete		G^7 + A9
G$^{7\,(\flat 5)}$	incomplete		G^7 + d5; optional: add a 9th
G$^{7\,(\sharp 5)}$	incomplete		G^7 + A5; optional: add a 9th
G$^{7\,(\sharp 11)}$	complete		G^7 + M9 + A11; optional: add a 13th
G^{13}	either		G^7 + M9 + M13
G$^{7\,(\flat 13)}$	incomplete		G^7 + M9 + m13

Though there are countless ways to voice extended chords, a quick way to get satisfying results is to put the root, seventh, and third in the bass clef and the remaining tones in the treble clef. Perform these examples of extended dominant harmonies.

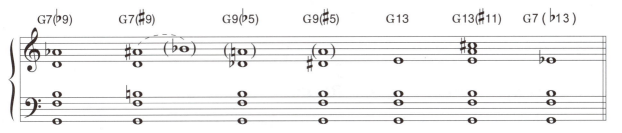

Exercise 26.2: Performing Extended Chords

Perform each chord below using several different voicings. Some chords can feature four parts, but many will require more than four.

(a) Bmi^7

(b) C$\sharp$ma^9

(c) F$^{7\,(\flat 9)}$

(d) A$^{7\,(\sharp 11)}$

(e) A$\flat$ma$^9_6$

(f) Dma^9

(g) B$\flat$mi^9

(h) E$\flat^{7\,(\flat 13)}$

(i) Emi^{11}

(j) F$\sharp^{13}$

(k) Ami^9

(l) E$^{7\,(\sharp 9)}$

(m) Cmi^7

(n) G^{add6}

(o) D$^{7\,(\sharp 5)}$

Text Painting

Composers use **text painting** to mirror the meaning of words or emotions in music. Sometimes text painting is quite literal, such as setting the word "high" to the highest melodic pitch in the phrase. Other times, it is more general, capturing the overall emotion of the text. Text painting can express subtle ideas as well, such as irony (e.g., setting the word "high" to the *lowest* melodic pitch).

Exercise 26.3: Text Painting

Track 1.36:   George David Weiss and Bob Thiele, "What a Wonderful World"

Listen to an excerpt from this song, which we studied in Chapter 24, and answer the questions below.

(a) How does the harmonization of the melody reflect the overall sense of the text?

(b) How does the music mirror the meaning of the words "think to myself"?

(c) Where does the hook occur?

Jazz Rhythm

The rhythm of jazz and blues is often "swung." We notate swung jazz in simple quadruple, but perform as if it were compound quadruple with accents on the weak parts of the beat.

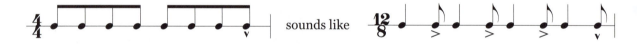

In jazz, listen for many syncopations, accents, and melodic anticipations.

Exercise 26.4: Performing Jazz Rhythms

Perform the jazz rhythms below, in a slow tempo. Perform again in a fast tempo.

II. CALL AND RESPONSE

Here, we'll perform twelve-bar blues progressions, in the characteristic three four-measure subphrases. Over the harmonies of the first subphrase, your teacher will perform a **riff**—a short melodic-rhythmic idea. Respond with the same riff over each of the two remaining subphrases.

Options for performing your response
Maintain the pitch, rhythm, and tempo of the call.

- Sing pitch only (with solfège syllables, scale-degree numbers, note names, or Roman numerals and figures).
- Sing rhythm only.
- Sing pitch and rhythm.
- Sing the progression in arpeggios.
- Conduct (or tap) while singing rhythm only, singing both pitch and rhythm, or singing the progression in arpeggios.
- Play on the keyboard or your instrument.

Options for writing your response

- solfège syllables
- scale-degree numbers
- note names
- note heads only
- rhythmic notation only
- notes and rhythm
- pop-music chord symbols

III. CONTEXTUAL LISTENING

EXAMPLE 1: Billy Joel, "She's Always a Woman to Me"

This song is not included on your CD. Instead, your teacher will place a recording on reserve in your listening room. We analyzed part of the chorus in Chapter 19's "Contextual Listening." Now we will listen to the entire song, focusing primarily on its text painting.

1. After the introduction, how do both meter and harmony symbolize the ambivalent nature of the woman to whom the song refers? (Hints: Conduct as you listen. Focus on the bass line to determine the chords.)

2. How does the composer paint the meaning of the words "she never gives out"?

3. In the lyrics below, each separate circle represents a different chord. In the key of V, which chord progression accompanies the circled lyrics?

And she never gives (in)
(She just changes her) (mind).

   (a) V: ii–V^7–I

   (b) V: IV–V^7–I

   (c) V: N–V^7–I

   (d) V: ♭VI–V^7–I

4. How does the music mirror the meaning of the words "She just changes her mind"?

5. Near the end, beginning with the lyrics "She is frequently kind," how is meter used to emphasize further the notion of the ambivalent nature of the woman?

6. Each time we hear the hook, where in the song does it occur?

7. Consider each verse to be **a** and each chorus to be **b.**
   Which best describes the form of the song?

   (a) **a a b a**

   (b) **a a ||: b a :||**

   (c) **||: a b :||**

   (d) **a b a b a**

EXAMPLE 2, TRACK 1.46

Listen to a phrase from an art song by Amy Beach, and complete the exercises below.

Wind o' the Westland blow, blow,
Bring me the dreams of long ago,
Long, long ago.

1. Which is the excerpt's meter signature?

    (a) $\frac{3}{4}$ (b) $\frac{4}{4}$ (c) $\frac{6}{8}$ (d) $\frac{9}{8}$

2. Which technique is featured in the bass line?

    (a) pedal point

    (b) Alberti figure

    (c) basso continuo

    (d) walking bass

3. Write the melody with solfège syllables.

4. Write the melody with scale-degree numbers.

5. Notate the pitches and rhythm of the melody on the staff below. Begin on B♭4. Use the appropriate clef, meter signature, bar lines, key signature, and accidentals. Beam notes appropriately given your choice of meter.

6. List several ways Beach's music conveys the meaning or emotion of the text.

Part V Musical Form and Interpretation

EXAMPLE 3, TRACK 1.47

Study the text to an excerpt from an art song by Fanny Hensel before listening for the first time. Then answer the questions below.

Ach Veilchen, armes Veilchen, wie blühst du aus dem Schnee?
(O violet, poor violet, how do you bloom in the snow?)
Im kurzen Sonnenweilchen, dann langem Winterweh, dann langem Winterweh.
(In the sun for a brief moment, then in long winter's pain, then in long winter's pain.)

1. Which is the rhythm of the accompaniment throughout much of the excerpt?

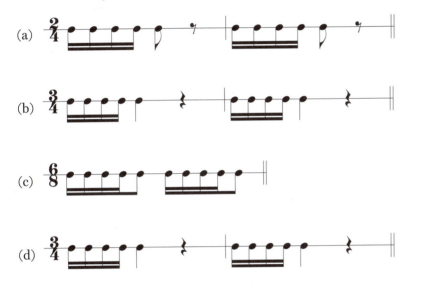

2. Write the melody with solfège syllables.

3. Write the melody with scale-degree numbers.

4. Write the bass pitches that occur on the beat with solfège syllables.

5. Write the bass pitches that occur on the beat with scale-degree numbers

6. (a) Notate the pitches and rhythm of the melody and the bass pitches that occur on the beat on the staves below. Begin on B♭4 and E♭3, respectively. There is no need to double the bass one octave lower. Use the appropriate clef, meter signature, bar lines, key signature, and accidentals. Beam notes appropriately given your choice of meter.

   (b) At each change of harmony, write the Roman numerals and figures beneath the bass pitch in your answer above.

7. The excerpt consists of a single phrase. Briefly describe techniques Hensel uses to expand this phrase.

8. How does Hensel evoke the meaning of "dann langem Winterweh" ("then in long winter's pain") at the end of the excerpt?

9. List two ways that Hensel signifies the meaning of "weh" ("pain").

EXAMPLE 4, TRACK 1.48

Much instrumental jazz is derived from song. Listen to an excerpt from one such composition by Count Basie, and complete the exercises below. All of the exercises refer to the music that happens *after the introduction.*

1. After the introduction, which of the following best represents the jazz rhythm of the trumpet?

2. From which scale are the pitches of the melody chosen?

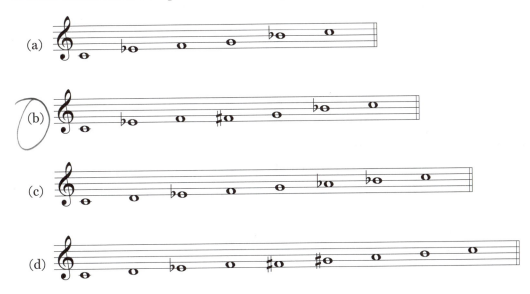

3. The initial melodic segment, or riff (four measures plus pickup), is heard six times during the excerpt. Notate the concert pitches of this riff on the staff below, beginning with E♭4. Write an appropriate clef and accidentals.

4. Now notate the pitches of this riff for B♭ trumpet, beginning with F4. Write an appropriate clef and accidentals.

5. Midway through the excerpt, the piano echoes the trumpet's riff. Notate the pitches of the four-measure piano riff on the staff below. Begin with E♭4. Write an appropriate clef and accidentals.

6. Notate the pitches of the piano riff for the E♭ alto saxophone. Begin with C5. Write an appropriate clef and accidentals.

7. In the second half of the excerpt, which of the following best describes the texture?

   (a) chordal homophony

   (b) heterophony

   (c) fugal imitation

   (d) accompanied call and response

8. While the trumpet plays, tap the beat and listen to the bass pitches at the beginning of each measure. Write the chord roots that sound on beat 1 in each of the measures below.

| 1 | 2 | 3 | 5 | 7 | 9 | 10 | 11 |

EXAMPLE 5, TRACK 1.49

This art song is from Schubert's cycle *Die schöne Müllerin* (*The Beautiful Maid of the Mill*).
The cycle tells the story of young love unrequited. We studied the melody and harmony of
the beginning of the song in Chapter 25. Now we focus on the song's text painting.

Poem by Wilhelm Müller (1794–1827)

Der Müller:

Wo ein treues Herze
In Liebe vergeht,
Da welken die Lilien
Auf jedem Beet;

Da muß in die Wolken
Der Vollmond geh'n,
Damit seine Tränen
Die Menschen nicht seh'n;

Da halten die Englein
Die Augen sich zu
Und schluchzen und singen
Die Seele zur Ruh.

Der Bach:

Und wenn sich die Liebe
Dem Schmerz entringt,
Ein Sternlein, ein neucs,
Am Himmel erblinkt;

Da springen drei Rosen,
Halb rot und halb weiß,
Die welken nicht wieder,
Aus Dornenreis.

Und die Engelein schneiden
Die Flügel sich ab
Und geh'n alle Morgen
Zur Erde herab.

Der Müller:

Ach Bächlein, liebes Bächlein,
Du meinst es so gut:
Ach Bächlein, aber weißt du,
Wie Liebe tut?

Ach unten, da unten
Die kühle Ruh!
Ach Bächlein, liebes Bächlein,
So singe nur zu.

The Miller:

Where a true heart
In love wastes away,
There wilt the lilies
In every bed;

There into the clouds must
the full moon go,
so that her tears
people do not see;

There angels
shut their eyes
and sob and sing
the soul to rest.

The Brook:

And when Love
conquers heartache,
a little star, a new one,
flickers in Heaven;

There spring three roses,
half red and half white,
never to wilt again,
on thorny stalks.

And the angels cut
their wings off
and go every morning
down to Earth.

The Miller:

Ah, little brook, dear little brook,
you mean so well,
Ah, little brook, but do you know,
what love does?

Ah, below, there below,
is cool rest!
Ah, little brook, dear little brook,
so just sing on.

1. Which is the overall form of the song?

   (a) binary

   (b) rounded binary

   (c) ternary

   (d) rondo

Exercises 2–7 refer to the beginning of the song.

2. Listen to the beginning, and list several ways Schubert musically portrays the miller's mood.

3. How does the motive that is sung to the word "Herze" mirror the meaning of the poetry?

4. The high point of phrase 1's melody occurs on "Liebe." How does Schubert's choice of melodic pitch reflect the meaning of the poetry?

5. How does Schubert associate "Lilien" with "Herze"? Why is this significant?

6. At the words "Da muß in die Wolken der Vollmond geh'n," how does Schubert paint a musical picture of the moon moving behind the clouds?

7. At the word "Tränen," how does Schubert change the motive first sung to the word "Herze"? Given the meaning of "Tränen," how is this significant?

Exercises 8–13 refer to the music from the middle to the end of the song.

8. What musical clues indicate when the brook sings?

9. How does Schubert's music portray the hopeful attitude of the brook?

10. How does the "Herze" motive change when the brook sings "Liebe"? What is the significance of this change?

11. What is the significance of the brook's highest melodic pitches and the words to which they are set? How do these high pitches contribute to the brook's hopeful attitude? How do these pitches compare with the miller's highest melodic pitches at the end?

12. Now listen to the end of the song, focusing on the words "Ach Bächlein, liebes Bächlein, so singe nur zu." Citing musical clues, describe how the miller has been influenced by his conversation with the brook. (Hint: Compare the setting of "Tränen" from the beginning with that of "Bächlein" near the end.)

13. How might your ideas about Schubert's text painting influence your performance of the song?

Study and perform each melody below to help get ideas for your improvisations and compositions. Harmonize the melodies: in Melodies 1–3, with the indicated chords; and in the melodies from earlier chapters, with chords appropriate to the nature of the song. Try including some of the extended chords we learned in this chapter.

Melody 1 Harold Arlen, "Blues in the Night"
Transcribe this melody into simple-quadruple meter.

Melody 2 Charlie Parker, "Billie's Bounce"
How has the blues progression been embellished here?

Melody 3 Thelonious Monk, "Straight, No Chaser"
How has the blues progression been embellished here?

Melodies from previous chapters:

Chapter 4, Melody 6   "St. James Infirmary"
Chapter 6, Melody 6   Richard Rodgers, "People Will Say We're in Love"
Chapter 6, Melody 7   Cole Porter, "I Love You"
Chapter 7, Melody 4   Franz Schubert, "Der Lindenbaum"
Chapter 8, Melody 3   Jerry Bock and Sheldon Harnick, "Sunrise, Sunset"
Chapter 8, Melody 4   Richard Rodgers, "If I Loved You"
Chapter 8, Melody 5   Amy Beach, "Oh Were My Love Yon Lilac Fair!"
Chapter 11, Melody 2   John Hewitt, "All Quiet Along the Potomac To-night"
Chapter 11, Melody 3   Jerome Kern, "The Song Is You"
Chapter 13, Melody 3   Irving Berlin, "White Christmas"
Chapter 14, Melody 3   Hoagy Carmichael, "Stars Fell on Alabama"
Chapter 15, Melody 4   Amy Beach, "Forgotten"
Chapter 15, Melody 6   Hugo Wolf, "Das verlassene Mägdlein"
Chapter 16, Melody 3   "Amazing Grace"
Chapter 17, Melody 1   "On the Erie Canal"
Chapter 20, Melody 3   Amy Beach, "Chanson d'Amour"
Chapter 25, Melody 1   Franz Schubert, "Die Liebe hat gelogen"

V. IMPROVISATION

Team Improvisations

1. Use the blues progression in section I, page 150, as the basis for a team improvisation. While one person realizes the chord progression on keyboard or guitar, a soloist improvises, drawing on the pitches of the blues scale. Switch parts and perform again.

Variations

- Play the progression in the style of an Elvis Presley song (e.g., "Hound Dog").
- Embellish the harmonies with extensions, and perform a riff-based improvisation like Example 4 (track 1.48), from "Contextual Listening."
- Transpose the progression to the keys of B♭, E♭, and F.

2. Each person in class transcribes a different popular song, notating the melody and pop-chord symbols. Then one person plays the chord progression from a classmate's song while another improvises a solo over it. Switch roles and perform again.

Strategies

- Most performers take great liberties when interpreting a song. Thus, in your transcription, you may simplify the rhythm and remove obvious melodic embellishments, leaving only the essence of the melody.
- Transcribe the bass line and remove any melodic embellishments; this will be the foundation of the harmonies you write. If the harmonies seem elaborate, you may simplify them as well, as long as you retain their original quality and function.
- Find a fake book to see how others have transcribed popular songs into **lead sheets** (a shorthand score for popular songs, giving the melody, chord symbols, and sometimes lyrics). Listen to a recording of the song and compare it with its lead sheet, noting how it is embellished both melodically and harmonically.
- When performing, try this common **A B A** plan: Student 1 plays the chord progression of the entire tune three times. During the first and third times, student 2 performs the "head" (the melody). During the second time, student 2 improvises a solo. Optional: Add an introduction and coda to this plan.

Solo Improvisation

Take the progression below as the basis for the verse of a contemporary popular song in a rock style. Embellish the outline as you sing your improvisation.

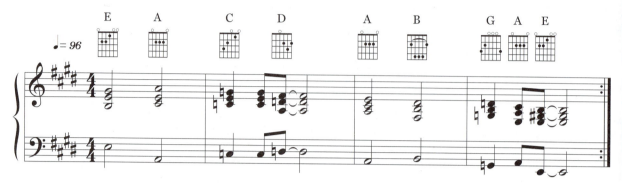

Variations

- Improvise a chorus, then play ‖: verse, verse, chorus :‖.
- Improvise a new verse that also features nothing but root-position major triads. Try to limit yourself to a maximum of three or four different chords.

VI. COMPOSITION

Taking ideas from your improvisations, compose a blues tune, a classic popular song, or a contemporary popular song. Write your own lyrics or collaborate with another student. Prepare to perform your song from a lead sheet on which the melody, lyrics, and chord symbols appear.

Strategies for Creating Lyrics

- Keep the language simple and direct.
- Most popular songs are about love—finding love, being in love, losing a love.
- Ballads often tell a story. Use the verse for the narration and the chorus to encapsulate the emotional impact of the story.
- The texture and dynamics of verses are usually lighter than those of the chorus; the verses build toward the chorus. The chorus builds toward the bridge.
- Include a hook in the chorus, the lyrics of which should be the song's title.
- Repeat the lyrics of the hook to the same melody and chords each time.
- In some music, like blues and rock, it is customary to use slang and poor grammar ("You ain't nothin' but a hound dog," "My momma done told me," etc.). In other songs, the lyrics can employ more sophisticated language and cosmopolitan references.
- When writing lyrics for the blues, try a sentence structure. Subphrases 1 and 2 state a "problem," and subphrase 3 states a consequence of the problem.

Sample blues lyric

	I		IV	I
Subphrase 1:	My baby done left me,		my baby is gone.	

	IV		I
Subphrase 2:	My baby done left me, didn't even pick up the phone.		

	V		IV	I
Subphrase 3:	Now that s/he left me,		I'm so alone.	

Strategies for Creating the Music

- Model your song on the song you transcribed in section V (Team Improvisations," #2).
- Use a standard form appropriate to the type of song you are composing.
- For contemporary pop songs, keep the chords simple and few in number.
- Create a tonal contrast in the chorus of contemporary pop songs or the bridge of classic pop songs.
- The melodies and chords on lead sheets are usually very simple; performers bring the music to life by embellishing them.
- For classic pop songs, tonicize different scale degrees using ii–V progressions.
- Create a "turnaround" between repetitions of the same music. A turnaround is a chord progression at the end that elides with the beginning of the repeated phrase. (For example, at the first cadence, perform iii^7–vi^7–ii^7–V^7. The iii chord substitutes for I in what would have been a PAC.)
- In all pop songs, parallelism, modal mixture, and harmonic retrogressions are normal and stylistic.
- Incorporate aspects of text painting that are musically appropriate to your lyrics.

CHAPTER 27 Variation and Rondo

Overview

In Chapter 27, we will learn to recognize by ear sectional and continuous variations as well as different types of rondos.

Outline of topics covered

I. KEY CONCEPTS
Sectional Variations
Continuous Variations
Rondo
II. CALL AND RESPONSE
Figural Variations

III. CONTEXTUAL LISTENING
IV. MELODIES FOR STUDY
V. IMPROVISATION
Continuous Variations
Solos and duets
Solos, duets, and trios

VI. COMPOSITION
Sectional Variations
Figural-variation duet
Character-variation solo

I. KEY CONCEPTS

Sectional Variations

Many movements or pieces are based on modified repetitions of an entire songlike small form (such as an **a a b a** phrase structure, a parallel period, or a rounded binary form). These are called **sectional variations**. The phrase structure and harmonic outline of the original small form—the theme—usually remain consistent in the variations, but composers might change just about anything else!

What usually stays the same:

- phrase structure
- outline of the harmonic structure

What often changes:

- mode (major to minor, for example)
- melodic figuration (in a **figural variation**, the same melodic figure appears throughout)
- timbre (or orchestration)
- texture, including textural inversions (e.g., the melody moves from the highest to the lowest voice)
- articulation
- dynamics
- rhythmic beat division
- tempo
- character
- register

Sectional variations frequently appear back-to-back, but sometimes there are interludes, transitions, or retransitions between them. (Transitions move the music to a new tonal area, whereas retransitions modulate back to the original key and theme.) Composers of Classical and Romantic music almost always use the entire structure in each variation. In more recent works, composers might truncate the structure of some variations, including only the first or second half of the theme, for example.

Exercise 27.1: Hearing Sectional Variations

Track 1.50

The following exercises are based on a theme and five variations for piano by Beethoven. First listen to the entire movement, then concentrate on the theme and each variation in turn.

Exercises 1–4 refer *only* to the theme, which may be divided into two large sections. Section 1 consists of four phrases. Sketch a phrase diagram to help you as you listen.

1. Which is the design of section 1's phrases?

    (a) **a a b a**   (c) **a b a c**

    (b) **a b a b**   (d) **a b c d**

2. Which is section 1's overall phrase structure?

    (a) two parallel periods

    (b) two contrasting periods

    (c) one parallel double period

    (d) one contrasting double period

3. Now listen to the design of the entire theme. Which is the design of the theme's sections?

   (a) **A A′**   (b) **A B**   (c) **A A′ B A′**   (d) **A B A C A**

4. Once again, consider the entire theme. Is its form (a) sectional or (b) continuous?

5. Now compare each variation with the theme, and list answers to the two questions below. For ideas of what to listen for, refer to the bulleted lists on page 175. Once you've finished, listen to the entire movement again.

	What remains the same?	*What is changed?*
Variation 1		
Variation 2		
Variation 3		
Variation 4		
Variation 5		

Continuous Variations

Continuous variations are usually based on a short, phrase-length theme, in contrast to the binary or ternary small forms of sectional variations. This "theme" is either a recurring bass line (a **ground bass**) or a recurring harmonic progression. The variations often feature phrase overlaps and other musical features that give them their continuous effect, in contrast to the "full stop" PACs typical of sectional variations.

Two terms you will hear for the different compositional techniques used in continuous variations are **passacaglia** (for the recurring ground bass) and **chaconne** (for the recurring progression). To remember which is which, associate *bass* with the first four letters of *pass*acaglia. Remember also that the chaconne technique is still practiced today. When musicians improvise solos over the blues progression or the chord changes of a jazz "standard," they are creating the contemporary equivalent of a chaconne.

Exercise 27.2: Hearing a Passacaglia (Ground Bass)

Track 1.51

The following exercises are based on an excerpt from a vocal duet with basso continuo by Monteverdi. Focus your listening on the repeating bass line. Then listen to how the upper parts create lovely contrapuntal lines against the bass.

1. Write the repeating portion of the bass line with solfège syllables.

2. Write the repeating portion of the bass line with scale-degree numbers.

3. Notate the pitches of the repeating portion of the bass line on the staff below. Begin on G2. Write the appropriate clef, key signature, and accidentals.

4. Briefly describe how the vocal part that enters second relates to the first.

Rondo

The plan of a rondo is simple: a refrain alternates with contrasting sections. We might sketch the plan like this:

	A	**B (C, D)**		**A**		
||:	Refrain	Contrasting section	:||	Refrain	Coda (optional)	||
		(usually two or three repetitions)				

Thus, typical rondo designs are **A B A C A** and **A B A C A D A**. If the rondo is also a palindrome (the same pattern forward and backward; for example, **A B A B A** or **A B A C A B A**), we may call it an **arch form,** or an **arch rondo.**

The character of rondos is often spirited and their tempos fast. Compared with the refrain, the contrasting sections are usually in a different key or mode (such as the parallel minor) and typically feature different melodic ideas.

Rondos may be composite forms; for example, the refrain might be a binary form. Recurrences of the refrain may be abbreviated. Some rondos include retransitional passages that lead back to the tonic-key refrain; these passages often feature interesting motivic development. Rondos often conclude with a coda.

Exercise 27.3: Hearing Rondo Form

Track 1.52

Let's revisit a work we studied previously (by Mendelssohn) to learn to hear rondo form. Listen to the entire work, and answer the questions below.

- If you hear the direct repetition of a section, that means it's *one* section, not two.
- To hear the contrasting section(s), listen for both (1) change of key and (2) change of thematic idea.

_____

1. How many sections do you hear?

   (a) 3   (b) 4   (c) 5   (d) 7

2. Which is the piece's section design?

   (a) **A B A′**   (c) **A B A′ B A″**

   (b) **A A′ B A″**   (d) **A B A′ C A″ B A‴**

3. Is there a coda?

II. CALL AND RESPONSE

Figural Variations

1. Your teacher will perform a phrase.
2. Respond with the outer voices.
3. The teacher will specify one or more types of embellishing tone.
4. Respond with a figural variation of the melody that includes the embellishing tone(s).

Options for performing your response
Maintain the pitch, rhythm, and tempo of the call.

- Sing pitch only (with solfège syllables, scale-degree numbers, note names, or Roman numerals and figures).
- Sing rhythm only.
- Sing pitch and rhythm.
- Sing the progression in arpeggios.
- Conduct (or tap) while singing rhythm only, singing both pitch and rhythm, or singing the progression in arpeggios.
- Play on the keyboard or your instrument.
- If the teacher performs an antecedent phrase, respond with a consequent phrase.

Options for writing your response
- solfège syllables
- scale-degree numbers
- note names
- note heads only
- rhythmic notation only
- notes and rhythm
- outer voices (or all parts) with Roman numerals and figured bass

III. CONTEXTUAL LISTENING

EXAMPLE 1, TRACK 1.53

The following exercises are based on a movement from a piano sonata by Haydn. First listen to the entire movement. As you listen, draw a diagram to help you remember the movement's structure.

1. Which is the excerpt's meter signature?

   (a) $\frac{2}{4}$

   (b) $\frac{3}{4}$

   (c) $\frac{6}{8}$

   (d) $\frac{9}{8}$

Exercises 2–9 refer only to the music of phrase 1. Phrase 1 is repeated.

2. Phrase one concludes with which type of cadence?

   (a) HC in the key of V

   (b) IAC in the key of I

   (c) PAC in the key of V

   (d) deceptive cadence in the key of I

3. Beginning on *sol*, write the melody with solfège syllables. Write **tr** for trill.

4. Beginning on $\hat{5}$, write the melody with scale-degree numbers. Write **tr** for trill.

5. Notate the pitches and rhythm of the melody on the staves below, beginning on A4. Write the appropriate clef, meter signature, bar lines, key signature, and accidentals. Beam notes appropriately given your choice of meter.

6. Melodic pitches 5 and 6 create which type of suspension? (Hint: Recall that suspensions are named according to the intervals above the bass pitch.)

    (a) 2–3

    (b) 4–3

    (c) 7–6

    (d) 9–8

7. Melodic pitches 12 and 13 create which type of suspension?

    (a) 2–3

    (b) 4–3

    (c) 7–6

    (d) 9–8

8. In the middle of phrase 1, the chromatic pitch is which type of embellishing tone?

    (a) passing

    (b) neighboring

    (c) suspension

    (d) anticipation

9. The end of phrase 1 employs which type of $^6_4$ chord?

    (a) passing

    (b) neighboring

    (c) cadential

    (d) arpeggiated

Questions 10–14 refer only to the music that immediately follows phrase 1, which we will call segment 2. Segment 2 is repeated.

10. Compare the beginning of segment 2 with the beginning of phrase 1. How is segment 2's initial motive related to phrase 1's initial motive?

    (a) Segment 2's motive is rhythmically augmented.

    (b) Segment 2's motive is transposed down one octave.

    (c) Segment 2's motive is inverted.

    (d) Segment 2's motive employs wider melodic intervals.

11. The first two chords of segment 2 create which progression?

    (a) V_5^6–I

    (b) vii$^{\circ 4}_3$–I^6

    (c) V_3^4/ii–ii^6

    (d) V_5^6/V–V

12. In the last phrase of segment 2, the beginning of the melody is doubled in which of the following ways?

    (a) thirds only

    (b) sixths only

    (c) thirds, then sixths, then thirds

    (d) sixths, then thirds, then sixths

13. The last phrase of segment 2 employs which secondary dominant chord?

    (a) V_3^4/iii

    (b) V_2^4/IV

    (c) V_5^6/V

    (d) V^7/vi

14. Segment 2 concludes with which of the following?

    (a) a cadential $^6_4$ that leads to a PAC in the tonic

    (b) a modulation to the relative-minor key

    (c) a falling-fifth sequence

    (d) a textural inversion (the melody occurs in the lower part)

*Questions 15–16 refer only to the **B** section, which immediately follows segment 2 and sounds in the parallel-minor key.*

15. Which is the **B** section's opening chord progression?

    (a) i–V^7–VI

    (b) i–V$_5^6$–i

    (c) i–V$_3^4$–i^6

    (d) i–V$_2^4$–i^6

16. The first half of the **B** section modulates to which key?

    (a) III

    (b) IV

    (c) V

    (d) VI

Questions 17–18 refer to the entire movement.

17. Which is the form of the movement's **A** section?

    (a) simple binary

    (b) rounded binary

    (c) simple ternary

    (d) composite ternary

18. Which is the form of the entire movement?

    (a) rounded binary

    (b) ternary

    (c) theme and variations

    (d) rondo

EXAMPLE 2, TRACK 1.54

The following exercises are based on a movement from a string quartet by Haydn. Listen to the entire movement, then answer the questions as directed.

1. Which is the excerpt's meter signature?

(a) $\frac{2}{4}$

(b) $\frac{3}{4}$

(c) $\frac{6}{8}$

(d) $\frac{9}{8}$

Exercises 2–6 refer only to the music of phrase 1. Phrase 1 is repeated.

2. Phrase 1 concludes with which type of cadence?

(a) half

(b) imperfect authentic

(c) perfect authentic

(d) deceptive

3. Write the melody with solfège syllables.

4. Write the melody with scale-degree numbers.

5. Notate the pitches and rhythm of the melody on the staves below. Begin on G5. Use the appropriate clef, meter signature, bar lines, key signature, and accidentals. Beam notes appropriately given your choice of meter.

6. From the middle of phrase 1, the harmonies are based on which progression?
   Hint: The middle is suddenly louder.

(a) falling fifths

(b) falling thirds

(c) ascending 5–6

(d) ascending fifths

Questions 7–11 refer to phrase 2. Phrase 2 is also repeated.

7. At the beginning of phrase 2, the motive is developed in all of the following ways except which?

    (a) It is inverted.

    (b) It is doubled in thirds.

    (c) It is transposed to the dominant.

    (d) It appears in a middle part instead of the highest.

8. Which is the only secondary dominant that occurs in phrase 2?

    (a) vii°^{7}/ii

    (b) V$^4_3$/IV

    (c) V$^6_5$/V

    (d) vii°^{7}/vi

9. Near the end of phrase 2, the motive returns in the highest part. At that point, which linear intervallic pattern occurs?

    (a) 5–10

    (b) 10–5

    (c) 10–6

    (d) 10–10

10. Phrase 2 concludes with which progression?

    (a) IV–I–V

    (b) V$^6_5$–I–V

    (c) ii–V–I

    (d) ii^6–V^7–I

11. Phrases 1 and 2 comprise which larger structure?

    (a) parallel period

    (b) contrasting period

    (c) phrase group

    (d) double period

Questions 12–18 refer to the music of phrase 3. Phrase 3 also repeats.

12. In which key does phrase 3 begin?

    (a) i

    (b) ii

    (c) iii

    (d) vi

13. Relative to the key in your answer to #12, phrase 3 modulates to which key?

    (a) III

    (b) iv

    (c) v

    (d) VI

In #14–#17, begin notating your answers in the key of the local tonic (the answer to #12). Then indicate the modulation, and change your syllables or numbers to the new key (the answer to #13).

14. Write the bass line with solfège syllables.

15. Write the bass line with scale-degree numbers.

16. Write the melody with solfège syllables.

17. Write the melody with scale-degree numbers.

18. (a) Notate the pitches and rhythm of the melody and bass line of phrase 3 on the staves below. Begin on A4 and A2, respectively. Use the appropriate clef, meter signature, bar lines, key signature, and accidentals. Beam notes appropriately given your choice of meter.

(b) Beneath each bass pitch in your answer above, write the Roman numerals and figures of the harmony. Indicate the modulation, and continue your chord symbols in the new key.

Questions 19–22 refer to the music immediately following the repetition of phrase 3.

19. The original motive returns in which part of the texture?

(a) highest   (b) middle   (c) lowest

20. The third entrance of the original motive features which type of motive development?

(a) fragmentation

(b) rhythmic augmentation

(c) melodic inversion

(d) change in articulation

21. At the fifth entrance of the original motive, which type(s) of motive development occur(s)? Hint: The fifth entrance includes the chromatic pitch *fi* ($\sharp\hat{4}$).

    (a) sequence and suspension simultaneously

    (b) normal form and inverted form simultaneously

    (c) fragmentation

    (d) rhythmic diminution

22. Just before the grand pause (long rest in all parts), which type of motive development occurs?

    (a) fragmentation

    (b) rhythmic augmentation

    (c) melodic inversion

    (d) change in articulation

Now listen several times to the entire movement. Sketch a diagram of the form to help you answer questions 23–25.

23. Which is the form of the movement's **A** section?

    (a) simple binary

    (b) rounded binary

    (c) simple ternary

    (d) composite ternary

24. Which is the form of the entire movement?

    (a) rounded binary

    (b) ternary

    (c) theme and variations

    (d) rondo

25. During the coda, which of the following does *not* occur?

    (a) motive fragmentation

    (b) call and response

    (c) secondary dominants

    (d) modulation to V

MUSIC NOTEPAD

EXAMPLE 3, TRACK 1.55

Listen to an excerpt from a piano work by Chopin, and complete the exercises below.

1. Which is the excerpt's meter signature?

   (a) $\frac{2}{4}$

   (b) $\frac{3}{4}$

   (c) $\frac{6}{8}$

   (d) $\frac{9}{8}$

Exercises 2–6 refer only to the first half of the excerpt.

2. Write the bass line with solfège syllables.

3. Write the bass line with scale-degree numbers.

4. Write the melody with solfège syllables. You may leave out the grace notes.

5. Write the melody with scale-degree numbers. You may leave out the grace notes.

6. (a) Notate the pitches and rhythm of the melody and bass line on the staves below. Again, leave out the grace notes. Begin on C♯5 and A3, respectively. Write the appropriate clef, meter signature, bar lines, key signature, and accidentals. Beam notes appropriately given your choice of meter.

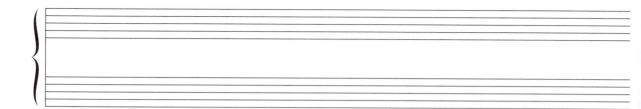

(b) Beneath each bass pitch in your answer above, write the Roman numerals and figures of the harmony.

(c) From the beginning until the half cadence, identify each dissonant embellishing tone in the melody in your answer above with P or N.

Exercises 7–12 refer only to the second half of the excerpt.

7. Write the bass line with solfège syllables.

8. Write the bass line with scale-degree numbers.

9. Write the melody with solfège syllables (leaving out the grace notes).

10. Write the melody with scale-degree numbers (leaving out the grace notes).

11. (a) Notate the pitches and rhythm of the melody and bass line on the staves below (leaving out the grace notes). Begin on C5 and A3, respectively. Write the appropriate clef, meter signature, bar lines, key signature, and accidentals. Beam notes appropriately given your choice of meter.

(b) Beneath each bass pitch in your answer above, write the Roman numerals and figures of the harmony.

12. What is varied in the second half of the excerpt when compared with the first?

(a) the mode

(b) the figuration

(c) the timbre

(d) the meter

MUSIC NOTEPAD

EXAMPLE 4, TRACK 1.56

The following exercises are based on an excerpt from a ballet by Copland. We are familiar with the beginning of this theme from our previous listening. Now we will hear the entire theme followed by five variations.

Exercises 1–8 refer only to the theme.

1. In the first half of the theme, which describes the accompaniment of the clarinet melody?

    (a) Violins sustain pitches *sol* ($\hat{5}$) and *do* ($\hat{1}$).

    (b) Violins sustain the pitches of the V chord.

    (c) Violins play the melody in augmentation.

    (d) Violins play the melody in canon.

2. Write the melody of *phrases 3 and 4* with solfège syllables.

3. Write the melody of *phrases 3 and 4* with scale-degree numbers.

4. Notate the melodic pitches and rhythm of *phrases 3 and 4* on the staves below. Begin on E♭5. Use the appropriate clef, meter signature, bar lines, key signature, and accidentals. Beam notes appropriately given your choice of meter.

5. At the beginning of phrase 3, which instruments double the clarinet melody?

    (a) violin and flute

    (b) oboe and violin

    (c) flute and piano

    (d) cello and oboe

6. Which is the phrase design of the theme?

   (a) **a a′ b a″**   (c) **a b a′ c**

   (b) **a a′ b c**   (d) **a b c d**

7. Which is the phrase structure of the theme?

   (a) two parallel periods

   (b) parallel double period

   (c) parallel period followed by contrasting period

   (d) contrasting double period

8. Which is the form of the theme?

   (a) simple binary

   (b) rounded binary

   (c) ternary

   (d) rondo

After the initial statement of the theme, there is a brief modulatory interlude. Variation 1 begins after this interlude, with the clarinet in its high register. Questions 9–11 refer to Variation 1.

9. Compared with the key of the theme, Variation 1's key is transposed by which of the following?

   (a) up a step

   (b) up a third

   (c) down a step

   (d) down a third

10. At the beginning of Variation 1, the clarinet melody is doubled by which instrument?

    (a) violin

    (b) bassoon

    (c) flute

    (d) piano

11. How much of the theme is featured in this variation?

    (a) phrases 1 and 2 only

    (b) phrases 2, 3, and 4

    (c) phrase 3 and 4 only

    (d) all phrases

Questions 12–14 refer to Variation 2. Note that Variation 2 consists of only three phrases.

12. At the beginning of Variation 2, which of the following occurs?

    (a) chromatic variations of the theme

    (b) figural variations of the theme

    (c) theme in inversion

    (d) piano ostinato in the accompaniment

13. At the beginning of phrase 2, how is the theme developed?

    (a) melodic inversion

    (b) canon at the octave

    (c) rhythmic diminution

    (d) fragments used in a sequence

14. Copland does not use all the theme's phrases in Variation 2. Which describes the portions of the theme he does include?

    (a) phrase 1 with one note change; varied repetition of phrase 1; phrase 2

    (b) phrase 1 with one note change; phrase 3, phrase 4

    (c) phrase 2; phrase 3; varied repetition of phrase 3

    (d) phrase 2; phrase 3; phrase 4

After Variation 2, there is a short, modulatory transition. Questions 15–17 refer to Variation 3, which begins after the transition in a faster tempo.

15. Compared with Variation 2, which is the transposition of the key of Variation 3?

    (a) up a third

    (b) up a fourth

    (c) a tritone

    (d) down a fourth

16. Which describes the texture of Variation 3?

    (a) nonimitative polyphony

    (b) chordal homophony

    (c) heterophony

    (d) monophony

17. In Variation 3, how much of the theme is featured?

   (a) phrases 1 and 2 only

   (b) phrases 2, 3, and 4

   (c) phrases 3 and 4 only

   (d) all phrases

Questions 18–21 refer to Variation 4, which begins slower suddenly.

18. At the very beginning of this variation, listen carefully to the flute and bassoon. Which describes the way Copland develops the theme?

   (a) The flute plays the **a** phrase while the bassoon plays the **b** phrase.

   (b) The flute plays the **b** phrase while the bassoon plays the **a** phrase.

   (c) The flute and bassoon play the **a** phrase, doubled in octaves.

   (d) The flute and bassoon play the **b** phrase, doubled in octaves.

19. Which is the role of the strings?

   (a) They accompany the winds with sustained chords.

   (b) They accompany the winds with pizzicato chords.

   (c) They play the bass line.

   (d) They rest.

20. How many phrases comprise Variation 4?

   (a) one phrase

   (b) two phrases

   (c) three phrases

   (d) all of the theme

21. Which is the last harmonic interval?

   (a) unison/octave   (b) third   (c) fourth   (d) fifth

The remaining exercises refer to Variation 5, which is louder and in a slow, majestic tempo.

22. Write the bass line with solfège syllables.

23. Write the bass line with scale-degree numbers.

24. Beginning on C, notate the pitch classes and rhythm of the bass line on the staves below. You may write in any octave. Use the appropriate clef, meter signatures, bar lines, key signature, and accidentals.

25. Variation 5 consists of which part of the theme?

(a) the first half

(b) the middle (phrases 2 and 3)

(c) the second half

(d) all of it

Part V Musical Form and Interpretation

EXAMPLE 5, TRACK 1.57

Listen to three phrases from a symphony by Brahms, and complete the exercises below.

1. Which is the excerpt's meter signature?

   (a) $\frac{2}{4}$ (b) $\frac{3}{4}$ (c) $\frac{6}{8}$ (d) $\frac{9}{8}$

Exercises 2–8 refer only to the theme, which is the music of phrase 1.

2. Write the bass line with solfège syllables.

3. Write the bass line with scale-degree numbers.

4. Write the melody with solfège syllables.

5. Write the melody with scale-degree numbers.

6. (a) Notate the pitches and rhythm of the melody and bass line on the staves below. Begin on B3 and E3, respectively. (There is no need to double the bass line one octave lower.) Write the appropriate clef, meter signature, bar lines, key signature, and accidentals.

   (b) Beneath each bass pitch in your answer above, write the Roman numerals and figures of the harmony.

7. The penultimate melodic pitch is which type of embellishing tone?

   (a) passing

   (b) anticipation

   (c) retardation

   (d) chordal skip

8. At the end of the melody, which rhythmic feature occurs?

   (a) hemiola

   (b) anacrusis

   (c) three against two

   (d) asymmetrical meter

Exercises 9–12 refer to the music of phrase 2.

9. Using solfège syllables, write the bass pitch that occurs on each downbeat. Hint: Listen for the pizzicati in the double basses.

10. Using scale-degree numbers, write the bass pitch that occurs on each downbeat. Hint: Listen for the pizzicati in the double basses.

11. Transcribe your answers to #9 and #10 into pitch classes and rhythm on the staff below. Begin on E2. (There is no need to double the bass line one octave lower.) Assume each pitch lasts for the entire measure. Write the appropriate clef, meter signature, bar lines, key signature, and accidentals.

12. Compare the first melodic subphrase of phrases 1 and 2. In phrase 2's first subphrase, the melody includes which embellishing tones?

   (a) passing tones only

   (b) passing tones and a suspension

   (c) neighbor tones and a suspension

   (d) suspensions only

Exercises 13–17 refer to the music of phrase 3.

13. Write the bass line with solfège syllables.

14. Write the bass line with scale-degree numbers.

15. Notate the pitch classes and rhythm of the bass line on the staff below. Begin on E2. (There is no need to double the bass line one octave lower.) Write the appropriate clef, meter signature, bar lines, key signature, and accidentals.

16. The melody of phrase 3 may be divided into short subphrases, each of which begins with a characteristic pattern of three intervals. Which are the generic pitch intervals of this motivic pattern?

    (a) second–third–second

    (b) second–fourth–second

    (c) third–fourth–third

    (d) third–fifth–second

17. During phrases 2 and 3, which rhythmic feature occurs?

    (a) hemiola

    (b) changing meter

    (c) three against two

    (d) syncopation

The last question refers to the entire excerpt.

18. Considering your answers to all previous exercises, which type of variations does Brahms employ in this movement?

    (a) chaconne

    (b) passacaglia (ground bass)

    (c) figural variations

    (d) character variations

For each of the melodies below, prepare to do any of the following:

- Sing on scale-degree numbers or solfège syllables.
- Sing or play the melody in its parallel key.
- Transpose to other keys on your instrument.
- Identify chords and their inversions implied in the melody.
- Harmonize with chords we have learned since Chapter 12.
- Discuss aspects of phrase rhythm and phrase expansion.
- Improvise variations appropriate to the melody.

Also be prepared to answer any of the following questions:

- What type of cadence is implied at the end of each phrase?
- What is the key signature for the parallel-key versions?
- Which embellishing tones are implied in the melody?
- From which scale is the melody derived?
- Is there an implied tonicization or modulation?
- Which melodic pitches or implied chords are a product of modal mixture?

Melody 1 Wolfgang Amadeus Mozart, Clarinet Quintet, K. 581, fourth movement
Look at the clarinet's key signature on the top staff. Which type of clarinet does Mozart
call for? In addition to improvising variations, treat the first eight measures as a refrain, and
create a rondo.

Melody 2   Brahms, Variations on an Original Theme for Piano, Op. 21, No. 1
In addition to improvising variations, treat the first eight measures as a refrain, and create
a rondo.

Perform the next three melodies as duets. One person realizes the accompaniment (the
ground basses of the Purcell or the chords of the Strauss), while the other improvises
melodic variations.

Melody 3   Henry Purcell, ground bass from "A New Ground," an arrangement of "Here
the Deities Approve," from *Musick's Hand-Maid*
Because of its harmonic rhythm, perform this melody no faster than *andante*.

Melody 4   Purcell, ground bass from "Ground in Gamut," from *Musick's Hand-Maid*

Melody 5   Johann Strauss Jr., "The Beautiful Blue Danube" (adapted)
Revisit this waltz from Chapter 6 (Melody 8). Harmonize the phrase, concluding with an augmented-sixth chord in the key of vi.

V. IMPROVISATION

Continuous Variations

SOLOS AND DUETS

Determine the harmonic and melodic implications of the bass line below, then perform a series of continuous variations.

- Perform the bass line by itself. Then on the first repetition, sing a simple melody in counterpoint.
- On each successive repetition, make your melody increasingly elaborate.
- After your most elaborate embellishment, recapitulate the simple (first) melody as the last variation.
- Conclude this last variation on the tonic.

D:

Variations

- Perform as a duet instead. While one person performs the ground bass, the other performs the melody.
- Perform with instruments other than keyboard and voice. Change to a key suitable for both instruments.
- Perform in the parallel minor.

SOLOS, DUETS, AND TRIOS

Following the instructions above (for "Solos and Duets"), improvise a series of continuous variations on the outline below.

- *Solos:* Play the outline at the keyboard, and improvise a melody. Sing with solfège syllables or scale-degree numbers.
- *Duets:* One person improvises a keyboard accompaniment from the outline while the other improvises a melody. Switch parts and perform again.
- *Trios:* Two different instrumentalists improvise on the outline while a third improvises a melody above. Change parts so that each performer has a turn improvising the melody.

d: i   10-10 LIP —————————— V   VI ii⁶ V i

VI. COMPOSITION

Sectional Variations

FIGURAL-VARIATION DUET

After you have completed and checked your answers to "Contextual Listening" Example 3 (track 1.55), compose three figural variations based on the phrase structure of the first half of this excerpt. Perform your variations while a partner accompanies you, playing from the bass line and Roman numerals taken in dictation. Switch roles and accompany your partner's performance.

- For your performance, play Chopin's melody, then each of your variations.
- Perform your melody on your instrument. If you sing, use solfège syllables and scale-degree numbers.
- Make your figurations increasingly elaborate.
- Optional: Add a codetta after your last variation.

CHARACTER-VARIATION SOLO

After you have completed and checked your answers to "Contextual Listening" Example 4 (track 1.56), compose three character variations based on the theme. Prepare to perform the variations on your instrument.

- Retain the theme's phrase structure and harmonic outline.
- Review the bulleted list *What often changes* on page 175.
- Create an **A B A** structure. For example, Variations 1 and 3 might be fast, and Variation 2 be slow.
- Optional: Add a codetta.

CHAPTER 28

Sonata-Form Movements

Overview

This chapter is the culmination of much of what we have learned about tonal music. Among other things, motives, phrases, periods, modulations, sequences, and small forms all contribute to the creation of a sonata-form movement. In this chapter, we will learn to recognize the parts of a sonata form by ear, then demonstrate our understanding by composing a sonata-form movement.

Outline of topics covered

I. KEY CONCEPTS
Exposition
Development
Recapitulation
Coda

II. CALL AND RESPONSE

III. CONTEXTUAL LISTENING

IV. MELODIES FOR STUDY

V. IMPROVISATION

VI. COMPOSITION
Sonata-Form Movement for Piano

I. KEY CONCEPTS

The term **sonata** has three meanings in music. In medieval times, the word meant an instrumental piece, as opposed to a sung piece. "Sonata" is also the term we apply to a genre of multimovement works: from the instrumental sonata (for piano, violin, or cello, for example) to the string quartet, piano trio, concerto, and symphony, which is a sonata for orchestra.

Here, we focus on the third meaning, which refers to the **form** of an individual movement. **Sonata form** developed from rounded binary form. As sonata-form movements grew into larger and more sophisticated works, they also assumed some characteristics of ternary form.

The sections below list the parts of a sonata form and listening strategies for each. These are general strategies; not all of them apply to every sonata-form movement.

EXPOSITION

The **exposition** is analogous to the **A** section of a rounded binary or ternary form, except that it always includes more than one key area. It is made up of several subsections, including F, t, S, and (optionally) CL, as described below.

F: The **first theme group** (**F**) establishes the tonic key.

Listen for:
- tonally stable music, such as a phrase or period in the tonic key
- important motives, including both melodic and harmonic patterns

t: The **transition** (**t**) moves the composition from the tonic key area to a related key.

Listen for:
- modulation to V (in major-key movements) or III (in minor-key movements)
- tonally unstable music, such as sequences, LIPs, and the like
- a half cadence in the new key at the end of the transition
- a rest at the end of the transition
- material based on motive(s) of F (**dependent transition**)
- new motivic material (**independent transition**)

S: The **second theme group** (**S**) establishes a key closely related to the tonic.

Listen for:
- a half cadence in the new key; S follows this half cadence
- a rest at the end of the transition; S immediately follows the rest
- tonally stable music such as period structures, in the key of V (major-key movements) or III (minor-key movements)
- new theme(s), though some sonata-form movements repeat F's theme(s) during S
- changes in dynamics, register, articulation, texture, or any other elements we have learned to associate with structural division in music

CL: If present, the **closing theme** (**CL**) is generally the last part of the second theme group (and is in the same key). CL may serve as a codetta to the sonata's first section.

Listen for:
- music that reinforces the second key
- coda-like music
- repeated perfect authentic cadences in the second key
- music that sounds like a larger-scale cadential extension
- "bravura"—flashy or virtuosic—passages

In Classical and early Romantic sonata-form movements, listen for a repeat of the exposition.

DEVELOPMENT

Appearing in the same location as the **B** section of a rounded binary or ternary form, the **development** may contain modulatory and sequential passages; it often develops motives from the exposition. The German term for "development" is *Durchführung* — a "leading through." Like most music, sonata-form movements employ motivic development from the outset of the composition. "Leading through" reinforces the idea of tonal digression and the eventual return to the tonic key.

Listen for:
- tonally unstable music, like sequences and LIPs
- more chromaticism
- possible tonicizations of other keys
- more motivic development of ideas from the exposition

r: The **retransition** (**r**) is the music occurring at the end of the development, immediately preceding the recapitulation. It prepares for this return by prolonging the V chord in the tonic key.

Listen for:
- the V chord, often preceded by its dominant or an A^6 chord
- a thinning of texture
- V to change from a key area with its own leading tone back to the dominant chord
- a dominant pedal point
- a *ritardando* and a release of tension

RECAPITULATION

The **recapitulation** is the return of themes from the exposition in the tonic key.

Listen for:
- F, S, and CL to recur
- F, S, and CL all to be in the tonic key
- changes to t that prevent it from modulating

CODA

If present, the **coda** brings a sense of closure to the movement. A coda is to the movement what a cadential extension is to the phrase.

Listen for:
- those items listed in CL above
- pedal points
- plagal extensions

In sonatas by Beethoven and later composers, listen for more development, and even new themes!

II. CALL AND RESPONSE

Since sonata-form movements bring together many of the ideas we have studied thus far, your teacher will review several previous "Call and Response" sections. Further practice in hearing these components will improve your recognition of them in the "Contextual Listening" section. (In the chapters listed below, review the "Key Concepts" sections as well.)

Concept	Chapters
A. Motive development	9, 13, 18
B. Phrase structure and organization	12, 17, 20
C. Tonicization and modulation	19, 21, 22

MUSIC NOTEPAD

Part V Musical Form and Interpretation

III. CONTEXTUAL LISTENING

While listening to each example below, refer to the sonata-form chart at the beginning of the chapter for reminders of what to listen for.

EXAMPLE 1, TRACK 2.1

Listen to a movement from a piano sonata by Haydn, and complete the exercises below.

1. Which is the excerpt's meter signature?

   (a) $\frac{2}{4}$ (b) $\frac{3}{4}$ (c) $\frac{6}{8}$ (d) $\frac{9}{8}$

Exercises 2–7 refer only to the music of phrase 1, which is the first theme group (F). The phrase ends with silence.

2. Write the melody with solfège syllables. Write *tr* for trill.

3. Write the melody with scale-degree numbers. Write *tr* for trill.

4. Write the bass line with solfège syllables.

5. Write the bass line with scale-degree numbers.

6. (a) Notate the pitches and rhythm of the melody and bass line on the staves below. Begin on G4 and E2, respectively. Use the appropriate clef, meter signature, bar lines, key signature, and accidentals. Beam notes appropriately given your choice of meter.

(b) Beneath each bass pitch in your answer above, write the Roman numerals and figures of the harmony.

(c) Identify each dissonant embellishing tone in the melody in your answer above with P or N.

7. This movement is based on a three-pitch melodic motive, which begins as a descending third. We'll call this motive x. Circle each occurrence of motive x in your answer to #6. Prepare to explain the relationships between them.

Exercises 8–11 refer only to t, the music of the transition. The transition immediately follows phrase 1 and ends with an ascending scale, a descending arpeggio, and a brief silence.

8. Is the transition (a) dependent or (b) independent?

9. The transition's sequence is based on which progression?

(a) falling fifths   (c) ascending 5–6

(b) falling thirds   (d) ascending fifths

10. After the sequence, a two-beat idea (with a trill) is heard three times. Beginning with this idea, with which chord progression does the transition conclude?

(a) III: I–ii$^6_5$–I–ii$^6_5$–I–ii$^6_5$–vii°^{7}/V –V –vii°^{6}/V– V^6–V

(b) III: I–IV–I–IV–I–IV– V^7/V –V –V^7/V –V –V^6–V

(c) III: I–V–I–V–I–V– vii°^{7}/V –V –V$^6_4$–V^6–V

(d) III: I–vi–I–vi–I–vi– V^7/V –V –ii^6–V^6–V

11. List ways in which you hear motive x used during the transition.

Exercises 12–18 refer only to S, the music of the second theme group. This passage follows the transition and extends to the repeat.

In #12–#15, write the Roman numeral of the secondary key followed by a colon. Then notate your answers *in that key.*

12. Write the melody for the first phrase of S with solfège syllables.

13. Write the melody for the first phrase of S with scale-degree numbers.

14. Write the bass line for the first phrase of S with solfège syllables.

15. Write the bass line for the first phrase of S with scale-degree numbers.

16. Notate the pitches and rhythm of phrase 1's melody and bass line on the staves below. Begin on D5 and G2, respectively. (There is no need to double the first bass pitch one octave lower.) Use the appropriate clef, meter signature, bar lines, key signature, and accidentals. Beam notes appropriately given your choice of meter.

17. Phrase 1 of S concludes with which harmonic progression?

    (a) I–V^7–I

    (b) ii–V$^{8-7}_{4-3}$–I

    (c) IV–V–I

    (d) vi–V$^{6-5}_{4-3}$–I

18. How does phrase 2's design relate to phrase 1's design?

    (a) exact repetition of phrase 1

    (b) same beginning, different conclusion

    (c) different beginning, same conclusion

    (d) different beginning, different conclusion

19. Compare motive x from the closing theme (CL) with motive x from the beginning of S (the first three melodic pitches). The CL motive is

   (a) a transposition of S;

   (b) a rhythmic augmentation of S;

   (c) the inversion of S;

   (d) unrelated to S.

Questions 20–27 refer only to the music of the development.

20. The beginning of the development is in which key? (Hint: Listen to the beginning of the movement, then the beginning of the development.)

   (a) parallel major

   (b) relative major

   (c) dominant

   (d) submediant

21. The beginning of the development is derived from which of the following?

   (a) F (first theme group)

   (b) t (transition)

   (c) S (second theme group)

   (d) CL (closing theme)

22. At the beginning of the development, which type of $^6_4$ chord occurs?

   (a) passing

   (b) neighboring

   (c) cadential

   (d) arpeggiating

23. After a brief pause, the development is suddenly louder. Which key is tonicized here?

   (a) I

   (b) III

   (c) V

   (d) VI

24. From which music is this new section (after the brief pause) derived?

    (a) F (first theme group)

    (b) t (transition)

    (c) S (second theme group)

    (d) CL (closing theme)

25. From which music is the retransition derived?

    (a) F (first theme group)

    (b) t (transition)

    (c) S (second theme group)

    (d) CL (closing theme)

26. Which describes the music of the retransition?

    (a) The texture is inverted (what was originally high now sounds low, and what was low now sounds high).

    (b) The dynamics change; it begins soft and crescendos to the cadence.

    (c) A melodic sequence in the bass descends by thirds.

    (d) All of the above.

27. The retransition concludes on which chord?

    (a) I

    (b) V

    (c) V^6

    (d) V^6/V

Questions 28–32 refer only to the recapitulation.

28. How does F in the recapitulation compare with its original statement in the exposition?

    (a) F is identical.

    (b) F recurs in a different key.

    (c) F is truncated and elides with t.

    (d) F has a long cadential extension.

29. The transition, t, cadences on which chord?

    (a) III

    (b) V

    (c) V/V

    (d) VI

30. S returns in which key?

    (a) i

    (b) III

    (c) iv

    (d) V

31. In S's second phrase, the sequence features which LIP?

    (a) 6–5

    (b) 6–6

    (c) 10–5

    (d) 10–10

32. In the middle of CL, which key is tonicized?

    (a) I

    (b) III

    (c) V

    (d) VI

EXAMPLE 2, TRACK 2.2

Listen to a movement from a piano sonata by Mozart, and complete the exercises below.

1. Which is the excerpt's meter signature?

   (a) $\frac{2}{4}$ (b) $\frac{3}{4}$ (c) $\frac{6}{8}$ (d) $\frac{9}{8}$

Exercises 2–7 refer only to the music of phrase 1 of the first theme group.

2. Write the melody with solfège syllables.

3. Write the melody with scale-degree numbers.

4. (a) Notate the pitches and rhythm of the melody on the staves below. Begin on F4. Use the appropriate clef, meter signature, bar lines, key signature, and accidentals. Beam notes appropriately given your choice of meter.

   (b) Draw a bracket over melodic pitches 10–16. Call these pitches motive x. We will come back to motive x in later questions.

5. At the beginning, which best describes the lower part?

   (a) basso continuo

   (b) broken-chord figuration

   (c) walking bass

   (d) passacaglia

6. At the beginning of *the second half* of phrase 1, which describes the bass line?

   (a) rhythmic augmentation of melody

   (b) creates a pedal point

   (c) imitates the melody

   (d) Alberti bass

7. Which is phrase 1's cadential progression?

(a) ii⁶–V⁷–I

(c) V⁶₄₋₅₃–I

(b) IV–V–I

(d) vi–V⁷–I

Phrases 2 and 3 of the first theme group feature dotted rhythms and a chordal texture. Exercises 8–16 refer only to the music of these two phrases.

8. Write the melody with solfège syllables.

9. Write the melody with scale-degree numbers.

10. Write the bass line with solfège syllables.

11. Write the bass line with scale-degree numbers.

12. (a) Notate the pitches and rhythm of the melody and bass line on the staves below. Begin on C6 and A4, respectively. Use the appropriate clef, meter signature, bar lines, key signature, and accidentals. Beam notes appropriately given your choice of meter.

(b) In your answer above, write Roman numerals and figures under bass pitches where there are changes of harmony.

13. Phrase 2 concludes with which cadence type?

    (a) HC   (c) PAC

    (b) IAC   (d) deceptive

14. Phrase 3 concludes with which cadence type?

    (a) HC   (c) PAC

    (b) IAC   (d) deceptive

15. Which is the phrase structure of phrases 2 and 3?

    (a) parallel period

    (b) contrasting period

    (c) parallel double period

    (d) independent phrases

16. Compared with phrase 2, by which means is phrase 3 expanded?

    (a) introduction

    (b) internal repetition

    (c) internal sequence

    (d) cadential extension

Question 17–21 refer only to t, the music of the transition.

17. The beginning of the transition tonicizes which key?

    (a) ii   (c) V

    (b) IV   (d) vi

18. In the key of your answer to #17, which is the opening chord progression?
    The implied harmony of the anacrusis is shown in parentheses.

    (a) $(V_3^6)-I-V_4^6-I^6$

    (b) $(V_3^6)-I-vii^{ø6}_3-I^6$

    (c) $(V_3^6)-i-vii^{°6}_3-i^6$

    (d) $(V_3^6)-i-V_3^4-i^6$

19. The arrival on V in the new key of S is preceded by which of the following chords?

    (a) V: $ii^{ø4}_3$

    (b) V: iv^6

    (c) V: V^7/V

    (d) V: A^6

20. The arrival on V in the new key is prolonged by which means?

    (a) plagal extension

    (b) repeated ii–V progressions

    (c) sequence

    (d) suspensions

21. Is the transition (a) dependent or (b) independent?

Exercises 22–29 refer only to S, the music of the second theme group. S is made up of four phrases.

22. Write the melody of the first half of S (the first two phrases) with solfège syllables. Omit the grace notes.

23. Write the melody of the first half of S (the first two phrases) with scale-degree numbers. Omit the grace notes.

24. Notate the pitches and rhythm of the melody of the first half of S on the staves below. Begin on E5. Use the appropriate clef, meter signature, bar lines, key signature, and accidentals. Beam notes appropriately given your choice of meter.

25. Phrase 1 of S concludes with which cadence type?

    (a) HC   (b) IAC   (c) PAC   (d) plagal

26. Phrase 2 of S concludes with which cadence type?

    (a) HC   (b) IAC   (c) PAC   (d) plagal

27. How does phrase 3 relate to phrase 1 of S? Phrase 3 is

    (a) a variation that features neighbor tones and two-against-three rhythm;

    (b) a variation that features passing tones and different harmonies;

    (c) a contrast that features similar melodic material, but different harmonies;

    (d) a contrast that features different melodic material, rhythm, and harmonies.

28. Phrase 4 of S concludes with which cadence type?

    (a) HC   (b) IAC   (c) PAC   (d) plagal

29. Phrases 1–4 of S comprise which larger structure(s)?

    (a) two parallel periods

    (b) two contrasting periods

    (c) one parallel double period

    (d) one contrasting double period

Eliding with the cadence of phrase 4 of S, a transition leads to the closing theme group. We can call this transition t². Questions 30–35 refer only to the music of t²

30. In the key of V, which is the opening chord progression?

    (a) I–ii–V⁷–i

    (b) I–V⁷–i–V⁷

    (c) I–vi–ii⁶–V

    (d) I–vii°⁷–i–vii°⁷

31. A sequence leads to this transition's cadence. On which progression is the sequence based?

    (a) falling fifths

    (b) falling thirds

    (c) ascending 5–6

    (d) ascending fifths

32. The sequence features which LIP? (Hint: The LIP begins on chord 2 of the sequence.)

    (a) 7–6

    (b) 10–5

    (c) 10–7

    (d) 10–10

33. The end of the sequence features which rhythmic device?

    (a) syncopation

    (b) hemiola

    (c) two-against-three beat divisions

    (d) rhythmic augmentation of S's theme

34. Briefly describe how this sequence relates to motive x.

35. The end of this transition remains in the key of V. Its cadence is extended by many repetitions of which two cadential chords?

   (a) iv^6–V   (c) V$^6_5$/V–V

   (b) N^6–V   (d) vii°^{7}/V–V

Exercises 36–43 refer only to the music of the closing theme group.

36. Write phrase 1's melody with solfège syllables.

37. Write phrase 1's melody with scale-degree numbers.

38. Write phrase 1's bass line with solfège syllables.

39. Write phrase 1's bass line with scale-degree numbers.

40. (a) Notate the pitches and rhythm of phrase 1's melody and bass line on the staves below. Begin on A4 and F3, respectively. Use the appropriate clef, meter signature, bar lines, key signature, and accidentals. Beam notes appropriately given your choice of meter.

   (b) In your answer above, write Roman numerals and figures under bass pitches where there are changes of harmony

41. Phrase 1 concludes with which cadence type?

    (a) HC

    (b) IAC

    (c) PAC

    (d) plagal

42. List all the ways in which phrase 2 of CL is expanded.

43. Briefly describe how the very end of the exposition relates to motive x.

Exercises 44–50 refer only to the music of the development.

44. Write phrase 1's melody with solfège syllables.

45. Write phrase 1's melody with scale-degree numbers.

46. Write phrase one's bass line with solfège syllables.

47. Write phrase 1's bass line with scale-degree numbers.

48. (a) Notate the pitches and rhythm of phrase 1's melody and bass line on the staves below. Begin on G4 and E3, respectively. Use the appropriate clef, meter signature, bar lines, key signature, and accidentals. Beam notes appropriately given your choice of meter.

(b) In your answer above, write Roman numerals and figures under bass pitches where there are changes of harmony.

49. Phrase 1 concludes with which cadence type?

(a) HC   (c) PAC

(b) IAC   (d) deceptive

50. How does phrase 2 relate to phrase 1?

(a) identical melody and harmony

(b) melodic variation with identical harmony

(c) harmonic variation with identical melody

(d) different melody and harmony

The beginning of the retransition elides with the cadence of phrase 2 of the development. Questions 51–54 refer only to the music of the retransition.

51. On which music is the beginning of the retransition based?

(a) phrase 1 of F (first theme group)

(b) t (the transition)

(c) phrase 1 of S (second theme group)

(d) t² (transition between S and CL)

52. During the retransition, a four-chord harmonic progression occurs twice—first in the key of ii, then in the key of vi. Which of the following is that progression?

(a) ii°–i⁶–V⁶–i

(c) vii°⁶–i⁶–vii°⁷–i

(b) V⁶₄–i⁶–vii°⁷–i

(d) vii°⁶₅–i⁶–V⁶₃–i

53. Which are the two chords of the retransition's cadence?

(a) vi: ii⁶–V

(c) vi: It⁶–V

(b) vi: iv⁶–V

(d) vi: N⁶–V

54. At the end of the retransition's cadential extension, which chord occurs?

(a) ii   (b) IV   (c) V⁷   (d) vi

The final questions refer only to the music of the recapitulation.

55. Compare the first theme group (F) of the recapitulation with the first theme group in the exposition. Which describes F in the recapitulation?

(a) It is identical to F in the exposition.

(b) It has same beginning, but the end is truncated.

(c) The beginning is truncated, but the end is the same.

(d) Each part of F is truncated.

56. Compare the transition (t) in the recapitulation with the transition in the exposition. Which describes t in the recapitulation?

(a) It is identical to t in the exposition.

(b) It is the same length, but cadences on V.

(c) It is longer and cadences on V.

(d) It contains a falling-fifth sequence.

57. Compare the second theme group (S) in the recapitulation with the second theme group in the exposition. Which describes S in the recapitulation?

(a) transposed to the tonic

(b) second half is varied

(c) same length

(d) all of the above

58. Beginning with the transition to the closing theme group (t²), compare the entire end of the recapitulation with the end of the exposition. Which does *not* occur?

(a) The transition to CL (t²) is longer.

(b) The music of CL is transposed to the tonic.

(c) CL includes the same melody and harmony.

(d) CL includes a codetta.

IV. MELODIES FOR STUDY

For each of the melodies below, prepare to do any of the following:

- Sing on scale-degree numbers or solfège syllables.
- Sing or play the melody in its parallel key.
- Transpose to other keys on your instrument.
- Improvise a variant vocally or on your instrument.
- Identify chords and their inversions implied in the melody.
- Harmonize with chords we have learned since Chapter 12.
- Discuss aspects of phrase rhythm and phrase expansion.

Also be prepared to answer any of the following questions:

- What type of cadence is implied at the end of each phrase?
- What is the key signature for the parallel-key version?
- Which embellishing tones are implied in the melody?
- From which scale is the melody derived?
- Is there an implied tonicization or modulation?
- Which melodic pitches or implied chords are a product of modal mixture?

In addition, use the melodies below as models to help you compose your own sonata-form movement. Perform the grace notes in each example *on* the beat.

Melody 1   Mozart, Piano Sonata in A minor, K. 310, first movement

Melody 2 Haydn, Piano Sonata No. 45 in E♭ Major, first movement

V. IMPROVISATION

To help prepare your sonata-form composition in section VI, review and practice the improvisation exercises in these earlier chapters.

Chapter 17: "Consequent Phrase" and "Team Improvisations" (p. 405)
Chapter 18: Improvisations 1 and 2 (pp. 437–38)
Chapter 20: "Consequent Phrases with Phrase Expansions" (p. 491)
Chapter 21: "Consequent Phrases That Include Phrase Expansions" (p. 25)
Chapter 22: "Modulatory Periods" (p. 68)

VI. COMPOSITION

Sonata-Form Movement for Piano

We now compose a small movement for piano in sonata form. This will be done in several steps; each step is related to compositions you completed in previous chapters. Model your new work on the "Contextual Listening" examples in this chapter. Prepare to perform your movement in class, or work with a pianist who will read it for you.

Exposition: First theme group and transition

1. Choose a major key and a meter type.
2. In phrase 1:
   (a) Establish the tonic key.
   (b) Introduce the motive of F, the first theme group.
   (c) Conclude with a PAC in I.

3. In phrase 2 (t):
   (a) Begin with the motive of phrase 1 (F), thus creating a dependent transition.
   (b) Use a sequence, LIP, or other means to modulate to V.
   (c) Conclude with a HC *in the key of V.*

Exposition: Second theme group

1. Make a list of the attributes of F (character, register, dynamics, articulation, texture, tempo, type of accompaniment, harmonic rhythm, etc.).
2. Choose the *opposite* of three or more of these attributes to help you create a motive for S.
3. Use this new motive to compose a parallel period *in the key of V.*
4. In phrase 2 of your period:
   (a) Create an internal expansion by repeating a subphrase.
   (b) Conclude with a PAC in V.
   (c) Compose a cadential extension (codetta) that contains a "flourish."

Development

Compose two phrases.
1. In phrase 1:
   (a) Begin in the key of V.
   (b) Use an embellished form of F's motive.
   (c) Conclude with an IAC in V.
2. In phrase 2:
   (a) Begin like phrase 1.
   (b) Create a falling-fifth sequence.
   (c) Conclude with the progression A^6–V *in the key of I.*

Recapitulation

1. Copy phrase 1 of F.
2. Rewrite t so that it cadences on V instead of V/V.
3. Transpose S to the key of the tonic.

Variation
Complete this project in a *minor* key. Which elements change?

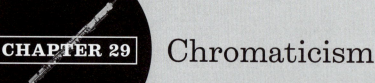

CHAPTER 29 Chromaticism

Overview

In Chapter 29, we will consider a new way to prolong major triads and learn to chromaticize several voice-leading patterns with which we are already familiar.

Outline of topics covered

I. KEY CONCEPTS

Common-Tone Embellishing Chords

Chromatic Voice Exchanges and the Chromaticized Cadential $^6_4$

Chromatic Sequences

Chromatic falling fifths

Chromatic falling thirds

Ascending 5–6 sequences

II. CALL AND RESPONSE

III. CONTEXTUAL LISTENING

IV. MELODIES FOR STUDY

V. IMPROVISATION

VI. COMPOSITION

Ragtime Piece

Instrumental Duet

I. KEY CONCEPTS

Common-Tone Embellishing Chords

Perform the three chords below, then play chord 2 only. It *sounds* like a diminished seventh chord, but does not function like one. (If it did, it would lead to a D-minor chord.)

Common-tone diminished seventh chord

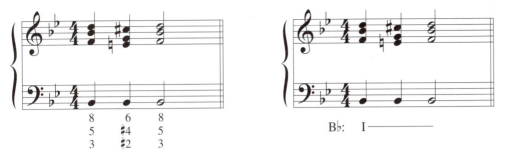

$$\begin{array}{ccc} 8 & 6 & 8 \\ 5 & {\sharp}4 & 5 \\ 3 & {\sharp}2 & 3 \end{array}$$

B♭: I ——————————

When we harmonize the chromatic neighbor tones that prolong a major chord, as above, we get a **common-tone diminished seventh chord** (**CT°7**). When analyzing the chord, we may notate all the figures (as above), but all we need to do to indicate the function of the chord is write the Roman numeral of the chord that is prolonged.

Now perform the chords below, then play chord 2 only. It *sounds* like an augmented-sixth chord, but does not function like one. (If it did, it would resolve to a dominant chord in D minor.)

Common-tone German augmented-sixth chord

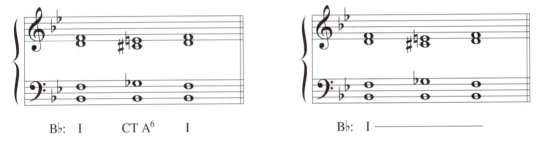

B♭: I   CT A⁶   I   B♭: I ——————————

When we embellish a tonic harmony with chromatic neighbors ♯2̂, ♯4̂, and ♭6̂, a **common-tone German augmented-sixth chord** (**CT A⁶**) results. Note that scale-degrees ♯2̂ and ♯4̂, are found in both the CT°7 and CT A⁶, but the CT A⁶ also includes ♭6̂.

Many people call such chords as CT°7 and CT A⁶ **apparent chords.** Apparent chords are embellishing rather than structural, and are really just the product of voice-leading or melodic prolongation. They harmonize passing or neighbor tones, making these dissonances sound more consonant.

Here's how to play a CT°7 chord.

Upper voice: Play neighbor tones *mi–ri–mi* (3̂–♯2̂–3̂).
Upper voice: Play neighbor tones *sol–fi–sol* (5̂–♯4̂–5̂).
Upper voice: Play *do–la–do* (1̂–6̂–1̂).

Bass voice: Play *do–do–do* (1̂–1̂–1̂).

Here's how to play a CT A⁶ chord.

Upper voice: Play neighbor tones *mi–ri–mi* (3̂–♯2̂–3̂).
Upper voice: Play neighbor tones *sol–fi–sol* (5̂–♯4̂–5̂).
Upper voice: Play neighbor tones *sol–le–sol* (5̂–♭6̂–5̂).

Bass voice: Play *do–do–do* (1̂–1̂–1̂).

The first chord may be left out in each progression.

Exercise 29.1: Performing Common-Tone Diminished Seventh and Common-Tone Augmented-Sixth Chords

Following the voice-leading in the two examples above, (1) expand each of the following major chords with a common-tone diminished seventh chord. Perform the given chord, then the CT°7, then the given chord again. Sing with solfège syllables and scale-degree numbers. Then (2) expand the major chord with a common-tone augmented-sixth chord.

1. F
2. D
3. E♭
4. B
5. C♯

6. A♭
7. G
8. B♭
9. A
10. F♯

Chromatic Voice Exchanges and the Chromaticized Cadential $^6_4$

Perform the progression below, and listen for the voice exchange (VE) and cadential $^6_4$.

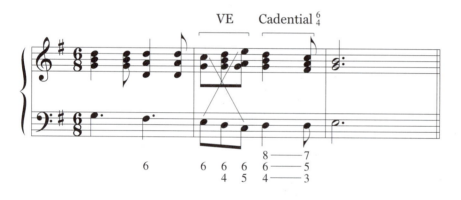

Now as you perform the variation below, listen for the chromatic VE and the chromatic alteration of the cadential $^6_4$.

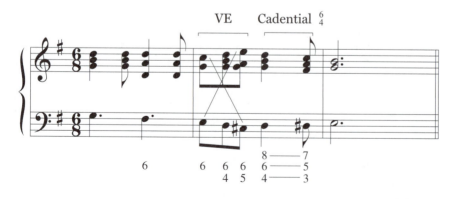

A chromatic VE creates a cross relation (C is exchanged with C♯); in a progression like the one above, this is normal voice-leading. The chromatic pitch in the VE might be the leading tone of a secondary dominant-function chord.

A chromaticized cadential $^6_4$ results from a chromatic passing tone in the bass (D♯ in our example). When a cadential $^6_4$ is altered in this way, we can notate its beginning, leaving dashes after the $^6_4$ to show that its resolution is interrupted. Three ways to continue the notation are shown below.

Bracket notation   *Slash notation*   *Colon notation*

$\overline{\begin{array}{cc} \text{vii}^{\circ 7} & \text{i} \end{array}}$

V^6_{4-} vi V^6_{4-} $\text{vii}^{\circ 7}$/vi–vi V^6_{4-} vi: $\text{vii}^{\circ 7}$ i

Chromatic voice exchanges may also occur when we use modal mixture or an augmented-sixth chord. As you perform the progressions below, sing each of the outer voices to highlight the sound of the voice exchange. The $^6_4$ chords within each voice exchange are passing chords.

With mixture   *With an augmented-sixth chord*

   VE   VE   VE

F: I–V^6_4–I^6–IV–I$^6_4$–iv^6–V^{8-7}_{4-3}–I   g: i–iv^7–i$^6_4$–Gr^6–V^{6-5}_{4-3}–i

Chromatic Sequences

As we move toward an important moment in a phrase, or move from one key to another, we can use all or part of a sequence to help create tension. And we can make a sequence even more dramatic by chromaticizing one or more of its chords.

CHROMATIC FALLING FIFTHS

In Chapter 22's "Call and Response" section, we learned that the falling-fifth progression is the most common and convenient way to modulate to new keys. The process involves two steps: (1) choose a portion of the sequence that concludes with the tonic chord of the new key; then (2) chromaticize the penultimate chord, thus creating a secondary dominant in the new key.

In the example below, a chromaticized "ii" becomes V in the key of the dominant.

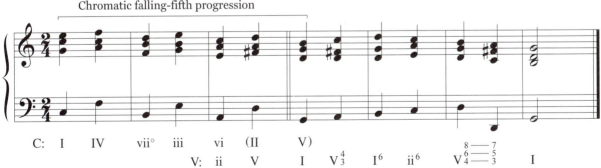

Chromatic falling-fifth progression

C: I   IV   vii°   iii   vi   (II   V)

                               V: ii   V   I V^4_3 I^6 ii^6 $\text{V}^{8-7}_{6-5}_{4-3}$ I

CHROMATIC FALLING THIRDS

In a falling-third sequence, chords 1–2, 3–4, and 5–6 can sound like tonic-dominant progressions if we chromaticize chord 4 by raising its third. Since chords 4–5 create a deceptive resolution in vi, we must remember to move upper voices contrary to the bass and double the third in chord 5. Perform the sequence below with and without the G♯ in measure 2, and listen for the difference.

Use the voice-leading typical of all deceptive resolutions.

Another common way to chromaticize this sequence is to substitute V_3^6/vi or vii°⁷/vi for chord 2.

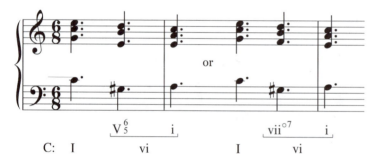

ASCENDING 5–6 SEQUENCES

Though most sequences that we hear descend, there are two common ascending sequences: the ascending-fifth sequence (I–V–ii–vi), which occurs only occasionally, and the 5–6 sequence, which is quite common. The 5–6 sequence rises by step.

Diatonic 5–6 Sequence: If we use root-position chords and rise by step, we get parallel fifths and octaves. Perform the progression below and listen for the parallel octaves and fifths in measures 1–2.

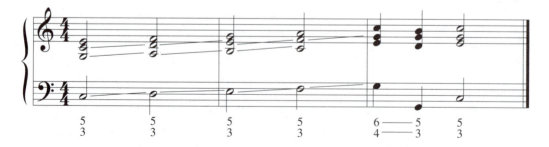

To rise by step but avoid these obvious parallels, we apply a 5–6 technique. Perform the diatonic progression below, and listen for the 5–6 motion in the tenor voice. Listen as well to how the soprano voice "reaches over" to create contrary motion against the rising bass. You can also create variations by performing either eighth note of each eighth-note pair in the soprano; in this case, each eighth note becomes a quarter note like the rest of the chord.

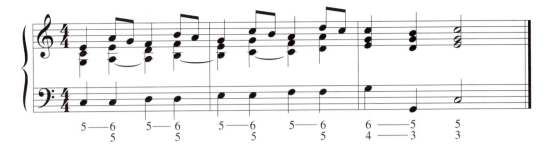

Chromatic 5–6 Sequence: Chromaticizing the bass line makes the ascending 5–6 sequence more dramatic because it creates fifth-related secondary dominants. The chromatic 5–6 sequence is the most common ascending sequence. As you perform the example below, refer to the strategies underneath.

Concentrate on a different strategy each time you repeat the progression. Create variations by performing either eighth note of each eighth-note pair in the soprano.

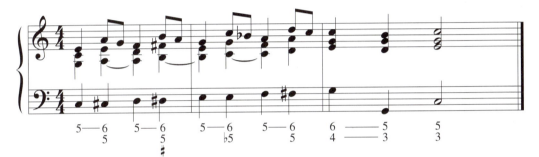

Strategies

Listen for:

- an ascending chromatic bass line
- ascending, fifth-related secondary dominants
- two-chord units that rise by step
- the 5–6 motion
- linear intervallic patterns 10–6–5 when performing what is written, 10–6 when performing only the first eighth note of each pair, and 10–5 when performing only the second eighth note of each pair
- a line that "reaches over" to create contrary motion against a rising bass

---

Exercise 29.2: Performing Ascending 5–6 Sequences

Using the two examples above as models, perform diatonic and chromatic 5–6 sequences beginning on each of the tonic chords below. Perform three different soprano lines, as in the examples above (with two eighth notes, then each eighth note in turn). Sing each part with solfège syllables and scale-degree numbers.

1. B♭ Major   2. D Major   3. G Major   4. E♭ Major   5. A Major   6. F Major

II. CALL AND RESPONSE

Your teacher will perform a melody or chord progression.

A. If you hear a melody:
    (1) Respond with the call.
    (2) Create a bass line that accompanies the call.
    (3) Create a four-part harmonization of the call.

B. If you hear a progression:
    (1) Respond with the call.
    (2) Then respond with an embellished form of the progression that features a chromaticized cadential $^6_4$, CT$^{\circ 7}$ chord, or chromatic voice exchange.

Options for performing your response

Maintain the pitch, rhythm, and tempo of the call.

- Sing pitch only (with solfège syllables, scale-degree numbers, note names, or Roman numerals and figures).
- Sing rhythm only.
- Sing pitch and rhythm.
- Sing the progression in arpeggios.
- Conduct (or tap) while singing rhythm only, singing both pitch and rhythm, or singing the progression in arpeggios.
- Play on the keyboard or your instrument.

Options for writing your response

- solfège syllables
- scale-degree numbers
- note names
- note heads only
- rhythmic notation only
- notes and rhythm
- four parts (or just outer voices) with Roman numerals and figured bass

III. CONTEXTUAL LISTENING

EXAMPLE 1, TRACK 2.3

Listen to an excerpt from a keyboard work by Handel, and complete the exercises below.

1. Which is the meter signature of the excerpt?

    (a) $\frac{2}{4}$ (b) $\frac{3}{4}$ (c) $\frac{9}{8}$ (d) $\frac{12}{8}$

2. Which is the section design of the entire movement?

    (a) **A A**   (b) **A A'**   (c) **A B**   (d) **A B A'**

3. Which is the form of the entire movement?

    (a) simple binary   (c) simple ternary

    (b) rounded binary   (d) composite ternary

    - If your answer was (a) or (b), complete #4 and #5, then skip to #8. (Do not complete #6–#7.)
    - If your answer was (c), skip to #8. (Do not complete #4–#7.)
    - If your answer was (d), skip to #6. (Do not complete #4–#5.)

4. Is the binary (a) sectional or (b) continuous?

5. Are the sections balanced?

6. (a) Which is the form of section 1?

    (1) parallel period

    (2) contrasting period

    (3) simple binary

    (4) rounded binary

    If your answer was (3) or (4), complete parts (b) and (c).

    (b) Is the binary (1) sectional or (2) continuous?

    (c) Are the sections balanced?

7. (a) Which is the form of section 2?

    (1) parallel period

    (2) contrasting period

    (3) simple binary

    (4) rounded binary

    If your answer was (3) or (4), complete parts (b) and (c).

    (b) Is the binary (1) sectional or (2) continuous?

    (c) Are the sections balanced?

Exercises 8–17 refer only to section 2, phrase 1.

8. Using a neutral syllable, sing the bass pitches. By the end of the phrase, which scale degree do they tonicize? _____

Strategy

Sustain this tonicized pitch and listen to the beginning of the excerpt again. After you hear the original tonic pitch, sing up or down the scale until you reach the newly tonicized pitch.

9. Write the Roman numeral of the tonicized scale degree. _____ This is the key to which the phrase modulates.

10. With solfège syllables, write the melodic pitches that occur on each of the first six downbeats.

11. With scale-degree numbers, write the melodic pitches that occur on each of the first six downbeats.

12. With solfège syllables, write the bass pitches that occur on each of the first six downbeats.

13. With scale-degree numbers, write the bass pitches that occur on each of the first six downbeats.

14. To which type of scale do these bass pitches belong?

  (a) major

  (b) ascending melodic minor

  (c) natural (descending melodic) minor

  (d) chromatic

15. (a) Transcribe your answers to #10–#13 on the staff below. Begin on C5 (melody) and A3 (bass). Use the appropriate clef, meter signature, bar lines, key signature, and accidentals.

(b) In your answer above, write the generic harmonic intervals that occur between the outer voices.

(c) Which linear intervallic pattern do they form? _____ — _____

16. Which sequence occurs in the phrase?

(a) falling fifths

(b) falling thirds

(c) ascending 5–6

(d) ascending fifths

17. (a) On the staves below, notate *all* the pitches and rhythm of the melody and bass line in the first phrase of section 2. Begin on C5 and A3, respectively. Write the appropriate clef, meter signature, bar lines, key signature, and accidentals. Beam notes appropriately given your choice of meter.

(b) Beneath each bass pitch in your answer above, write the Roman numerals and figures of the harmony. Show any secondary-dominant relationships, and, at the appropriate location, indicate the modulation.

(c) Identify each dissonant embellishing tone in the melody in your answer above as passing (P), neighbor (N), anticipation (A), or suspension (S).

18. (a) On the staff below, notate the pitches and rhythm of *section 1's* melody and bass line. Begin on F5 and F3, respectively. Write the appropriate clef, meter signature, bar lines, key signature, and accidentals. Beam notes appropriately given your choice of meter. Write *tr* for trills.

(b) Beneath each bass pitch in your answer above, write the Roman numerals and figures of the harmony. Show any secondary-dominant relationships.

(c) Identify each dissonant embellishing tone in the melody in your answer above as passing (P), neighbor (N), anticipation (A), or suspension (S).

19. (a) On the staves below, notate the pitches and rhythm of the melody and bass line for the last phrase in the excerpt. Begin in the bass on D3 with a two-beat lead-in. The melody begins on C5. Write the appropriate clef, meter signature, bar lines, key signature, and accidentals. Beam notes appropriately given your choice of meter.

(b) Beneath each bass pitch in your answer above, write the Roman numerals and figures of the harmony. Show any secondary-dominant relationships.

(c) Identify each dissonant embellishing tone in the melody in your answer above as passing (P), neighbor (N), anticipation (A), or suspension (S).

EXAMPLE 2, TRACK 2.4

This excerpt from a keyboard prelude by Bach features three-part harmony that is realized in an arpeggiated texture. The repeated figuration is reminiscent of the figural variations we studied in Chapter 27. For our purposes, we will divide the music into four segments:

- Segment 1 begins with a sequence and ends with the first melodic pitch of segment 2.

- Segment 2 begins with a three-step sequence (descending bass arpeggios alternate with scale passages).

- Segment 3 begins with a four-pitch bass line that's repeated; the segment continues with a sequence, and ends with a scale.

- Segment 4 includes the last nine bass pitches, the last of which is the cadential bass pitch.

1. Which is the excerpt's meter type?

   (a) simple triple

   (b) simple quadruple

   (c) compound duple

   (d) compound triple

2. Write the Roman numeral of the key to which the excerpt modulates. _____

Exercises 3–8 refer only to the music of segment 1.

3. Write the bass line with solfège syllables.

4. Write the bass line with scale-degree numbers.

Assume that the highest voice is sustained instead of arpeggiated and has the same rhythmic value as each bass pitch.

5. Write the melody with solfège syllables.

6. Write the melody with scale-degree numbers.

7. (a) Notate the pitches and rhythm of the melody and bass line on the staff below. Begin on D5 and B♭3, respectively. Write the appropriate clef, meter signature, bar lines, key signature, and accidentals. Beam notes appropriately given your choice of meter.

(b) Beneath each bass pitch in your answer above, write the Roman numerals and figures of the harmony.

(c) Identify each dissonant embellishing tone in the melody in your answer above with P or N.

8. On which sequence is segment 1 based?

   (a) falling fifths　　　　(c) ascending 5–6

   (b) falling thirds　　　　(d) ascending fifths

Questions 9–12 refer only to the music of segment 2.

9. In the bass line, the first four-pitch arpeggio outlines which chord?

   (a) I　　(b) ii　　(c) V　　(d) vi

10. The fifth bass pitch (the beginning of the scale) is the root of which chord?

    (a) I　　(b) ii　　(c) V　　(d) vi

11. Compared with the first bass arpeggio, the second bass arpeggio occurs at which generic interval?

    (a) down a second　　　　(c) up a second

    (b) down a third　　　　(d) up a third

12. Which best describes segment 2's sequence?

    (a) two-chord units that descend by second

    (b) two-chord units that descend by third

    (c) two-chord units that ascend by second

    (d) two-chord units that ascend by third

Exercises 13–17 refer only to the music of segment 3. At the appropriate moment, write the Roman numeral of the new key and change your syllables or numbers. Pay close attention to the melodic patterns in both the melody and bass line of the sequence. These patterns will help you determine the main melody and bass pitches of the scale that follows.

13. Write the bass line with solfège syllables.

14. Write the bass line with scale-degree numbers.

15. Write the melody with solfège syllables.

16. Write the melody with scale-degree numbers.

17. (a) Transcribe your answers to #13–#16 into notation on the staves below. Begin on D4 (melody) and B♭2 (bass). Write the appropriate clef, meter signature, bar lines, key signature, and accidentals. Beam notes appropriately given your choice of meter.

(b) Write the harmonic pitch intervals between the melody and bass in the staves above. After the repeated four-pitch unit, which linear intervallic pattern occurs during the sequence?

(1) 6–6   (3) 10–5

(2) 7–6   (4) 10–6

(c) Which is the name of the sequence?

    (1) falling fifths   (3) ascending 5–6

    (2) falling thirds   (4) ascending fifths

The final exercises refer only to the music of segment 4. For each answer, be sure to write the Roman numeral of the newly tonicized key.

18. Write the bass line with solfège syllables.

19. Write the bass line with scale-degree numbers.

Assume that the highest voice is sustained instead of arpeggiated and has the same rhythmic value as each bass pitch.

20. Write the melody with solfège syllables.

21. Write the melody with scale-degree numbers.

22. (a) Transcribe your answers to #18–#21 into notation on the staff below. Begin on B♭4 (melody) and E2 (bass). Write the appropriate clef, meter signature, bar lines, key signature, and accidentals. Beam notes appropriately given your choice of meter.

    (b) Beneath each bass pitch in your answer above, write the Roman numerals and figures of the harmony.

    (c) During the first four bass pitches, which linear intervallic pattern occurs?

        (1) 5–6   (3) 7–6

        (2) 5–10   (4) 10–10

EXAMPLE 3, TRACK 2.5

Listen to a two-phrase excerpt from a chamber work by Brahms, and complete the exercises below.

1. Which is the excerpt's meter signature?

   (a) $\frac{2}{4}$ (b) $\frac{3}{4}$ (c) $\frac{4}{4}$ (d) $\frac{9}{8}$

Exercises 2–6 refer only to phrase 1.

2. Write the bass pitches that occur on each downbeat with solfège syllables. Listen for the cello pizzicati.

3. Write the bass pitches that occur on each downbeat with scale-degree numbers. Listen for the cello pizzicati.

4. Write the violin melody with solfège syllables. Write ~ for the turn.

5. Write the violin melody with scale-degree numbers. Write ~ for the turn.

6. (a) Notate the pitches and rhythm of the melody and bass line on the staves below. Begin on B4 and G2, respectively. Write the appropriate clef, meter signature, bar lines, key signature, and accidentals. Beam notes appropriately given your choice of meter.

(b) Beneath each bass pitch in your answer above, write the Roman numerals and figures of the harmony.

(c) Identify each dissonant embellishing tone in the melody in your answer above with P or N.

The remaining exercises refer only to phrase 2, which begins when the opening motive returns.

7. Write the bass line with solfège syllables. Listen for the cello pizzicati at the beginning of the phrase.

8. Write the bass line with scale-degree numbers. Listen for the cello pizzicati at the beginning of the phrase.

9. Notate the pitches of the bass line on the staves below. Begin on G3. Write the appropriate clef, meter signature, bar lines, key signature, and accidentals. Beam notes appropriately given your choice of meter.

10. At the beginning of phrase 2, how is the melody developed?

    (a) The melody overlaps with another melodic statement.

    (b) The melody is doubled in sixths.

    (c) The melody is in a canon at the octave.

    (d) The melody sounds in the lowest part.

11. The first three harmonies of phrase 2 belong to which key?

    (a) relative minor

    (b) parallel minor

    (c) dominant

    (d) submediant

12. Which type of sequence occurs during phrase 2?

    (a) falling fifths

    (b) falling thirds

    (c) ascending 5–6

    (d) ascending fifths

13. Which is the linear intervallic pattern at the beginning of the sequence?

    (a) 6–6

    (b) 7–10

    (c) 10–6

    (d) 10–10

14. Phrase 2 concludes with which cadence?

    (a) HC in I

    (b) PAC in I

    (c) HC in V

    (d) PAC in V

15. Briefly summarize the phrase expansion used in phrase 2. Refer to your answers to previous questions for ideas.

EXAMPLE 4, TRACK 2.6

Listen to a four-phrase excerpt from a piano rag by Scott Joplin, and complete the exercises below.

1. Write the bass line with solfège syllables. Group the syllables according to phrases.

2. Write the bass line with scale-degree numbers. Group the numbers according to phrases.

3. Write the melody with solfège syllables. Group the syllables according to phrases.

4. Write the melody with scale-degree numbers. Group the numbers according to phrases.

5. (a) Notate the pitches and rhythm of the melody and bass line in $\frac{2}{4}$ meter on the staves below. Begin on E♭6 and E♭2, respectively. Write the appropriate clef, bar lines, key signature, and accidentals. Beam notes appropriately given the meter.

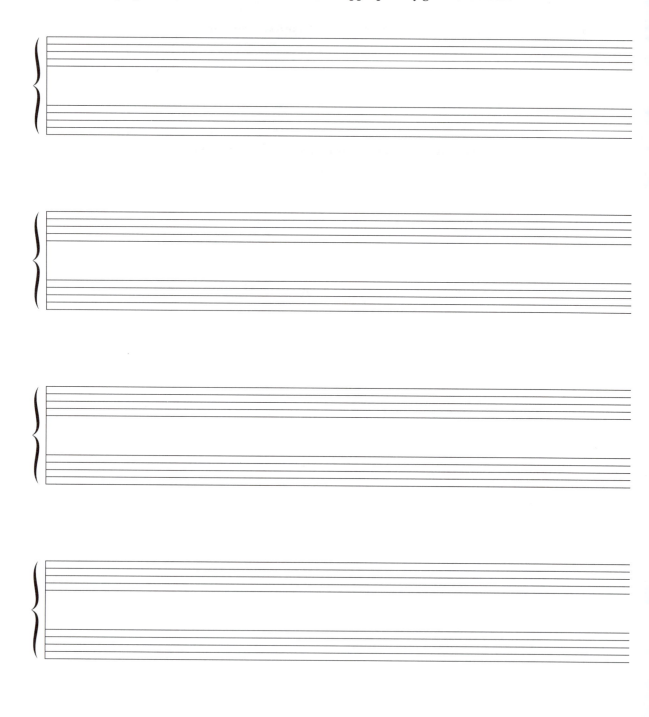

(b) Beneath each bass pitch in your answer above, write the Roman numerals and figures of the harmony. Show tonicizations and modulations.

(c) Circle each common-tone diminished seventh chord.

6. Phrase 1 concludes with which cadence type?

    (a) Phrygian

    (b) plagal

    (c) IAC

    (d) deceptive

7. Phrase 2 concludes with which cadence type?

    (a) IAC in the tonic

    (b) PAC in the tonic

    (c) IAC in the new key

    (d) PAC in the new key

8. Phrase 3 concludes with which cadence type?

    (a) Phrygian

    (b) plagal

    (c) IAC

    (d) deceptive

9. Phrase 4 concludes with which cadence type?

    (a) IAC in the tonic

    (b) PAC in the tonic

    (c) IAC in the new key

    (d) PAC in the new key

10. Which is the excerpt's phrase structure?

    (a) parallel period

    (b) contrasting period

    (c) parallel double period

    (d) contrasting double period

EXAMPLE 5, TRACKS 2.7–9

The exercises below are based on a work for piano by Chopin. Listen to the entire composition (track 2.7), then excerpts 1 (track 2.8) and 2 (track 2.9), then the entire composition again.

1. Which is the meter type of the piece?

   (a) simple duple
   (c) compound duple

   (b) simple quadruple
   (d) compound triple

Exercises 2–7 refer only to the music of excerpt 1 (track 2.8).

2. The third melodic pitch is which type of embellishing tone?

   (a) passing tone
   (c) consonant skip

   (b) neighbor tone
   (d) anticipation

3. The fifth melodic pitch is which type of dissonant embellishing tone?

   (a) passing tone
   (c) incomplete neighbor

   (b) consonant skip
   (d) anticipation

4. (a) Notate the pitches of the bass line on the staves below. Begin on E♭3. Write the appropriate clef and key signature (or accidentals).

   (b) Write the Roman numerals and figures beneath each bass pitch in your answer above.

5. In the middle of the texture, the moving parts prolong the harmonies with which embellishing tones?

   (a) passing tones

   (b) lower neighbor tones

   (c) upper neighbor tones and a passing tone

   (d) double neighbor tones and a consonant skip

6. The form of excerpt 1 is best represented by which of the following diagrams?

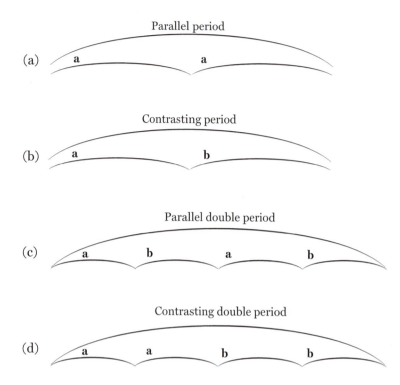

(a) Parallel period — a a

(b) Contrasting period — a b

(c) Parallel double period — a b a b

(d) Contrasting double period — a a b b

Now listen to excerpt 2 (track 2.9).

7. Excerpt 2's harmonic progression is based on which progression?

   (a) falling fifths

   (b) ascending fifths

   (c) falling thirds

   (d) ascending thirds

8. Excerpt 2 concludes with which type of cadence?

   (a) HC

   (b) IAC

   (c) PAC

   (d) deceptive

9. At the cadence, the melody is embellished by which of the following?

   (a) cadential $^6_4$

   (b) suspension

   (c) retardation

   (d) consonant skips

10. Listen to excerpt 1 (track 2.8) and sing the tonic pitch. Keep singing *do* (1̂) and replay excerpt 2 (track 2.9). Which pitch is tonicized in excerpt 2?

    (a) dominant

    (b) relative major

    (c) Neapolitan

    (d) major tonic

Listen once again to the entire work (track 2.7), and answer the following questions.

11. Compared with the phrases at the beginning, the last phrase in the piece is expanded by which means?

    (a) rhythmic augmentation

    (b) a circle-of-fifths progression

    (c) an internal repetition and a cadential extension

    (d) canonic imitation

12. Which is the section design of the piece?

    (a) **A**

    (b) **A B**

    (c) **A B A**

    (d) **A B A C A**

13. Which is the form of the piece?

    (a) one-part

    (b) simple binary

    (c) rounded binary

    (d) ternary

Musical Form and Interpretation

IV. MELODIES FOR STUDY

For each of the melodies below, prepare to do any of the following:

- Sing on scale-degree numbers or solfège syllables.
- Sing or play the melody in its parallel key.
- Transpose to other keys on your instrument.
- Improvise a variant vocally or on your instrument.
- Identify chords and their inversions implied in the melody.
- Harmonize the melody with chords we have learned since Chapter 12.
- Discuss aspects of phrase rhythm and phrase expansion.

Also be prepared to answer any of the following questions:

- What type of cadence is implied at the end of each phrase?
- What is the key signature for the parallel-key version?
- Which embellishing tones are implied in the melody?
- From which scale is the melody derived?
- Is there an implied tonicization or modulation?
- Which melodic pitches or implied chords are a product of modal mixture?

Melody 1 "My Country, 'Tis of Thee" (traditional; words by Samuel Francis Smith)
Over the word "liberty" in your harmonization, use a chromatic cadential $^6_4$ followed by a deceptive resolution.

Melody 2 Joe Burke, "Tiptoe Through the Tulips"
Harmonize this melody with a chromatic 5–6 sequence. On beat 4 of measure 4, use a borrowed chord.

Melody 3 Frank Perkins and Mitchell Parish, "Stars Fell on Alabama"
Harmonize the chromatic neighbor tones with common-tone diminished seventh chords.

Melody 4   Richard Rodgers, "Sixteen Going on Seventeen," from *The Sound of Music*
Harmonize the beginning of most phrases with common-tone diminished seventh chords.
In measure 20, include a voice exchange followed by a cadential $^6_4$ in measure 21. What is
unusual about the phrase rhythm at the end?

Melody 5   Brahms, String Sextet No. 2 in G Major, fourth movement (violin 1 part)
In your harmonization, create an ascending 5–6 sequence in measures 6–7. Modulate to V.

Melody 6   Richard Strauss, *Don Quixote* (adapted)
Perform this excerpt as a duet. Adjust the range to a comfortable octave.

V. IMPROVISATION

While one person plays a ragtime accompaniment based on the outline below, a second improvises a melody. The accompanist should also improvise, embellishing the outline and imitating the soloist when possible. Each performer should prepare to solo or accompany. After performing your rag several times, write a Roman-numeral analysis to help you transpose it to G Major and E♭ Major.

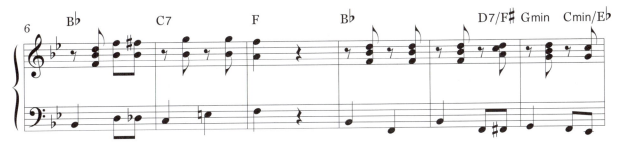

Strategies

- According to Scott Joplin, rags should never be played fast. Try a nice strolling tempo of around MM = 72–76.
- Create a motive that features rhythms characteristic of rags, such as these four:

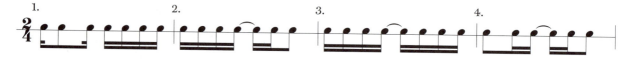

- Perform the motive each time the opening chord progression recurs.
- Transform the motive in other places.
- In measure 8, one or both performers should create a lead-in to the next phrase. (Tip: The bass is a good place to play the lead-in!)

VI. COMPOSITION

Ragtime Piece

Now use ideas from your improvisation to write a rag, modeled on the sounds and style of Scott Joplin.

A: Begin with the music of the improvisation outline above. (This section will repeat, by means of first and second endings.)

B: Compose a new, contrasting section. (This section will also repeat, with first and second endings.)

A′: Recapitulate the music of the outline. (This section will be played only once.)

Score your rag for (1) a brass ensemble of trumpets, horns, trombones, and tuba, or (2) a woodwind ensemble of flutes, clarinets, and saxophones (alto, tenor, and baritone). If the instruments are available, perform your arrangements in class; if not, create a MIDI version instead.

Musical Challenge!

In Chapter 23, we learned that rags are typically composite binaries—two large sections, each of which is a binary form. Once you have completed this assignment, therefore, you have actually composed just *half* of a rag. Complete the entire rag by composing a second binary section (**A B**) in the key of IV.

Instrumental Duet

Realize the progression below in four parts, in keyboard style. Once you are satisfied with your voice-leading, use the progression as the basis of a work for a solo instrument and piano. You may augment the rhythmic values, change the meter, use different types of phrase expansions, and so on, but keep it in a major key. Consider making the progression a theme and adding several figural variations.

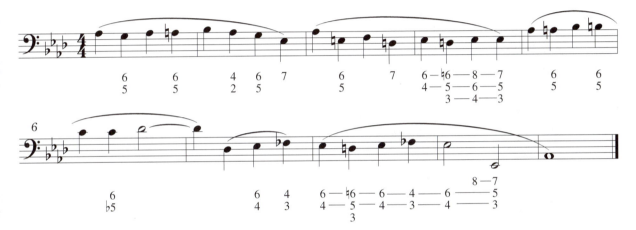

Into the Twentieth Century

CHAPTER 30 Modes, Scales, and Sets

Overview

In this chapter, we will perform and learn to recognize aurally some of the most common sounds in music of the twentieth and twenty-first centuries.

Outline of topics covered

I. KEY CONCEPTS

Sounds of the Twentieth and Twenty-first Centuries

Performing modes

Creating and performing new scales

Performing pentatonic scales

Performing octatonic scales

Performing whole-tone scales and related sounds

Integer notation

II. CALL AND RESPONSE

III. CONTEXTUAL LISTENING

IV. MELODIES FOR STUDY

V. IMPROVISATION

VI. COMPOSITION

I. KEY CONCEPTS

Sounds of the Twentieth and Twenty-first Centuries

During the last century, composers began to explore ways to use familiar sounds in unfamiliar ways. Many of their techniques are still employed today.

PERFORMING MODES

One common practice of twentieth-century composers was to include modes in their works, and thereby create compositions whose character contrasted with that of tonal music. To review the sounds of modes, revisit some of the works we studied in volume 1.

Chapter 4:   "Contextual Listening" #2 (p. 93)
             "Contextual Listening" #4 (p. 97)
             Debussy, "Passepied" (p. 104)
             "Canoeing Song" (p. 104)
Chapter 5:   "Contextual Listening" #4 (p. 117)
             "The Butterfly" (p. 122)
Chapter 10: "When Johnny Comes Marching Home" (p. 239)
Chapter 11: "Morrison's Jig" (p. 261)
Chapter 17: "On the Erie Canal" (p. 403)

Exercise 30.1: Reviewing Modes

Before completing the exercises below, review Chapter 4 (especially the section on "Diatonic Modes," p. 82). Then perform the modes indicated below, playing and singing both up and down from the given final. Remember, we may call the first pitch *do* ($\hat{1}$) and sing with chromatic solfège syllables, or we may sing modes as rotations of the major scale (and sing the Dorian mode, for example, from *re* to *re* [$\hat{2}$ to $\hat{2}$]).

(a) F Lydian   (e) E Mixolydian   (i) A Dorian

(b) D Phrygian   (f) G♯ Phrygian   (j) B♭ Lydian

(c) G Dorian   (g) C Lydian   (k) A♭ Mixolydian

(d) F♯ Aeolian   (h) B Dorian   (l) D♯ Phrygian

CREATING AND PERFORMING NEW SCALES

Another way twentieth-century composers found to create new sounds was to put familiar patterns together in different ways. To understand this idea, let's use tetrachords to create some new scales.

Exercise 30.2: Creating and Performing New Scales

Combine the following tetrachords in different ways to make new scales. (For example, Phrygian plus harmonic produces the scale C D♭ E♭ F G A♭ B C.) Prepare to perform your solutions in class. As you listen to classmates perform, notate some of their ideas so that you have a collection of scales for later use in your "Improvisation" and "Composition" exercises.

(a) major   (b) minor   (c) Phrygian   (d) harmonic   (e) whole-tone

PERFORMING PENTATONIC SCALES

Although any five-note scale may be called pentatonic, we learned in Chapters 3 and 4 that there are two pentatonic scales frequently used by Western musicians: the *major pentatonic scale*, which sounds like *do–re–mi–sol–la–do* ($\hat{1}$–$\hat{2}$–$\hat{3}$–$\hat{5}$–$\hat{6}$–$\hat{1}$); and the *minor pentatonic scale*, which sounds like *do–me–fa–sol–te–do* ($\hat{1}$–♭$\hat{3}$–$\hat{4}$–$\hat{5}$–♭$\hat{7}$–$\hat{1}$). These scales may be recalled as rotations of the black keys on the piano, with the major pentatonic beginning on G♭ and the minor pentatonic on E♭. The minor pentatonic scale can also be heard in many blues pieces (see Chapter 26).

Before completing the exercises below, review these pentatonic works: from Chapter 3, "Amazing Grace" (p. 59) and Melody 8 (p. 74); from Chapter 4, Bartók's "Evening in Transylvania" (p. 81) and "Canoeing Song" (p. 104).

Exercise 30.3: Performing Pentatonic Scales

Perform major and minor pentatonic scales from each of these pitches. Consider the given pitch to be the tonic. Then think of its major or minor key signature to find the pitches of the pentatonic scale.

(a) A	(c) C	(e) B	(g) D	(i) C♯
(b) E	(d) F	(f) F♯	(h) G	(j) B♭

PERFORMING OCTATONIC SCALES

Though any eight-pitch scale is an **octatonic scale**, we usually reserve the name for the specific scale that is made up of alternating whole and half steps. A favorite of composers, the sound of the octatonic scale may be imagined in several ways.

W–H Octatonic Scales: To make an octatonic scale that begins whole-step half-step, perform two minor tetrachords whose beginnings are a tritone apart.

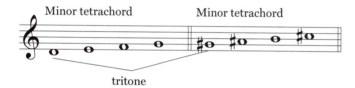

Creating octatonic scales this way has two advantages. First, we can hear the tetrachords as familiar sounds; after all, every minor scale begins this way! Second, the scales will be easier to read because we have grouped the pitches into familiar patterns. As with other scales, repeat the first pc at the top.

Another way: Begin the upper tetrachord one half step higher than the top pitch of the lower tetrachord.

Exercise 30.4: Performing W–H Octatonic Scales

Follow the steps below to perform W–H octatonic scales from the given pitches.

- To tune the scale, sing its pitch-interval names. Begin with the given pitch, then sing "whole–half–whole–half," and so on, or sing the intervals as integers (start on 0 and sing "0–2–1–2–1," etc.).
- To spell the scale, sing the solfège syllables or scale-degree numbers for each minor tetrachord as you play the scale: *do-re-me-fa, do-re-me-fa*; or 1̂–2̂–♭3̂–4̂, 1̂–2̂–♭3̂–4̂ (repeat *do* or 1̂ at the top of the scale).
- To reinforce both tuning and spelling, sing each note name as you play the scale.

(a) D	(d) B	(g) A♯	(j) F♯
(b) F	(e) E	(h) C♯	(k) A
(c) G♯	(f) G	(i) E♭	(l) C

H–W Octatonic Scales: To make H–W octatonic scales, play two *ti–do–re–me* ($\hat{7}$–$\hat{1}$–$\hat{2}$–$\flat\hat{3}$) tetrachords whose beginnings are a tritone apart. These are called **octatonic tetrachords.** These scales will also be easy to read because we have grouped the pitches into familiar patterns.

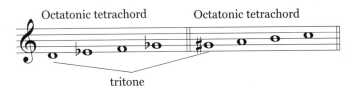

Again, repeat the first pc at the top of the scale.

Another way: Begin the upper octatonic tetrachord one whole step above the top pitch of the lower tetrachord.

Exercise 30.5: Performing H–W Octatonic Scales

Perform H–W octatonic scales from the same pitches in Exercise 30.4.

- To tune the scale, sing the interval pattern: "tonic–half–whole–half–whole" or "0–1–2–1–2," and so on.
- To spell the scale, sing "*ti–do–re–me, ti–do–re–me*" (or "$\hat{7}$–$\hat{1}$–$\hat{2}$–$\flat\hat{3}$, $\hat{7}$–$\hat{1}$–$\hat{2}$–$\flat\hat{3}$") as you play.
- To reinforce both tuning and spelling, sing each note name as you play the scale.

Diminished Scales: The sum of two fully diminished seventh chords one half step apart always yields an octatonic scale. This saturation of "diminished" quality is why many jazz musicians call the octatonic scale the **diminished scale.** Play a diminished seventh chord that includes the pitch C4. Then play each of the diminished seventh chords one half step away from C. (You may repeat the first pc at the top.)

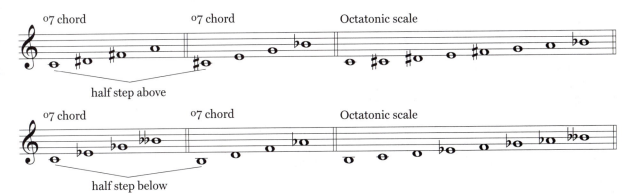

Exercise 30.6: Combining Chords to Create Octatonic Scales

1. Perform octatonic scales that are the combination of two diminished seventh chords one half step apart. Begin on the pitches from Exercise 30.4. Sing each note name as you play the scale.

2. Experiment to find other four-note chords that may be combined to create an octatonic scale. Perform these for the class.

Subsets of the Octatonic Scale: Composers may *imply* an entire collection by including only some of its pitches. For example, C–E–B♭ may substitute for the seventh chord C–E–G–B♭. The three-note group is a *subset* of the larger collection. The same concept applies to modes and scales.

A common way composers imply the octatonic collection is to play two major triads or dominant seventh chords a tritone apart.

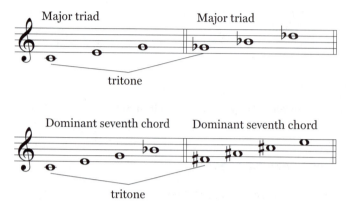

Experiment with this idea by playing the triads (or seventh chords) in different inversions, then reordering the pitches until you like the sound.

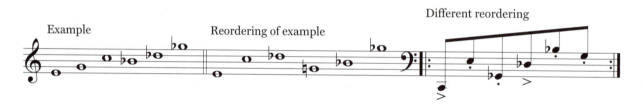

Exercise 30.7: Performing Subsets of the Octatonic Scale

1. Experiment to find other triad or seventh chords you can combine to create subsets of the octatonic scale. Prepare to perform your solutions in class.

2. Combine the octatonic tetrachord with the other tetrachords listed in Exercise 30.2. What new scales can you make? Do you notice that many of these new scales are also eight-tone scales?

All-Interval Tetrachords: Composers like to find patterns in scales that may be sequenced. For example, the sequence below is based on an all-interval tetrachord, represented in each group of four sixteenth notes. **All-interval** means that the tetrachord contains one instance of each interval class. An **interval class** (**ic**) represents all pitch intervals that can be made from one pair of pitch classes. There are six interval classes altogether, labeled ic 1 to ic 6.

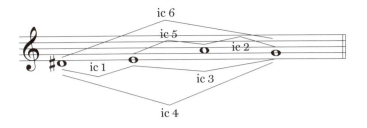

Exercise 30.8: Performing Melodic Sequences Using Octatonic Scales

Experiment until you discover at least five different melodic sequences using the pitches of the octatonic scale. Prepare to perform your solutions in class. As you listen to class-mates perform, notate some of their ideas so that you have a collection of melodic ideas for later use in your "Improvisation" and "Composition" exercises.

PERFORMING WHOLE-TONE SCALES AND RELATED SOUNDS

One way to make a whole-tone scale is to play two *do–re–mi* ($\hat{1}$–$\hat{2}$–$\hat{3}$) trichords one whole step apart. We can also think of them as beginning a tritone apart. Such methods help us to read the scale more easily.

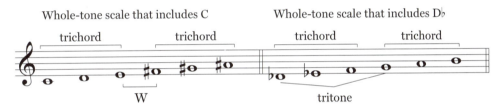

Another way: Combine two augmented triads whose roots are a whole step apart.

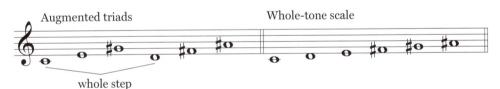

Exercise 30.9: Performing Whole-Tone Scales

Follow the steps below to perform whole-tone scales from the given pitches.

- To tune the scale, sing its pitch-interval names. Begin with the given pitch, then sing "whole–whole–whole," and so on, or sing the intervals as integers (start on 0 and sing "0–2–2–2," etc.). Another way is to sing chromatic solfège syllables or scale-degree numbers (*do–re–mi–fi–si–li–do*; $\hat{1}$–$\hat{2}$–$\hat{3}$–#$\hat{4}$–#$\hat{5}$–#$\hat{6}$–$\hat{1}$).
- To spell the scale, sing the solfège syllables or scale-degree numbers for each tri-chord: *do–re–mi, do–re–mi*; or $\hat{1}$–$\hat{2}$–$\hat{3}$, $\hat{1}$–$\hat{2}$–$\hat{3}$ (repeat *do* or $\hat{1}$ at the top of the scale).
- To reinforce both tuning and spelling, sing each note name as you play the scale.

(a) E   (c) B♭   (e) F   (g) D♭

(b) C♯   (d) A   (f) A♭   (h) B

Composers sometimes imply the sound of the whole-tone scale by featuring subsets. Here are two common whole-tone subsets to listen for.

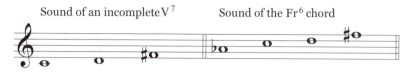

Sound of an incomplete V⁷   Sound of the Fr⁶ chord

Exercise 30.10: Performing Whole-Tone Subsets

Experiment to find whole-tone subsets that are not simply transpositions or inversions of those above. Prepare to perform your solutions in class.

INTEGER NOTATION

Scales like the octatonic and the whole-tone are awkward to spell; the octatonic scale includes two versions of the same basic note name (for instance, the scale could include both F♮ and F♯), while the whole-tone scale contains a diminished third (A♯–C, B–D♭, etc.). To simplify our understanding of such music, we can notate these and other sounds with integers. In integer notation, every pc that sounds like C (C, B♯, D♭♭, etc.) is called by the integer name 0 (zero), every pc that sounds like C♯/D♭ is called 1, and so on. We can also sing passages with integers instead of solfège syllables, scale-degree numbers, or letter names.

Exercise 30.11: Singing with Integer Names

Perform Exercises 30.4, 30.5, and 30.9 again. This time, sing your answers with integer notation.

II. CALL AND RESPONSE

Your teacher will perform a number of pitch patterns that feature pentatonic, octatonic, and whole-tone materials, then ask you to perform or write what you heard.

Options for performing your response
Maintain the pitch, rhythm, and tempo of the call.

- Sing pitch only (with solfège syllables, scale-degree numbers, note names, or pc integer names).
- Sing rhythm only.
- Sing pitch and rhythm.
- Conduct (or tap) while singing rhythm only or singing both pitch and rhythm.
- Play on your instrument.

Options for writing your response

- note names or pc integers
- interval succession (W–H, 2–1, etc.)
- note heads only
- rhythmic notation only
- notes and rhythm

III. CONTEXTUAL LISTENING

EXAMPLE 1, TRACK 2.10

Listen to an excerpt from a piano work by Lutosławski, and complete the exercises below.

1. Which term represents the texture of the excerpt?

   (a) monophony

   (b) chordal homophony

   (c) nonimitative polyphony

   (d) imitative polyphony

2. Which is the meter signature of the excerpt?

   (a) $\frac{2}{8}$

   (b) $\frac{3}{8}$

   (c) $\frac{4}{8}$

   (d) $\frac{5}{8}$

3. The excerpt begins with an introduction followed by two phrases. Compared with phrase 1, phrase 2

   (a) begins and ends the same;

   (b) begins the same but ends differently;

   (c) begins differently but ends the same;

   (d) begins and ends differently.

4. Notate the pitches and rhythm of the excerpt on the staves below. Write in all accidentals. The first pitches are given. If necessary, break the dictation into steps: rhythm, intervals, pitches, lower part, higher part, and so on.

5. On which collection is the excerpt based?

   (a) Mixolydian mode

   (b) pentatonic

   (c) whole-tone

   (d) octatonic

EXAMPLE 2, TRACK 2.11

Listen to a brief excerpt from an art song by Alban Berg, and complete the exercises below.

1. On which scale is this excerpt based?

   (a) pentatonic

   (b) octatonic

   (c) whole-tone

   (d) Lydian

2. Which is the meter type of the excerpt?

   (a) simple triple

   (b) simple quadruple

   (c) compound duple

   (d) compound triple

3. In the vocal line, which is the quality of the triad arpeggios?

   (a) major

   (b) minor

   (c) augmented

   (d) diminished

4. Notate the rhythm of the vocal line on the blank staff below.

5. Beneath the rhythm you notated in #4, write the sequence of pitch intervals in the vocal line. Write arrows up and down to show the direction of the intervals and contour of the melody.

6. Use your answers to #4 and #5 to notate the pitches and rhythm of the vocal melody on the staff below. Begin on E5, and write the appropriate clef and accidentals.

7. At the beginning, which is a correct notation of the piano's pitches?

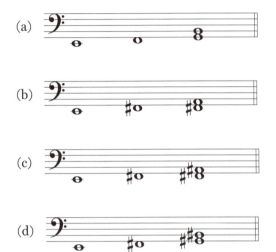

(a)

(b)

(c)

(d)

EXAMPLE 3, TRACK 2.12

Listen to an excerpt from a chamber work by Rebecca Clarke, and complete the exercises below.

1. Which is the meter signature of this excerpt?

    (a) $\frac{2}{4}$

    (b) $\frac{3}{4}$

    (c) $\frac{6}{8}$

    (d) $\frac{9}{8}$

2. On which type of scale is this excerpt based?

    (a) pentatonic

    (b) octatonic

    (c) whole-tone

    (d) Phrygian

3. At the end of each half of the excerpt, the viola sustains a long pitch. What is the quality of the chord that accompanies these sustained pitches?

    (a) major triad

    (b) augmented triad

    (c) major seventh chord

    (d) minor seventh chord

4. Notate the pitches and rhythm of the viola melody for the first half of the excerpt (to the first long sustained note) on the staves below. Begin on A4 in the appropriate clef for viola. Write in all accidentals. If necessary, break the dictation into steps: rhythm, intervals, pitches.

5. After the long sustained viola note, the melody you notated above repeats, transposed to a higher pitch. Compared with the beginning, by what interval has the composer transposed the repetition?

   (a) M3

   (b) P4

   (c) TT

   (d) P5

6. Transcribe the melody of the first half for alto saxophone. Begin on F♯5. Write the appropriate clef and accidentals.

EXAMPLE 4, TRACK 2.13

Listen several times to this composition for piano by Debussy before completing the exercises below.

1. The beginning of the piece is based on which scale or mode?

   (a) Lydian mode

   (b) pentatonic

   (c) whole-tone

   (d) octatonic

2. The opening theme is doubled at which interval?

   (a) m3　　(b) M3　　(c) TT　　(d) m6

3. When the bass first enters, which best represents its rhythm?

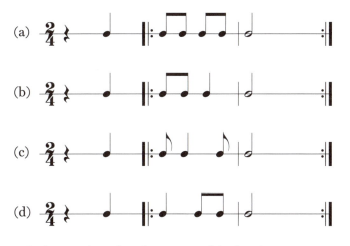

4. Which term describes the nature of the bass's repetition?

   (a) basso continuo　　　　(c) sequence

   (b) ostinato　　　　　　　(d) passacaglia

5. Immediately after the first entrance of the bass, a second theme enters in the middle register. Notate the pitches and rhythm of the initial statement of this melody in a single octave (ignore any octave doubling). Begin from the given pitch.

6. The opening theme is heard six times during the beginning of the composition. Which of the following best describes the texture of the piece during occurences 3–6?

(a) chordal homophony

(c) imitative polyphony

(b) nonimitative polyphony

(d) melody and accompaniment

7. After the initial statement of the second theme (which you notated in #5), the *beginning* of this second theme is repeated and combined with the first theme. Which of the following best describes the repetition of theme 2's beginning?

(a) exact

(b) transposed

(c) doubled using parallel chords

(d) inverted fragment

8. After theme 2's repetition and just before the entrance of a third theme, the bass line consists of pitches with long durations. Listen several times to the beginning of the bass line (recall #3), and compare these two places. How is the latter bass line related to the original statement of the bass line?

(a) rhythmic augmentation of the original

(b) rhythmic diminution of the original

(c) transposition of the original

(d) inversion of the original

9. About two and a half minutes in to the piece, there is a change of character and tempo. On which scale is this new section based?

(a) major

(b) natural (descending melodic) minor

(c) Phrygian mode

(d) pentatonic

10. Which is the role of the bass line throughout the composition?

(a) It has no consistent role.

(b) It serves as a pedal point.

(c) It defines the tonal centers of each section.

(d) It moves in contrary motion to the highest part.

11. Refer to your answers to the previous exercises to help answer this question. Which is the form of the composition?

(a) simple binary

(c) sonata

(b) ternary

(d) rondo

IV. MELODIES FOR STUDY

For each of the melodies below, prepare to do any of the following:

- Conduct and sing it in rhythm.
- Play it on an instrument.
- Identify scales or collections within melodic segments.
- Transpose the melody to other keys on your instrument.
- Identify the pitch intervals between successive notes.

Strategies for Singing

- Practice singing these melodies by performing the rhythm alone (while conducting), then slowly the pitch alone, then the pitch and rhythm together.
- To focus on intonation, sing on interval numbers (e.g., sing a whole step as "2," a minor third as "3," and so on).
- Once you feel confident of the pitches and intervals, sing in rhythm on "la," then with pc integer names.
- Modal or pentatonic melodies may be sung on solfège syllables or scale-degree numbers.
- For melodies that exceed your voice range, transfer pitches to octaves that are more easily sung; try to do so at natural breaks in the phrasing.

Melody 1 Debussy, "Général Lavine," from *Preludes*, Book II

Melody 2 Charles Ives, "September"

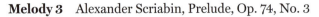

Melody 3 Alexander Scriabin, Prelude, Op. 74, No. 3

Melody 4 Debussy, "Bruyères," from *Preludes*, Book II

Melody 5 Germaine Tailleferre, Sonata in C♯ minor for Violin and Piano
This "free" use of diatonicism is sometimes called **pandiatonicism.**

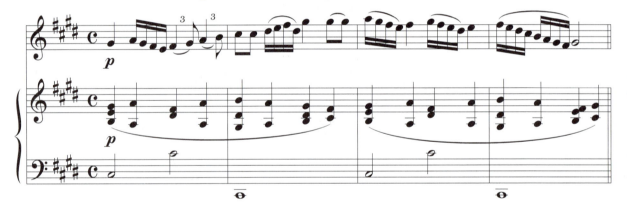

Melody 6 Rebecca Clarke, Sonata for Viola and Piano, first movement

Melody 7 Igor Stravinsky, "Danse infernale de tous les sujets de Kastchéi" ("Infernal Dance of King Kastchéi's Subjects"), from *L'oiseau de feu* (adapted)

V. IMPROVISATION

In this improvisation, we will create an **additive *crescendo*** and a **subtractive *diminuendo*—** two techniques often used by composers to create interesting textures.

First, choose one of the collections below, and perform it to get the sounds in your ears, voice, and fingers. Remember, the members of this scale are pitch classes and may be expressed in any octave.

- pentatonic (either the major or minor pentatonic)
- whole-tone (one of the two distinct collections of the scale)
- octatonic (one of the three distinct collections of the scale)
- any contrived scale you created in Exercise 30.2 or 30.8

1. Begin quietly with a brief motivic idea, which may be repeated and varied as the performer chooses. A second person then enters the improvisation, performing an idea that in some way complements the first. (This second idea might be contrasting in its rhythm, register, timbre, articulation, etc.) Other performers likewise enter one at a time until the texture is dense and the dynamics loud.
2. At the dynamic peak, a soloist joins the texture, singing or playing a slow, lyrical melodic line that will sharply contrast with the more chaotic background.
3. Gradually the ensemble reduces its dynamics, and performers drop out one by one.
4. The soloist concludes the improvisation with a brief cadenza.

Strategies

- Prepare to improvise with *all* of the scales listed above.
- Try incorporating some of the pitch patterns you created earlier in the exercises in section I.
- Include as many different instrumental timbres as you have available.
- Decide on the order of entries. For example, the teacher may cue the entry of each performer, or performers might enter in an order decided on in advance.
- Discern the tempo, meter, and character of the improvisation from the first performer.
- The soloist should listen to the texture and imitate motives heard in the background.

Variations

- At the high point, the teacher points to a new scale. As seamlessly as possible, all performers play the same melodic shapes, but now with the pcs of the new collection.
- Choose one scale, switch to a second, and return to the first to create an **A B A** design. Think of ideas you might include in your composition below.
- When the texture is full, listen for the music of a specific performer. Create a call and response between yourself and that performer.
- Before performing, decide on a word that describes the general character or mood of the improvisation (e.g., "frightening," "joyful," "melancholic"). Craft your improvisations to reflect this character.

Record your improvisations. Listen to the performances and analyze what you hear. Do you hear any "wrong" notes (i.e., notes not in the scale)? Who played them? Are there parts that turned out especially well? Transcribe them to see why they were successful. Consider using some of these ideas in your compositions.

VI. COMPOSITION

Compose a short work in **A B A′** form that features a soloist with an accompanying instrument (piano or other keyboard, computer with MIDI gear, etc.). From the list below, choose a collection that will represent the sound of each section of your piece.

- modes
- new scales you created in Exercise 30.2
- pentatonic scale
- octatonic scale
- whole-tone scale

Some elements you might vary in the recapitulation:

- melodic contour (inversion, same shape but wider leaps, etc.)
- melodic embellishment
- dynamics
- articulation
- register
- doubling (e.g., parallel chords)
- amount of repetition (e.g., sequences)
- transposition of scale or melody or both
- nature of the accompaniment (e.g., block chords vs. arpeggios)
- change of motivic rhythm

Strategies

In addition to using a different scale in the **B** section, think of other musical elements you might change to help listeners hear the form of your piece. For example, if the **A** section is fast, loud, staccato, and high, **B** might be slow, soft, legato, and low.

Although you could simply copy the material from section **A** and paste it at the end to create a recapitulation, composers seldom do this anymore. Usually they vary some musical elements in the recapitulation. For example, a melody might return with its contour inverted, in a more embellished form, or both.

Three examples

A section	**B** section	**A** section (varied)
1. Dorian mode	Pentatonic scale	Dorian mode (Invert contour of the melody.)
2. Whole-tone scale	Octatonic scale	Whole-tone scale (Double the melody using augmented triads.)
3. Lydian-Mixolydian mode	New scale	Lydian-Mixolydian mode (Sequence the melody; accompany the melody with arpeggios instead of block chords.)

Perform your compositions in class. Listeners should be able to determine the scale collections used, the form of the composition, and the nature of the variation in both the **B** section and the recapitulation. Listeners should also take dictation, notating the pitches and rhythm of motivic ideas in order to suggest additional ideas for each composer.

CHAPTER 31

Music Analysis with Sets

Overview

Earlier we learned to identify the sounds prevalent in common-practice music—triads and seventh chords. Since the beginning of the twentieth century, composers have included additional sounds in their palettes. Here, we explore some of these sounds (and their transpositions and inversions) through guided listening and performance.

Outline of topics covered

I. **KEY CONCEPTS**
  Identifying Sets
  Transposing Sets
  Inverting Sets
  Interval-Class Vectors

II. **CALL AND RESPONSE**
III. **CONTEXTUAL LISTENING**
IV. **MELODIES FOR STUDY**

V. **IMPROVISATION**
  Duets
VI. **COMPOSITION**

I. KEY CONCEPTS

Identifying Sets

A group of pitch classes, or pcs, is called a **pitch-class set** (**pcset**). A group of pitches is called a **pitch set**. Sets can be melodies, chords, or scales. To articulate their musical ideas, composers group pitches by register, articulation, dynamics, timbre, and so on. We listen for these associations to help us determine which pcs or pitches should be included in a set.

Often when musicians study sets, there is a temptation to depend on numbers and mathematical concepts at the expense of the aural and kinesthetic aspects of listening and performing. In the examples below, our fingers and ears will be our guides as we learn to identify and compare sets.

Perform the examples below, and listen to the sounds. Our ears (and eyes) reveal that the first two sonorities in each prelude, sets A and B, are the same, though reversed in order.

Alexander Scriabin, Prelude, Op. 59, No. 2   Scriabin, Prelude, Op. 67, No. 2

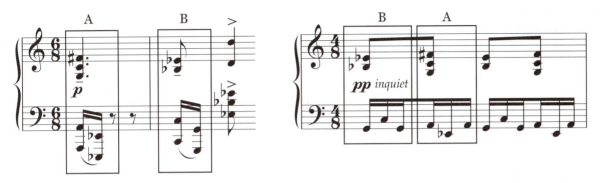

Since these preludes were composed years apart, we can conclude that Scriabin treats sets A and B as distinct sonorities, although ones not found in traditional music. (A is a nontriad sound; and while B *sounds* like a predominant chord in tonal music, it does not function as such.)

The pcs of set A are identical in each prelude, as are the pcs of set B. But what if we hear two sets whose sound is similar but whose pcs are different? How do we find the relationship between them?

Transposing Sets

Consider the highest line in the example below to be set C.

Scriabin, Prelude, Op. 59, No. 2 (mm. 1–3a)

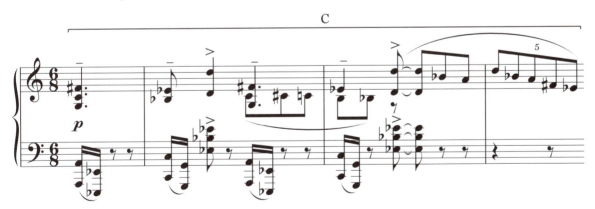

Play this line, and sustain its five *distinct* pitches, as shown below. Then play the pitches in order from lowest to highest.

Set C, original order   Play from lowest to highest.

Now play the example below. We'll call this combined melody and harmony set D.

Scriabin, Prelude, Op. 59, No. 2 (mm. 12–13a)

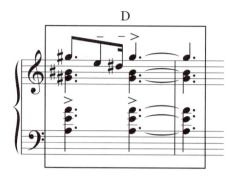

Sustain the pitches of set D to hear them as a chord. (We leave out the lower octave doublings of pcs A, E, and G♯ to keep all the pitches within the span of one octave.) Then play the pitches in order from lowest to highest.

Set D, original order   Play from lowest to highest.
(with duplicates left out)

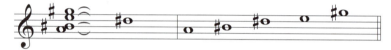

Play sets C and D as chords, then melodically from lowest to highest pitch, and compare them. Can you hear that D is a transposition of C by six semitones? Listen to the intervals of each to confirm this.

Set C, original order   Play from lowest to highest.   Set D, original order   Play from lowest to highest.

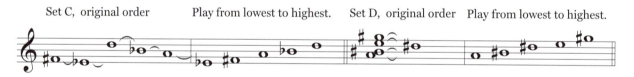

Until we become familiar with sounds like these, it may be hard to hear such relationships. One method that will help us hear how different sets are related is to find each set's **normal order**: its most compact form.

To find the normal order of set C, first play its pitches in order from lowest to highest, as before. Then play and notate each rotation of set C (move the lowest pitch to the top for each new rotation). The rotation that ascends from D is the normal order of set C because it has the smallest outside interval (from D to B♭). Write the pc integers beneath each pitch of the normal order. We can also notate the normal order with curly braces: C {2 3 6 9 t}.

Rotations of set C   Normal order

2   3   6   9   t

Now play the rotations of set D to find its normal order.

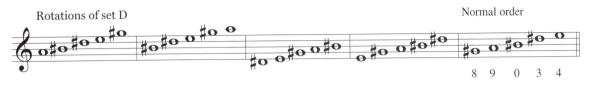

Rotations of set D

Normal order

8   9   0   3   4

We look for the rotation with the smallest outside interval, and find that it's the one that ascends from G♯: {8 9 0 3 4}.

Play the normal order of sets C and D, and listen to the succession of intervals for each: +1, +3, +3, +1. Sets whose normal orders have the same succession of intervals, like C and D, are related by transposition. Let's determine their exact transposition.

List the elements of set D (the second set we hear).	{8 9 0 3 4}
Subtract the elements of set C (the first set we hear).	− {2 3 6 9 t}
This reveals the number of semitones of transposition.	6 6 6 6 6

(If an element in set D is smaller than the element in set C that is being subtracted from it, we add 12 to D's element: rather than 0-6, 3-9, and 4-t, we subtract 12-6, 15-9, and 16-t.)

The result confirms what our ears told us earlier. Set D is a transposition of set C up six semitones. We notate this relationship as D = T_6C. T stands for "transposition," and the number after indicates the interval of transposition in semitones.

Inverting Sets

In the example below, consider the first five *distinct* pitches of the highest line to be set E.

Scriabin, Prelude, Op. 67, No. 2 (mm. 1–3)

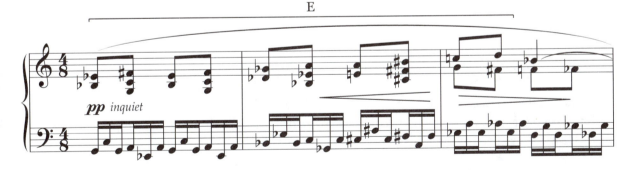

Play the distinct pcs of sets E and A (from p. 289), notated on the staff below. Play them melodically and harmonically, and compare their sounds. Can you hear that each is the sound of a fully diminished seventh chord plus another note?

Set E   Set A

Are sets E and A related? Let's find out. First, find the normal order of set A. Play the rotations of A, shown below.

Here, we find three rotations that have the same smallest outside interval. When this happens, we choose as "best" normal order the rotation that has the smallest intervals (often semitones) closely packed at one end or the other. In this case, the rotation that ascends from F♯ has a semitone between the first two pitches, making it the best normal order: { 6 7 9 0 3 }.

Now perform the rotations of set E to find its normal order.

Here too, three rotations have the same outside smallest interval. In this case, the rotation that ascends from F♯ has a semitone between the last two pitches, making it the best normal order: { 6 9 0 2 3 }.

What is the specific relationship between set A { 6 7 9 0 3 } and set E { 6 9 0 2 3 }? Compare their successive pitch intervals: for set A, the pitch intervals ascend +1, +2, +3, +3; and for set B, the pitch intervals ascend +3, +3, +2, +1. When the interval successions of two normal orders are identical but are *reversed* in order, the two sets are related by *inversion*.

We take these final steps to find their exact relationship:

List the elements of A.	{ 6 7 9 0 3 }
List the elements of E in reverse order	+ { 3 2 0 9 6 }
(because we already know E is related by inversion).	
Add the elements to reveal the relation.	9 9 9 9 9

We notate this relationship as E = T_9IA, where I indicates "inversion." The $_9$ is called the **index number** —the number we obtained when we added the pcs of the sets together.

It is helpful to remember that with transpositions we *subtract* the elements, and with inversions we *add* them. In performing these operations, if we get a number larger than 11 or smaller than 0, we subtract 12 or add 12 to keep the result between 0 and 11.

Interval-Class Vectors

Another way to determine relationships between sets is to compare their interval-class content. A quick way to identify an interval class (ic) is to find the shortest possible distance between two pcs as measured in semitones. At the keyboard, play trichords { 7 9 2 } and { 2 4 9 }. One possible realization is shown below.

The distance between pcs A and G might be 22, 10, or 2 semitones. Because 2 is the smallest distance, A and G are members of ic 2.

Now determine, by ear and eye, all the interval classes by playing each pair of pitches. In each trichord, we hear one ic 2 and two ic 5s.

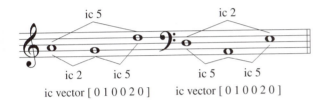

We summarize the interval-class content of any set in an **ic vector**. To make an ic vector, write the interval classes (1–6) in one row and the number of occurrences of each ic underneath.

Interval class:	1	2	3	4	5	6
Number of occurrences of each ic:	0	1	0	0	2	0

Once we have completed this tally, we take the bottom row as the ic vector: [0 1 0 0 2 0]. Because both {7 9 2} and {2 4 9} share the same ic vector, they share the same interval content, which means they sound alike.

In the five exercises that follow, we will identify sets from works by Anton Webern and Igor Stravinsky, and relate them by transposition and inversion. In each exercise, work through the process at the keyboard (or other instrument) in order to help you learn to recognize trichords (Webern) and tetrachords (Stravinsky) aurally and kinesthetically.

Exercise 31.1: Webern, "Nachts" ("At Night"), from *Sechs Lieder* (*Six Songs*), Op. 14

Perform the excerpt below. For each bracketed trichord set, find the normal order and ic vector. Then find the relationship between the sets specified.

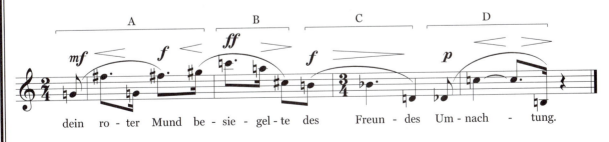

Translation: Your red mouth sealed the friend's madness.

(staff lines)

Set A   Normal order { ___ ___ ___ }   ic vector [___ ___ ___ ___ ___ ___]

Set B   Normal order { ___ ___ ___ }   ic vector [___ ___ ___ ___ ___ ___]

Set C   Normal order { ___ ___ ___ }   ic vector [___ ___ ___ ___ ___ ___]

Set D   Normal order { ___ ___ ___ }   ic vector [___ ___ ___ ___ ___ ___]

How are sets A and D related?

How are sets B and C related?

Exercise 31.2: Webern, "Wiese im Park," from *Four Songs for Voice and Orchestra*, Op.13

Perform the excerpt below. Find the normal order and ic vector for each bracketed trichord set, then answer the question that follows.

Translation: The many bluebells!

(staff lines)

Set E   Normal order { ___ ___ ___ }   ic vector [___ ___ ___ ___ ___ ___]

Set F   Normal order { ___ ___ ___ }   ic vector [___ ___ ___ ___ ___ ___]

How are sets E and F related?

Exercise 31.3: Stravinsky, "Action rituelle des ancêtres" ("Ritual Dance of the Elders"), from *The Rite of Spring*

Perform the excerpt below. Find the normal order and ic vector for each bracketed tetrachord set, then answer the questions that follow.

Set G   Normal order { ___ ___ ___ ___ }   ic vector [___ ___ ___ ___ ___ ___]

Set H   Normal order { ___ ___ ___ ___ }   ic vector [___ ___ ___ ___ ___ ___]

How are sets G and H related?

Combine the pcs of sets G and H to make a scale. What is the name of this scale?

Exercise 31.4: Stravinsky, "Rondes printanières" ("Spring Rounds") and "Action rituelle des ancêtres," from *The Rite of Spring*

Perform the excerpts below, find the normal order and ic vector for each bracketed tetrachord set, and answer the question that follows.

Set J   Normal order { ___ ___ ___ ___ }   ic vector [___ ___ ___ ___ ___ ___]

Set K   Normal order { ___ ___ ___ ___ }   ic vector [___ ___ ___ ___ ___ ___]

How are sets J and K related?

Exercise 31.5: Webern, Cantata, Op. 29

Perform the excerpt below, find the normal order and ic vector for each bracketed tetrachord set, and answer the questions that follow.

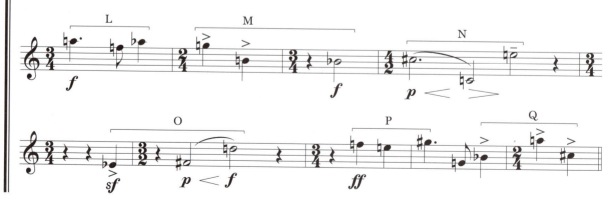

Set L   Normal order { ___ ___ ___ }   ic vector [___ ___ ___ ___ ___ ___]

Set M   Normal order { ___ ___ ___ }   ic vector [___ ___ ___ ___ ___ ___]

Set N   Normal order { ___ ___ ___ }   ic vector [___ ___ ___ ___ ___ ___]

Set O   Normal order { ___ ___ ___ }   ic vector [___ ___ ___ ___ ___ ___]

Set P   Normal order { ___ ___ ___ }   ic vector [___ ___ ___ ___ ___ ___]

Set Q   Normal order { ___ ___ ___ }   ic vector [___ ___ ___ ___ ___ ___]

How are sets M and L related?

How are sets N and L related?

How are sets O and L related?

How are sets P and L related?

How are sets Q and L related?

II. CALL AND RESPONSE

Your teacher will perform a number of pitch patterns, then ask you to perform or write what you heard.

Options for performing your response

Maintain the pitch, rhythm, and tempo of the call.

- Sing pitch only (with pc or interval numbers, or note names).
- Sing rhythm only.
- Sing pitch and rhythm.
- Conduct (or tap) while singing rhythm only or singing both pitch and rhythm.
- Play on your instrument.

Options for writing your response

- normal order
- note names or integers
- note heads only
- rhythmic notation only
- notes and rhythm

III. CONTEXTUAL LISTENING

For some of the questions in this section, you may need to consult Appendix 3 ("Set-Class Table").

EXAMPLE 1, TRACK 2.12

We listened to this excerpt of a chamber work by Rebecca Clarke in Chapter 30. Now that we know more about set theory, let's listen again and analyze her motive.

1. Consider the first four pcs of the string melody to be an unordered pcset. Call this tetrachord set A. Realize the pcs of set A as pitches on the staff below in ascending order. Write the integer beneath each pc.

2. Play and notate the four rotations of set A on the staff below. What is the normal

   order for set A? { ____ ____ ____ ____ }

3. Find the intervals between each pc in set A, and arrange them as an ic vector.

   The ic vector of set A is [____ ____ ____ ____ ____ ____].

EXAMPLE 2, TRACK 2.14

Listen to a piano work by Bartók that is based on a folk melody, and complete the following exercises.

1. Which is the meter signature for this excerpt?

   (a) $\frac{2}{4}$ (b) $\frac{3}{4}$ (c) $\frac{6}{8}$ (d) $\frac{9}{8}$

2. Which is the texture of the excerpt?

   (a) imitative counterpoint

   (b) nonimitative counterpoint

   (c) melody and accompaniment

   (d) chordal homophony

3. Notate the rhythm of the melody on the staves below. Assume the beat unit to be the quarter note. Write an appropriate meter signature and bar lines, and beam notes characteristically.

4. The melody is doubled at the octave. Notate the pitches and rhythm of the higher voice on the staves below. Begin on A4. Write the appropriate clef and accidentals. To work more quickly, use shortcuts to help you recall the internal repetitions.

5. The melody of the first three measures has only five distinct pitch classes. Use your answer to #4 to determine the normal order of this pentachord.

   (a) { 4 5 6 9 e }

   (b) { 9 e 4 5 6 }

   (c) { 3 4 6 9 e }

   (d) { 6 9 e 3 4 }

6. The end of the excerpt most resembles which traditional cadence? (Hint: Listen to the bass line.)

   (a) authentic

   (b) deceptive

   (c) plagal

   (d) Phrygian

7. (a) Listen to the first half of the excerpt again, up to and including the punctuating chord. Notate each distinct pitch class you hear (in both melody and bass) on the staff below. Rearrange these pitches to make a scale. Because the focal pitch of the entire excerpt is B, begin your scale on B. Use your answers to previous questions to help you.

   (b) With which tetrachord does the scale begin?

      (1) major

      (2) minor

      (3) harmonic

      (4) Phrygian

   (c) With which tetrachord does the scale end?

      (1) major

      (2) minor

      (3) harmonic

      (4) Phrygian

EXAMPLE 3, TRACKS 2.15–17

The exercises below are based on a work for piano by Debussy. First listen to track 2.15, and complete these exercises.

1. Which of the following is a correct notation of the *first* chord in the piece?

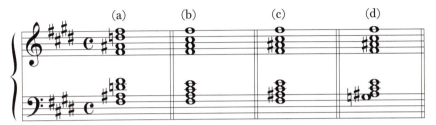

2. How is the *second* chord in the piece related to the first?

   (a) It is the subdominant chord.

   (b) It is a transposition of the first.

   (c) Its chord members are from the same whole-tone scale.

   (d) It supplies the remaining pitches of the chromatic collection.

3. Notate the pitches and rhythm of the melody on the staff below. The pitch and duration of the first note are given.

4. (a) Reorder the first five distinct pitch classes of the melody from #3 into a pentachord that begins on B. Notate your answer on the staff below.

   (b) What is the traditional name for the pentachord above?

       (1) major   (3) harmonic

       (2) minor   (4) Phrygian

   (c) What is the normal order of this pentachord?

       (1) {0 1 2 4 6}   (3) {e 1 2 4 6}

       (2) {1 2 4 6 e}   (4) {e 1 2 4 7}

Now listen to track 2.16, and complete #5–#9.

5. Notate the pitches and rhythm of the melody on the staff below. (The melody is in the middle register.) The pitch and duration of the first note are given.

6. The first four distinct pitch classes of the melody are from which tetrachord?

    (a) major   (c) harmonic

    (b) minor   (d) Phrygian

7. The parallel-chord triads in the highest register are of which quality?

    (a) major   (c) augmented

    (b) minor   (d) diminished

8. When considered together, the pitch classes of all four parallel-chord triads are members of which scale?

    (a) whole-tone   (c) octatonic

    (b) pentatonic   (d) harmonic minor

9. The final chord of the excerpt is of which quality?

    (a) major triad

    (b) minor triad

    (c) major seventh (MM⁷)

    (d) minor seventh (mm⁷)

Now listen to track 2.17, which is the same excerpt as track 2.16, but without the parallel-chord triads this time.

10. Which is a correct notation of the first chord?

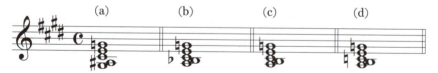

IV. MELODIES FOR STUDY

For each of the melodies below, prepare to do any of the following:

- Conduct and sing it in rhythm.
- Play it on an instrument.
- Identify sets or scales within melodic segments.
- Transpose the melody on your instrument.
- Identify the pitch intervals between successive notes.

Strategies for Singing

- Practice singing these melodies by performing the rhythm alone (while conducting), then slowly the pitch alone, then the pitch and rhythm together.
- Sing on interval numbers to focus on intonation (e.g., sing a whole step as "2," a minor third as "3," and so on).
- Once you feel confident of the pitches and intervals, sing in rhythm on "la," then on pc integers.
- For melodies that exceed your voice range, transfer pitches to octaves that are more easily sung; try to do so at natural breaks in the phrasing.

Melody 1   Charles Ives, "Premonitions"

Melody 2   Bartók, *Two Rumanian Dances*, Op. 8a, No. 1 (adapted)

Melody 3   Arnold Schoenberg, *Das Buch der hängenden Gärten (The Book of the Hanging Gardens)*, No. XIV

Melody 4   Alban Berg, Piano Sonata, Op. 1 (adapted)

Melody 5   Paul Hindemith, *Concert Music for Strings and Brass*, Op. 50

V. IMPROVISATION

Duets

We will improvise an **A B A** duet that moves from whole-tone sets to pentatonic sets, then back to whole-tone sets. Choose from the sets given below, moving from one scale to the next by means of the common trichord {6 8 t}. First, on your own, practice realizing these sets by singing and playing them to get the sounds in your ears, voice, and fingers. Remember to think of these realizations as pitch classes that may be expressed in any octave.

Whole-tone:

   {6 8 t}, {6 8 0}, {6 t 4}, {6 8 t 0}, {6 8 t 2}, {6 8 0 2}

Pentatonic:

{1 3 6}, {1 3 8}, {6 8 t}, {1 3 6 8}, {6 8 t 1 3}

"Pivot set" to move between collections: {6 8 t}

For the duet, one performer develops an ostinato based on one of the whole-tone sets. A second performer improvises a melody based on any of the remaining whole-tone sets. At a predetermined signal, such as a nod of the head, both perform only pcs from the "pivot" collection {6 8 t}. At a second signal, they move to the pentatonic sets and repeat the process (with one improvising an ostinato and the other a melody). Return to the whole-tone sets, again by means of {6 8 t}, giving the improvisation an **A B A** design.

Variations

- Add percussion to the ensemble. Use instruments if they are available, or improvise with pencils on notebooks, hand tapping, etc.
- Add a conductor. The performers must follow the gestures of the conductor, adjusting elements of their performance such as dynamics, tempo, and texture.

VI. COMPOSITION

Compose a short, single-section work that features a soloist with an accompanying instrument (piano or other keyboard, computer with MIDI gear, etc.). From the list below, choose a set that will represent the sound of your piece. Base all of your melodic and harmonic ideas on that single set, together with its transpositions and inversions.

{0 1 3 4}
{0 1 6 7}
{0 1 4 6}
{0 2 3 6 8}
{0 1 3 6 9}

Strategies

- As a precompositional strategy, transpose and invert your set to begin on each of the twelve pcs. Choose from among these possibilities those you think sound best.
- Consider using the order of the pcs in the set as the basis for organizing your transpositions or inversions. For example, say we chose this set, in this order: {t 7 0 6}. The whole notes in measures 2–5 below are the ordered elements of our original set.

Ordered set {t 7 0 6}   Transpositions based on the order of the original elements

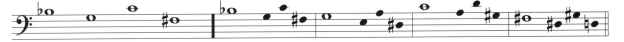

- Follow the previous suggestion, but use unordered pcsets instead (put the whole notes in the example above in any order).
- Remember, these are pcs. You may write them in any octave in the range of your instruments.

- As you hear in the listening examples, timbre is a very important element in recent music. Mark your scores with articulations, bowings, or special effects such as flutter-tonguing, harmonics, etc.
- Feature your sets both melodically and harmonically. (What chords can you make from your sets?)
- Can you make a scale with transpositions of your set?
- For extended instrumental techniques, consult with your soloist as well as an orchestration book, such as Samuel Adler's *The Study of Orchestration*, 3rd ed. (New York: Norton, 2002).
- For nontraditional ideas of how to notate music, consult Gardner Read's *Music Notation: A Manual of Modern Practice*, 2nd ed. (New York: Taplinger, 1979).

Perform your compositions in class. Listeners should also take dictation, notating the pitches and rhythm of motivic ideas in order to suggest additional ideas for the consideration of each composer.

Sets and Set Classes

CHAPTER 32

Overview

In Chapter 32, we continue our study of sets related by transposition and inversion. We will classify sets by their set-class names, and will learn to recognize the sound of certain set classes commonly featured in the works of twentieth- and twenty-first-century composers.

Outline of topics covered

I. KEY CONCEPTS

    Identifying Sets as Members of Set Classes

    Sets related by transposition

    Sets related by inversion

II. CALL AND RESPONSE

    Trichords

    Tetrachords

III. CONTEXTUAL LISTENING

IV. MELODIES FOR STUDY

V. IMPROVISATION

    Duets with Octatonic Scales and Subsets

VI. COMPOSITION

I. KEY CONCEPTS

Identifying Sets as Members of Set Classes

SETS RELATED BY TRANSPOSITION

If we take a pcset, such as { 2 3 6 9 t }, and write out all of its distinct transpositions ({ 3 4 7 t e }, { 4 5 8 e 0 }, etc.) and all distinct transpositions of its inversion { t 9 6 3 2 } as well, we have the **set class** (**SC**) for our pcset. Since it would be cumbersome to refer to this SC by listing all its members, we let one pcset represent the entire group. This is called its **prime form**.

As well as a prime form, each set class can be identified with a label: a hyphenated number like 4-13. These labels, which can be found in Appendix 3, were developed by music theorist Allen Forte; they are called "Forte numbers."

How do we find a particular set on Forte's list? To find out, let's return to the Scriabin prelude examples from Chapter 31. Play sets A, B, C, and D at the piano to become familiar with them again. Reorder them at the keyboard to review the principle of normal order.

Prelude, Op. 59, No. 2   Prelude, Op. 67, No. 2

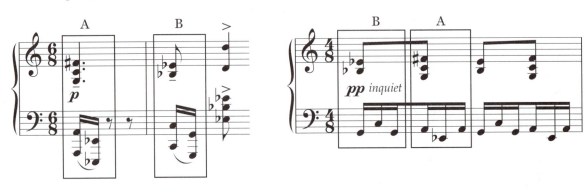

Prelude, Op. 59, No. 2

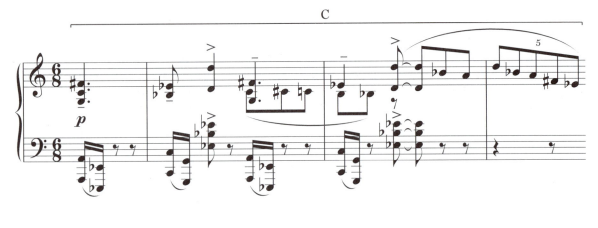

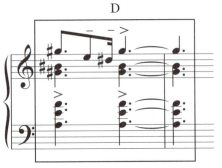

In Chapter 31, we discovered that set D is a transposition of C by six semitones. We also found the normal order for each of these sets. Once we know the normal order of a set, we can determine its prime form, and thus set class. Play the rotations of C again, as in Chapter 31, to determine its normal order.

Rotations of C   Normal order

2 3 6 9 t

Now, to find C's prime form, we call the first pc of the normal order 0. Play your pitch realization of this pentachord, { 2 3 6 9 t }, and count up the chromatic scale from the first note to each of the others, noting the number of semitones between them, as shown below. The interval numbers you get from this process also represent the pcs of the prime form. Like movable-*do* solfège, we might think of this technique as "movable zero."

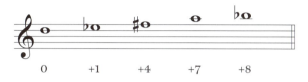

0   +1   +4   +7   +8

Thus, we learn that the prime form for set C is [0 1 4 7 8]. (The integers of a prime form are notated between square brackets.) If we look up [0 1 4 7 8] in Appendix 3, in the "PCs" column, we find that its set-class number is 5-22. The first part of the number (5) shows that this is a pentachord (five elements); the second (22) shows that this set is the twenty-second on the list of pentachords. The set class 5-22 represents all possible transpositions and inversions of [0 1 4 7 8], including Scriabin's { 2 3 6 9 t }.

Another way: All prime forms begin on C (= pc 0). Transpose the normal order of set C to begin on C, by adding ten to each element. (When transposing pcs, enharmonic spellings are all equivalent.) We write the pc integer numbers beneath each pitch. These integers are the prime form of the set.

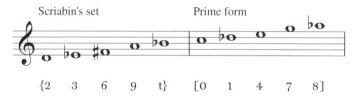

Scriabin's set   Prime form

{2   3   6   9   t}   [0   1   4   7   8]

Still another way: Using integer notation only, subtract the number of the first element from every element.

$$\begin{array}{r} \{2\ 3\ 6\ 9\ t\} \\ -\ \underline{2\ 2\ 2\ 2\ 2} \end{array}$$

prime form: 0 1 4 7 8

Now play the rotations of set D to find its normal order.

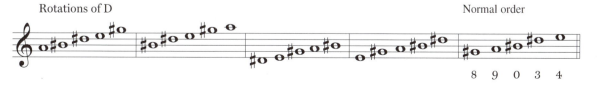

Rotations of D   Normal order

8 9 0 3 4

Call the first pc of the normal order 0, and count semitones to find the prime form. Play set D's prime form, and notate it on the staff below.

We learn that D also belongs to set class 5-22 [0 1 4 7 8]. Therefore, sets C and D are equivalent.

SETS RELATED BY INVERSION

Now let's find the set classes for inversionally related sets. Play the top line of the Scriabin excerpt below to hear set E.

Prelude, Op. 67, No. 2

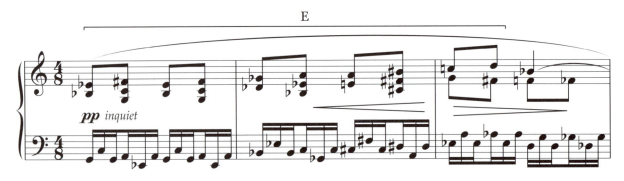

We will compare set E with set A (on p. 310). We found the normal order of both sets in Chapter 31: set E is { 6 9 0 2 3 } and set A is { 6 7 9 0 3 }.

What is the prime form of set A? Call the first pc of A's normal order 0. As you play upward from the first pitch, count the number of semitones between each pitch and the first one. Thus, we learn that A's prime form is [0 1 3 6 9].

Play the rotations of set E again. Recall that the best normal order had the smallest intervals to the right (or at the upper end of the rotation as we played it at the piano).

Because Forte's prime forms, however, all show the smallest intervals to the *left* of the set, we must invert E to find its prime form. To do this, we (1) play the normal order from highest to lowest pitch, (2) call the highest element 0, and (3) count the number of semitones *downward* between each pitch and the highest one.

Set E: The smallest interval is to the right.	Play E from the highest to the lowest pitch, counting the semitones between each pitch and the highest.

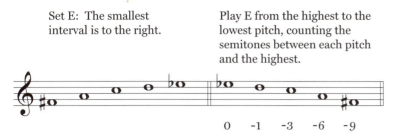

Like set A, set E's prime form is [0 1 3 6 9]. Both sets belong to SC 5-31.

In the five exercises that follow, we revisit the melodies by Anton Webern and Igor Stravinsky from Chapter 31's "Key Concepts." Practice singing the melodies as musically as possible. For the vocal/choral melodies, try singing the text; displace pitches by an octave as needed to stay within your vocal range.

Exercise 32.1: Webern, "Nachts" ("In the Night"), from *Six Songs for Voice and Chamber Orchestra*, Op. 14

For each bracketed set below, write in the prime form and Forte number.

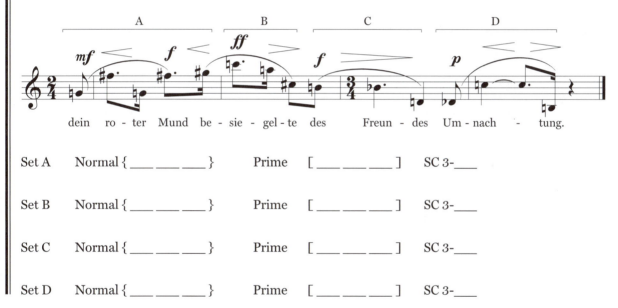

Set A	Normal { ___ ___ ___ }	Prime [___ ___ ___]	SC 3-___
Set B	Normal { ___ ___ ___ }	Prime [___ ___ ___]	SC 3-___
Set C	Normal { ___ ___ ___ }	Prime [___ ___ ___]	SC 3-___
Set D	Normal { ___ ___ ___ }	Prime [___ ___ ___]	SC 3-___

Exercise 32.2: Webern, "Wiese im Park" ("Meadow in the Park"), from *Four Songs for Soprano and Orchestra*, Op. 13

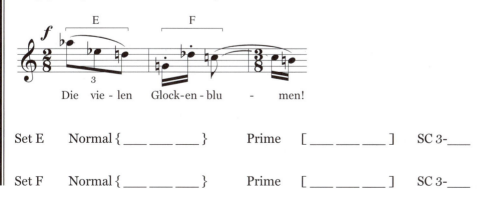

Set E	Normal { ___ ___ ___ }	Prime [___ ___ ___]	SC 3-___
Set F	Normal { ___ ___ ___ }	Prime [___ ___ ___]	SC 3-___

Exercise 32.3: Stravinsky, "Action rituelle des ancêtres" ("Ritual Action of the Ancestors"), from *The Rite of Spring*

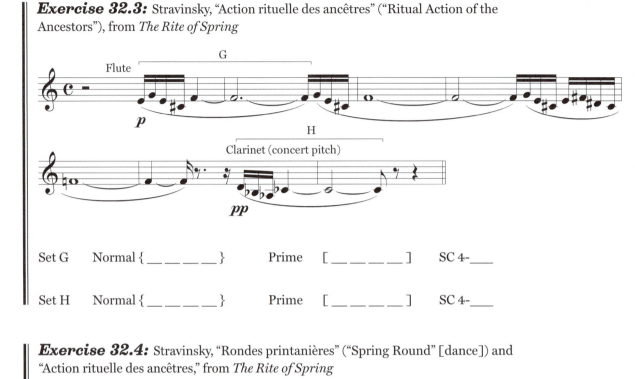

Set G   Normal { __ __ __ __ }   Prime   [__ __ __ __]   SC 4-___

Set H   Normal { __ __ __ __ }   Prime   [__ __ __ __]   SC 4-___

Exercise 32.4: Stravinsky, "Rondes printanières" ("Spring Round" [dance]) and "Action rituelle des ancêtres," from *The Rite of Spring*

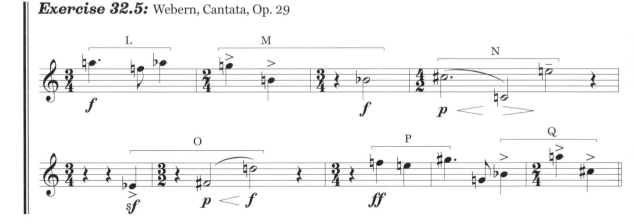

Set J   Normal { __ __ __ __ }   Prime   [__ __ __ __]   SC 4-___

Set K   Normal { __ __ __ __ }   Prime   [__ __ __ __]   SC 4-___

Exercise 32.5: Webern, Cantata, Op. 29

Set L   Normal { ___ ___ ___ }   Prime   [___ ___ ___]   SC 3-___

Set M   Normal { ___ ___ ___ }   Prime   [___ ___ ___]   SC 3-___

Set N   Normal { ___ ___ ___ }   Prime   [___ ___ ___]   SC 3-___

Set O   Normal { ___ ___ ___ }   Prime   [___ ___ ___]   SC 3-___

Set P   Normal { ___ ___ ___ }   Prime   [___ ___ ___]   SC 3-___

Set Q   Normal { ___ ___ ___ }   Prime   [___ ___ ___]   SC 3-___

II. CALL AND RESPONSE

Your teacher will perform a number of pitch patterns, then ask you to perform or write what you heard.

Options for performing your response
Maintain the pitch, rhythm, and tempo of the call.

- Sing pitch only (with pc or interval numbers, or note names).
- Sing rhythm only.
- Sing pitch and rhythm.
- Conduct (or tap) while singing rhythm only or singing both pitch and rhythm.
- Play on your instrument.

Options for writing your response

- normal order, prime form, or Forte SC number
- note names or integers
- note heads only
- rhythmic notation only
- notes and rhythm

TRICHORDS

Use the set-class lists below to help you identify the trichords and tetrachords you hear. Most can be associated with the sound of familiar modes and scale types. If you think of other associations for these SCs, add your ideas here.

Whole-tone trichords
3-6 [0 2 4]: whole-tone scale segment
3-8 [0 2 6]: incomplete Mm7
3-12 [0 4 8]: augmented triad

Pentatonic trichords
3-7 [0 2 5]: "Comin' Round the Mountain"
3-9 [0 2 7]: stacked fourths or fifths

"Triadic" trichords
3-10 [0 3 6]: diminished triad
3-11 [0 3 7]: minor triad (or major triad when the set is inverted)
3-12 [0 4 8]: augmented triad

Octatonic trichords
3-2 [0 1 3]: *mi–fa–sol*, $\hat{3}$–$\hat{4}$–$\hat{5}$ (when inverted: *do–ti–la*, $\hat{1}$–$\hat{7}$–$\hat{6}$)
3-3 [0 1 4]: *sol–le–ti*, $\hat{5}$–$\flat\hat{6}$–$\hat{7}$ (when inverted: *do–ti–le*, $\hat{1}$–$\hat{7}$–$\flat\hat{6}$)
3-5 [0 1 6]: "Viennese fourth chord" (one fourth, one tritone)

Chromatic trichords
3-1 [0 1 2]: "the" chromatic trichord
3-4 [0 1 5]: *ti–do–mi*, $\hat{7}$–$\hat{1}$–$\hat{3}$ (when inverted: *do–ti–sol*, $\hat{1}$–$\hat{7}$–$\hat{5}$)

TETRACHORDS

Traditional tetrachords
4-11 [0 1 3 5]: Phrygian tetrachord (major tetrachord when inverted)
4-7 [0 1 4 5]: harmonic tetrachord
4-10 [0 2 3 5]: minor tetrachord; may be octatonic

Traditional seventh chords
4-20 [0 1 5 8]: MM^7
4-27 [0 2 5 8]: Mm^7 and dm^7; may be octatonic
4-26 [0 3 5 8]: mm^7
4-28 [0 3 6 9]: dd^7

Whole-tone tetrachords
4-21 [0 2 4 6]: "the" whole-tone tetrachord
4-25 [0 2 6 8]: sound of Fr^6
4-24 [0 2 4 8]

All-interval tetrachords
4-Z15 [0 1 4 6]: octatonic subset
4-Z29 [0 1 3 7]: octatonic subset

Subsets of major and minor pentachords
4-14 [0 2 3 7]: *do–re–me–sol*, $\hat{1}$–$\hat{2}$–$\flat\hat{3}$–$\hat{5}$ (when inverted: *sol–fa–mi–do*, $\hat{5}$–$\hat{4}$–$\hat{3}$–$\hat{1}$)
4-22 [0 2 4 7]: *do–re–mi–sol*, $\hat{1}$–$\hat{2}$–$\hat{3}$–$\hat{5}$ (when inverted: *sol–fa–me–do*, $\hat{5}$–$\hat{4}$–$\flat\hat{3}$–$\hat{1}$)
4-23 [0 2 5 7]: "I Got Rhythm"; stacked fourths or fifths

Common tetrachords in nontonal literature

4-19 [0 1 4 8]: augmented M^7 or mM^7

4-8 [0 1 5 6]: two P4s a half step apart

4-16 [0 1 5 7]: first four notes of Japanese kumoijoshi scale

4-9 [0 1 6 7]: two TTs a half step apart; octatonic; one of the most frequently heard nontonal tetrachords

4-17 [0 3 4 7]: "split-third" triad; octatonic subset

Octatonic-scale subsets

4-3 [0 1 3 4]: the octatonic tetrachord

4-13 [0 1 3 6]

4-Z29 [0 1 3 7]: all-interval tetrachord

4-Z15 [0 1 4 6]: all-interval tetrachord

4-18 [0 1 4 7]

4-10 [0 2 3 5]: minor tetrachord

4-12 [0 2 3 6]:

4-27 [0 2 5 8]: Mm^7 and dm^7

4-17 [0 3 4 7]: split-third triad

4-28 [0 3 6 9]: dd^7

Chromatic or nearly chromatic tetrachords

4-1 [0 1 2 3], 4-2 [0 1 2 4], 4-4 [0 1 2 5], 4-5 [0 1 2 6], and 4-6 [0 1 2 7]

III. CONTEXTUAL LISTENING

For some of the exercises in this section, you may want to consult Appendix 3 for the prime forms and interval-class vectors.

EXAMPLE 1, TRACK 2.18

Listen to an excerpt from a choral work by Libby Larsen, and complete the following exercises.

1. Which is the meter type of the excerpt?

    (a) simple duple

    (b) simple triple

    (c) compound duple

    (d) compound triple

2. At the beginning, the women's voices are doubled at which harmonic interval?

    (a) M3

    (b) P4

    (c) P5

    (d) M6

3. The women sing "and the bridesmaids all wore" to which parallel harmonic intervals?

    (a) all thirds

    (b) 3–3–3–6–6–6

    (c) 6–6–6–3–3–3

    (d) all sixths

4. At the entrance of the men's voices ("bridesmaids all wore"), which is the quality of the chord?

    (a) major triad

    (b) minor triad

    (c) MM^7

    (d) mm^7

5. When the men first sing "green, green," the alternating harmonies are of which qualities?

    (a) minor triad, then Mm^7

    (b) minor triad, then mm^7

    (c) major triad, then MM^7

    (d) major triad, then mm^7

6. The last chord is of which quality?

    (a) major triad

    (b) minor triad

    (c) MM^7

    (d) mm^7

7. From the entry of the men's voices until the end of the excerpt, which is the mode?

    (a) Dorian

    (b) Phrygian

    (c) Lydian

    (d) Mixolydian

8. Notate the pitches and rhythm of the outer voices on the grand staves below. Begin on A4 in the sopranos. (Determine the first pitch in the basses from listening to the women.) Write the appropriate meter signature and key signature (or accidentals).

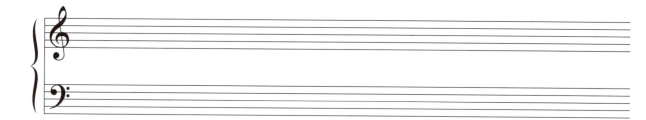

The first three pitches are an important motive in the work. Exercises 9–11 will help us hear some of the ways in which Larsen has treated this trichord.

9. The first trichord of the melody belongs to which set class?

    (a) [0 1 4]

    (b) [0 1 5]

    (c) [0 2 5]

    (d) [0 2 7]

10. Listen again from when the men sing until the end of the excerpt. Notate the lowest
    pitches of all the chords on the staff below. Write the appropriate clef and acciden-
    tals if necessary. Use answers to previous exercises to help you.

11. Show how the three distinct pitch classes from your answer to #10 are related to the
    opening melodic motive. Then summarize the connection between Larsen's melodic
    motive and her choice of harmonies. Illustrate your answer on the staff below.

EXAMPLE 2, TRACK 2.19

Listen to an excerpt from an art song by Messiaen, and complete the following exercises.

1. At the beginning, listen carefully to the lower part of the piano. For most of the excerpt, there are only four pitch classes in this lower part. The first pitch is C♯4. Notate the remaining three pitches on the staff below, and call all four pcs set A.

2. Play the rotations of set A at the keyboard, or notate them on the staff below. Find the normal order and prime form of set A. To which set class do these four pitches belong?

3. Set A is a subset of all the following scales *except* the

    (a) pentatonic;

    (b) whole-tone;

    (c) major;

    (d) octatonic.

4. Beginning on A♯4, notate the pitches of the singer's first "Alleluia" on the staff below. Write the appropriate clef and accidentals. Call all of the pitches set B. Call the first four distinct pitches set C.

5. Play the rotations of set B at the keyboard, or notate them on the staff below. Find the normal order and prime form. To which set class do these five pitches belong?

6. Find the intervals between each element in set C. Use this information to create its interval-class vector. Perform the intervals between the pcs, or realize set C as pitches on the staff below to help you visualize the process.

Set C's interval-class vector is [___ ___ ___ ___ ___ ___]

7. Which is another name for set C?

   (a) whole-tone tetrachord

   (b) Phrygian tetrachord

   (c) all-interval tetrachord

   (d) octatonic tetrachord

8. The performer sings "Alleluia" seven times, then concludes by singing just "ah." Notate the vocal pitches from this "ah" until the end on the staves below. Write the appropriate clef and accidentals. Begin on F♯4.

9. (a) Messiaen included a key signature when notating his composition. Examine the pitches in your answers to the previous questions. Which key signature(s) might make the most sense? Why?

   (b) If you had composed the work, would you have chosen to use a key signature or just written accidentals? Why?

10. On which scale is the excerpt based? (Refer to your answers to previous exercises to help.)

    (a) whole-tone

    (b) pentatonic

    (c) major

    (d) octatonic

11. Which is the final harmonic interval in the piano (in semitones)?

    (a) 7

    (b) 9

    (c) 10

    (d) 12

12. Which best describes the rhythmic relationship between voice and piano?

    (a) The voice and piano are rhythmically independent.

    (b) The voice follows the piano in a rhythmic canon.

    (c) The voice is a rhythmic augmentation of the piano.

    (d) The voice is a rhythmic diminution of the piano.

EXAMPLE 3, TRACK 2.20

Listen to an excerpt from an art song by George Crumb, and complete the exercises below.

1. Notate the pitches of the alto flute from the beginning until the soprano enters. Begin on B♭4, and write the appropriate clef and accidentals. Call the four distinct pitch classes set A.

2. Notate the pitches of the alto flute as flutists would see them in their music. The alto flute sounds a P4 below its written pitches.

3. Find the intervals between each pc in set A. Use this information to create its interval-class vector. Perform the intervals between the pcs, or realize set A as pitches on the staff below to help you visualize the process.

   Set A's interval-class vector is [___ ___ ___ ___ ___ ___].

4. Which is another name for set A?

   (a) whole-tone tetrachord

   (b) Phrygian tetrachord

   (c) all-interval tetrachord

   (d) octatonic tetrachord

5. Play the rotations of set A at the keyboard or notate them on the staff below. Find the normal order and prime form. To which set class does this tetrachord belong?

6. When she enters, the soprano sings the same motive four times. Which is the interval of this opening motive in semitones? (Hint: The third and fourth occurrences are easiest to hear.)

   (a) 1   (b) 2   (c) 3   (d) 4

7. After the soprano's first entrance, the flute plays again, adding one pitch to set A. Call set A plus this new pitch set B. Realize set B as pitches and play its rotations at the keyboard, or notate them on the staves below. What is the normal order for set B? To which set class does B belong?

8. After the flute performs set B, the antique cymbals repeat the first interval of the composition, to which one new pitch is added in the glockenspiel. Call this trichord set C. Realize the set as pitches and play its rotations at the keyboard, or notate them on the staff below. What is the normal order for set C? To which set class does C belong?

9. Beginning on D5, notate the five distinct pitches of the soprano on the staves below. Write the appropriate clef and accidentals. Call these pcs set D. Realize the set as pitches and play its rotations at the keyboard, or notate them on the staves below. What is the normal order for set D? To which set class does D belong?

10. Realize the pcs of sets B, C, and D as pitches in the order in which they appear. What is the musical significance of the soprano's last pitch?

Musical Challenges!

11. Listen to the soprano's last pitch several times. The percussion adds three pitches to
    hers to create a tetrachord. Call this tetrachord set E. While the soprano sustains her
    last pitch, the flute adds three pitches to create a different tetrachord. Call this tetra-
    chord set F.

    Realize each set as pitches and play the rotations at the keyboard, or notate
    them on the staves below. What are the normal orders for sets E and F? To which set
    classes do E and F belong?

12. How is set E related to set C?

13. How is set F related to set A?

MUSIC NOTEPAD

IV. MELODIES FOR STUDY

A. The two melodies that follow will help us learn the twelve trichord types.

For each of the melodies, prepare to do any of the following:

- Conduct and sing it in rhythm.
- Play it on an instrument.
- Identify trichords within melodic segments.
- Transpose the melody on your instrument.
- Identify the pitch intervals between successive notes.

B. Revisit the melodies in Chapter 31. Perform each as musically as possible. Identify at least four trichords in each melody by prime form or Forte number.

Strategies for Singing

- Sing on interval numbers to focus on intonation (e.g., sing a whole step as "2," a minor third as "3," and so on).
- Once you feel confident of the pitches and intervals, sing in rhythm on "la."

Once you have learned the trichords beginning on C, be sure to transpose melodies 1 and 2 to begin on each of the twelve pcs.

Melody 1 The Twelve Trichords (Pitches 1–3 in each trichord are the prime form; pitches 4–6 are an inverted form.)

Melody 2   Inverted Forms of the Twelve Trichords

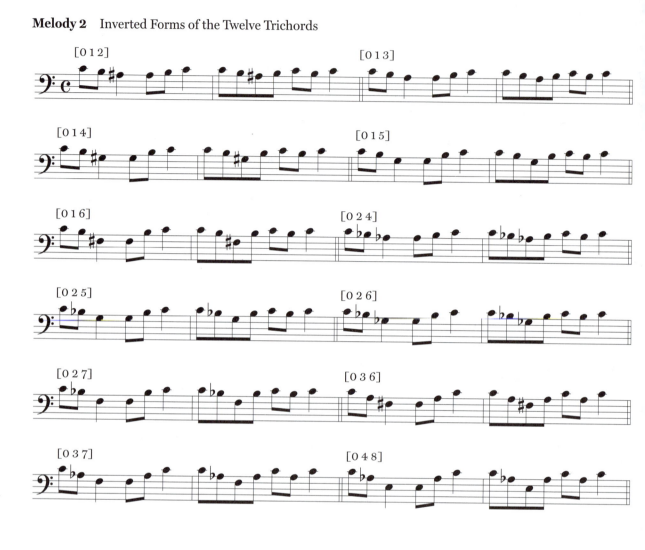

Duets with Octatonic Scales and Subsets

Choose one of the set classes below and realize it as pitches on a transparency or on the board. Write its transpositions and inversions as well. Add to this each of the three distinct versions of the octatonic scale (for example, W–H scales that include the pc C, C♯, or D). Perform all these examples to get the sounds in your ears, voice, and fingers. Remember to think of these realizations as pitch classes that may be expressed in any octave.

4-3 [0 1 3 4]   5-28 [0 2 3 6 8]
4-9 [0 1 6 7]   5-31 [0 1 3 6 9]
4-Z15 [0 1 4 6]

For the duet, one performer develops an ostinato based on some version of the set. A second performer listens to the pitches that sound and improvises a melodic line based on the octatonic scale that contains those pitches. If the accompanist changes to a different transposition or inversion of the set, the improviser should hear the change and adjust to a new octatonic scale if necessary.

Variations

- Relying on a predetermined signal, such as a nod of the head, the performers should switch their roles in the middle of the improvisation. Switch once more to give the improvisation an **A B A** design.
- Add percussion to the ensemble. Use instruments if they are available, or improvise with pencils on notebooks, hand tapping, etc. Listen to the melodic improviser and try to create a rhythmic canon.
- Add a second melodic improviser who must imitate the first improviser's melody, but in inversion. Feature pcs from the same octatonic scale as improviser 1.
- Add a conductor. The performers must follow the gestures of the conductor, adjusting elements of their performance such as dynamics, tempo, and texture.
- Add a speaker. The speaker might recite poetry or interject familiar maxims from musical history, such as Fux's "*Mi* contra *fa* est diabolus in musica" from *Gradus ad Parnassum*. (Today we might say, "The tritone is the devil in music!")

VI. COMPOSITION

Use the short piece you composed in Chapter 31 as the basis of a longer work in **A B A´** form. From the list below, choose a contrasting set class that will represent the sound of the **B** section of your piece. Vary the **B** section by means of contour, dynamics, motivic and rhythmic ideas, and mood.

4-3 [0 1 3 4]
4-9 [0 1 6 7]
4-Z15 [0 1 4 6]
5-28 [0 2 3 6 8]
5-31 [0 1 3 6 9]

For the **A´** section, feature the inversion of the original sets while returning to the contour, dynamics, and motivic and rhythmic ideas of the opening section. For ideas, review Chapter 30, section VI (particularly the list of elements you might vary in the recapitulation). Also review the compositional strategies given in Chapter 31, section VI.

Perform your compositions in class. Listeners should be able to detect the set classes used, the form of the composition, and the nature of the variation in both the **B** and **A´** sections. Listeners should also take dictation, notating the pitches and rhythm of motivic ideas in order to suggest ideas for the consideration of each composer.

CHAPTER 33

Ordered Segments, Serialism, and Twelve-Tone Rows

Overview

In this chapter, we will perform and learn to recognize aurally music that is composed of ordered pitch segments.

Outline of topics covered

I. KEY CONCEPTS
  Hearing Pitch Relationships
  Between Ordered Segments

II. CALL AND RESPONSE

III. CONTEXTUAL
  LISTENING

IV. MELODIES FOR STUDY

V. IMPROVISATION

VI. COMPOSITION

I. KEY CONCEPTS

Hearing Pitch Relationships Between Ordered Segments

A **segment** is an ordered sequence of pitches or pitch classes. Hearing pitch relationships between segments can be challenging, but there are strategies we can follow to make this easier. To learn these strategies, let's focus on a type of ordered segment that contains all twelve pitch classes: a **row.** The first time we hear a row in a piece, we call it P, meaning *prime.* Sing the row below, P, with pc integers (these are given beneath the staff) or note names. When singing pcs, sing 7 as "sev" and e as "lev."

Strategy

The strategy we earlier called "sing-check" is especially useful in passages that have challenging intervals. Give yourself the first pitch (C). Sing it, then try to sing the second. After singing pitch 2, check the pitch at the keyboard and correct yourself if necessary. Now try singing pitch 3, followed by a check at the keyboard, and so on.

Row P

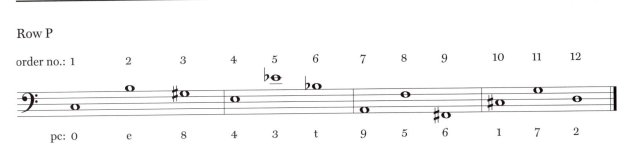

order no.:	1	2	3	4	5	6	7	8	9	10	11	12
pc:	0	e	8	4	3	t	9	5	6	1	7	2

Now let's learn how to hear transformations of P.

Listen for the interval sequence and direction.

1. Listen to the *beginning* of our row. P begins with a major seventh up and a minor third down. Because qualities like *major* and *minor* have little meaning in this music, we write the intervals in semitones, within angled brackets; thus, the opening intervals are <+11 −3>. We can also sing P with these interval numbers.

P (original ordered segment)

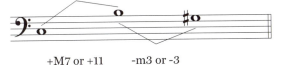

+M7 or +11   -m3 or -3

- When another segment begins with *the identical interval sequence,* we are hearing P or one of its transpositions.

Another form of P

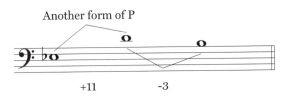

+11   -3

- When a segment features *the same interval sizes but opposite in direction,* we are hearing some form of I, the inverted form of P.

I (an inverted form of P)

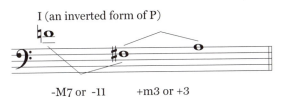

-M7 or -11   +m3 or +3

2. Listen to the *end* of the row. Assume we hear <+6 –5> at the end of P.

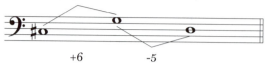

End of P

+6   –5

- When another segment begins with <+5 –6>, we are hearing some form of R, a retrograde of P. Listen to how *both sequence and direction are reversed.*

R (retrograde of the sequence at the end of P)

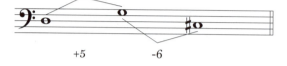

+5   –6

- When we hear a segment begin with <–5 + 6>, we are hearing some form of RI, a retrograde of the inversion of P. Listen to how *the ordered sequence is reversed.*

RI (retrograde of the inversion of the end of P)

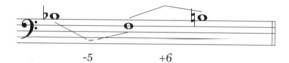

–5   +6

Analyze the pc intervals (pci) of the sequence.

1. Notate the pitches of an ordered segment.
2. Write the pc integer beneath each pitch.
3. Using integer notation and mod12 arithmetic, subtract the first pc from the second. This yields the pc interval between those pcs. For example, in our row the first pci is e (e – 0).
4. Continue until you find the pc interval between each pair of adjacent elements of the segment. In our row, the second pci is 9 (8 – e, or 20 – e mod 12), the third is 8 (4 – 8), and so on.

Row P

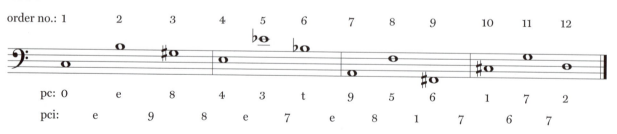

order no.: 1	2	3	4	5	6	7	8	9	10	11	12
pc: 0	e	8	4	3	t	9	5	6	1	7	2
pci:	e	9	8	e	7	e	8	1	7	6	7

5. When you hear other segments, compare their pci sequences with the one you wrote.

- P forms: P forms will have the *identical* pci sequence.
- I forms: Each element of the pci sequence is the *inverse* of the corresponding element in P. (To find the inverse, subtract the original from 12: 1 as opposed to e, 3 as opposed to 9, etc.)

- R forms: Compared with P, the pci sequence is both *reversed* and in *inverse*.
- RI forms: Compared with P, the pci sequence is *reversed*.

II. CALL AND RESPONSE

A. Your teacher will announce a starting pitch and perform an ordered pitch segment. Call this P. Respond with a repetition of P. The teacher will then ask for another form of P—a transposition (P), inversion (I), retrograde (R), or retrograde of the inversion (RI). Respond by performing or writing the form requested.

Each form of a segment has an integer in its name: e.g., P_7, I_2, R_4, RI_3.

- For P and I forms, the integer is the *first* pc in the segment.
- For R and RI forms, the integer is the *last* pc in the segment. Therefore, respond to R and RI calls in two steps.
  (1) Respond first with the P or I form.
  (2) Then play this P or I form backward.

B. Your teacher will announce and perform an ordered segment, P, then perform a transformation of P. Respond by performing, writing, or identifying the transformation.

Options for performing your response
Maintain the pitch, rhythm, and tempo of the call.

- Sing pitch only (with pc integers or note names).
- Sing pitches with interval numbers (start on 0; sing 7 as "sev" and e as "lev").
- Sing rhythm only.
- Sing pitch and rhythm.
- Conduct (or tap) while singing rhythm only or singing both pitch and rhythm.
- Play on your instrument.

Options for writing your response

- pc integers
- interval sequence and direction
- pitches
- pc intervals (pci) of the sequence
- note names
- note heads only
- rhythmic notation only
- notes and rhythm

Variation: Identify the pcset of trichord and tetrachord calls. Find the normal order and prime form.

MUSIC NOTEPAD

Part VI Into the Twentieth Century

III. CONTEXTUAL LISTENING

Your teacher may ask you to complete some or all of the exercises in each example below.

EXAMPLE 1, TRACK 2.21

The exercises below are based on an excerpt from a work for piano by Bartók.

1. At the beginning of the excerpt, which is the meter type?

   (a) simple triple   (c) compound duple

   (b) simple quadruple   (d) compound triple

Exercises 2–6 are based only on the higher part.

2. (a) The theme of the work is the first ten pitches in the higher part. *All later compar-isons will be made to this initial statement of the theme.* Notate the pitches and rhythm of the theme on the staff below. Begin on A4. Write the appropriate clef, meter signature, and accidentals.

   (b) Label the theme's first four pitches *segment 1* and the remaining six pitches *segment 2*.

   (c) Write the pitch interval between each pair of successive pitches of the theme. Write in semitones and include + for *above* and – for *below*. This will help you listen for changes in the theme, such as melodic inversion.

   < ___ ___ ___ ___ ___ ___ ___ ___ ___ >

   (d) If we consider segment 1 to be an *unordered* pcset, what is its normal order? What are its Forte number and prime form? (To find Forte numbers, consult Appendix 3.)

   (e) Think of every possible way to create trichord subsets of segment 1. Notate these subsets on the staff below. To which set class do these subsets belong?

   (f) If we consider segment 2 to be an *unordered* pcset, what is its normal order? What are its Forte number and prime form?

3. How is the second statement of the theme varied?

   (a) The pitches change in segment 1.

   (b) The pitches change in segment 2.

   (c) The rhythm changes in segment 1.

   (d) The rhythm changes in segment 2.

4. How is the third statement of the theme related to its first statement?

   (a) The pitches are transposed up a tritone.

   (b) There are more dotted rhythms.

   (c) The melodic contour is inverted.

   (d) The rhythm is augmented.

5. (a) Listen again, and compare statement 4 and those that immediately follow it with the original statement of the theme. Which compositional device does Bartók employ?

   (1) fragmentation

   (2) melodic inversion

   (3) rhythmic diminution

   (4) parallel chords

   (b) Beginning with this fourth statement and continuing through the ninth, the theme descends from the pieces's highest pitch, B♭5. Starting on this B♭, notate just the *first* pitch of each of these entrances on the staff below.

   (c) To which scale do these initial pitches belong?

   (1) pentatonic

   (2) whole-tone

   (3) harmonic minor

   (4) octatonic

6. Which best describes the compositional process in the final statement of the theme?

   (a) The contour of the theme is inverted.

   (b) The theme is rhythmically augmented.

   (c) The order of segments 1 and 2 is reversed.

   (d) The entire theme is heard in retrograde.

Listen to the excerpt again. Focus your listening on the lower part and its relationship to the theme statements in the higher part.

7. The first entrance of the lower part is

    (a) a rhythmic augmentation of the higher part;

    (b) a rhythmic diminution of the higher part;

    (c) an imitation of the higher part at the octave;

    (d) a melodic inversion of the higher part.

8. The second entrance of the lower part is

    (a) a melodic inversion of the higher part;

    (b) an imitation of the higher part a M6 below;

    (c) a rhythmic augmentation of the higher part;

    (d) a fragmentation of the higher part.

9. The third entrance of the lower part is

    (a) an imitation of the higher part a M9 below;

    (b) a melodic inversion of the higher part;

    (c) a rhythmic diminution of the higher part;

    (d) a fragmentation of the higher part.

10. The fourth through ninth entrances in the lower part

    (a) are rhythmic diminutions of the higher part;

    (b) are rhythmic augmentations of the higher part;

    (c) are melodic inversions of the higher part;

    (d) imitate the higher part at the octave.

11. The last three statements of the lower part are

    (a) melodic inversions of the higher part;

    (b) imitations of the higher part at the octave;

    (c) rhythmic diminutions of the higher part;

    (d) fragmentations of the higher part.

EXAMPLE 2, TRACK 2.22

Listen to the beginning of a twelve-tone composition for mixed chorus by Stravinsky, in which only the women's voices are heard. Then complete the following exercises.

> The dove descending breaks the air
> With flame of incandescent terror,
> Of which the tongues declare
> The one discharge from sin and error.

1. Notate the pitches and rhythm of both parts on the staves below in simple-triple meter. The first pitches of each part are given.

Strategies for Listening

- Listen to the excerpt many times.
- Focus your listening on each part separately and then together.
- Divide this task into steps.
    - (a) Sketch the rhythm above or below the staff, or lightly in the staff. This will guide you in placing the pitches.
    - (b) Notate an analysis of the interval succession. This will help you determine the pitches.
    - (c) Confirm your melodic pitches by checking them against the harmonic pitch intervals.
    - (d) Finally, transcribe the melodies onto the staff.

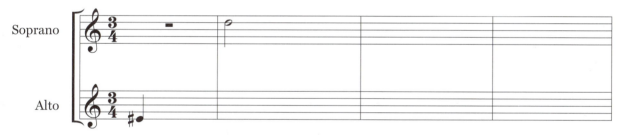

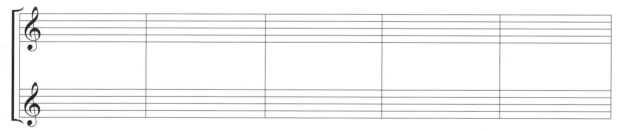

2. Knowing that composers might choose P, I, R, and RI row forms, study your notation above and see if Stravinsky's pitch relationships become apparent. Before we examine the excerpt in detail, write a verbal description of how Stravinsky treats his row.

3. (a) Notate the first twelve *distinct* pitches of the alto part on the staff below (to the text "The dove descending breaks the air"). Call these pitches P$_5$, meaning the row form that begins on pc 5.

(b) Write the pc integer beneath each pitch.

(c) Write the pc interval number between each successive pair of pc integers. This will help us compare this initial statement of the row with other statements.

(d) Write the row order numbers, 1–12, above each pitch. This will help us find our location in the row.

4. (a) Notate the first twelve distinct pitches of the soprano part on the staff below ("The dove . . . terror").

(b) Write the pc integer beneath each pitch.

(c) Write the pc interval number between each successive pair of pc integers.

(d) Write the row order numbers, 1–12, above each pitch.

(e) How is this second row related to P$_5$, the original row? Use any of the information above to help you answer this question.

5. (a) Notate the last twelve distinct pitches of the soprano part on the staff below ("Of which . . . error"). This music begins immediately after the music you analyzed in #4.

(b) Write the pc integer beneath each pitch.

(c) Write the pc interval number between each successive pair of pc integers.

(d) Write the row order numbers, 1–12, above each pitch.

(e) How is this row related to P_5, the original row? Use any of the information above to help you answer this question.

6. (a) Notate the distinct pitches of the end of the alto part on the staff below ("Of which . . . error"). Note that there are only eleven pitches.

(b) Write the pc integer beneath each pitch.

(c) Write the pc interval number between each successive pair of pc integers.

(d) Write the row order numbers, 1–11, above each pitch.

(e) How is this row related to P_5, the original row? Use any of the information above to help you answer this question.

(f) As the music continues beyond this excerpt, the altos sing the next pitch. With which pc would the altos begin their next phrase? Why?

7. (a) Examine the alto pitches in the middle of the excerpt ("air with flame of incandescent terror"). To which row form do they belong? (The row begins in the middle of the notes sung to "air.")

(b) Compare your answer with that of #3. How are the alto's first two row statements linked?

8. Create a 12 × 12 matrix based on Stravinsky's row. Notate the pcs with integers.

   (a) Transpose the first row (your answer to #3) to begin on pc 0 by subtracting 5 from each element in the row. Write this transposed row form in the top row of your matrix.

   (b) Write the I form of the row down the left column in the matrix. To find I, take the inverse of each pc in the top row.

   (c) Consider each pc in the left column the first pc of a new transposition of the row.

   (d) Check your work.
   - Make sure that the diagonal from top left to bottom right contains only zeros.
   - Make sure each row or column includes one each of the twelve pc integers. (No pcs may be duplicated.)

EXAMPLE 3, TRACK 2.23

Listen to an excerpt from an art song by Webern, and complete the exercises below.

Wie bin ich froh!   How happy am I!
noch einmal wird mir alles grün.   Once again all grows green about me.

1. Which is a correct notation of the rhythm at the beginning of the excerpt?

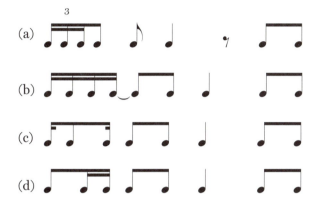

Strategy for Listening _____

When listening to twelve-tone music, it is customary to call the first row we hear P. However, Webern's first row sounds in the piano and includes a chord, so we can't determine the interval sequence. We therefore focus first on the singer's music to hear the interval sequence. Comparing this row with the piano music will help us determine which rows Webern uses in the accompaniment, at the beginning and throughout.

_____

2. (a) Notate the pitches of the voice on the staff below. Begin on G4. (You may want to notate the interval succession first, then transcribe the pitches onto the staff.)

(b) Write the pc integer beneath each pitch.

(c) Write the pc interval number between each successive pair of pc integers.

(d) Write the row order numbers, 1–12, above each pitch.

3. (a) Notate the first five pitches of the piano's music on the staff below. Begin with F♯3.

(b) Write the pc integer beneath each pitch.

(c) Write the pc interval number between each successive pair of pc integers.

(d) Write the row order numbers, 1–5, above each pitch.

4. (a) Compare the pc intervals of the piano's first segment with those at either end of the row in the voice part. (Refer to your answer to #2; you'll see that the piano music begins with one of those two interval series.) Following the interval series from #2, determine the remaining pcs of the first row heard in the piano. Realize your answer by notating the pcs (of the whole row) as pitches on the staff below.

(b) Write the pc integer beneath each pitch.

(c) Write the pc interval number between each successive pair of pc integers.

(d) Write the row order numbers, 1–12, above each pitch.

5. Now listen to the music of the piano again. Refer to what you learned in #4 to determine which of the chords below is a correct notation of the first chord heard in the piano. (Hint: The correct chord is the realized pcs of row order numbers 6–9.)

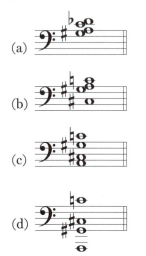

(a)

(b)

(c)

(d)

6. (a) Notate the five pitches of the piano that are played immediately after the voice's first note. Begin on G4. These pitches are the beginning of the piano's second row.

(b) Compare the beginning of this row with the other two row forms you discovered. In simple, nontechnical terms, how does this row form relate to what precedes it?

(c) Look at your answer to #4 (piano row 1), and compare this with your answer to part (a) (the beginning of piano row 2). Listen to the piano's music again, from the beginning. At what point do you hear the twelfth pitch of the piano's first row? What has Webern done to connect piano row 1 to piano row 2?

7. In #4, you determined the original form of the row (in the piano), P_6. Create a 12×12 matrix based on this row. Notate the pcs with integers.

(a) Transpose the first row (your answer to #4) to begin on pc 0 by subtracting 6 from each element in the row. Write this transposed row form in the top row of your matrix.

(b) Write the I form of the row down the left column in the matrix. To find I, take the inverse of each pc in the top row.

(c) Consider each pc in the left column the first pc of a new transposition of the row.

(d) Check your work.
   • Make sure that the diagonal from top left to bottom right contains only zeros.
   • Make sure each row or column includes one each of the twelve pc integers. (No pcs may be duplicated.)

8. Refer to your matrix to identify the row form you heard sung in the voice.

9. (a) Notate the last three pitches of the piano on the staff below. Begin on B3. Write the pc integer beneath each pitch.

(b) Look at your matrix and find a form of the row that concludes with these three pcs. What is the name of that row?

(c) Listen again to the piano music. Follow the rows as you listen. Can you hear the change from one row form to a second, and then back to the original?

EXAMPLE 4, TRACK 2.24

Listen to a song by Luigi Dallapiccola for soprano, E♭ clarinet, and B♭ clarinet. Though these clarinets are transposing instruments, we will notate them in concert pitch.

Laß deinen süßen Rubinenmund	Let not your sweet ruby mouth
Zudringlichkeiten nicht verfluchen;	Condemn me for being so importunate;
Was hat Liebesschmerz andern Grund,	What other reason does heartache have
Als seine Heilung zu suchen?	Than to look for its own healing?

1. (a) Notate the first twelve pitches of the voice on the staff below (to the text "Laß deinen süßen Rubinenmund"). Begin on E4. This original row is called P_4.

(b) Write the pc integer beneath each pitch.

(c) Write the pc interval number between each successive pair of pc integers.

(d) Write the row order numbers, 1–12, above each pitch.

2. (a) Notate the first twelve pitches of the B♭ clarinet (the first clarinet we hear) on the staff below. Begin on concert pitch C♯4.

(b) Write the pc integer beneath each pitch.

(c) Write the pc interval number between each successive pair of pc integers.

(d) Write the row order numbers, 1–12, above each pitch.

(e) How does this second row relate to the original row, P_4?

(f) Transpose the concert pitches in part (a) to the pitches that would appear in the B♭ clarinet part. (Tip: Add 2 to each integer in the row.)

3. (a) Notate the *last* twelve pitches of the B♭ clarinet on the staff below. (These pitches begin immediately after those in your answer to #2.) Begin on concert pitch D4.

(b) Write the pc integer beneath each pitch.

(c) Write the pc interval number between each successive pair of pc integers.

(d) Write the row order numbers, 1–12, above each pitch.

(e) How does this row relate to the original row, P_4?

4. Listen again to the beginning of the voice part and compare what you hear with the *beginning* of the B♭ clarinet part. What is the *rhythmic* relationship between these two parts?

5. Listen again to the beginning of the voice part and compare what you hear with the *end* of the B♭ clarinet part. What is the *rhythmic* relationship between these two parts?

6. In #1, you determined the original form of the row, P_4. Create a 12 × 12 matrix based on this row. Notate the pcs with integers.

(a) Transpose the first row (your answer to #1) to begin on pc 0 by subtracting 4 from each element in the row. Write this transposed row form in the top row of your matrix.

(b) Write the I form of the row down the left column in the matrix. To find I, take the inverse of each pc in the top row.

(c) Consider each pc in the left column the first pc of a new transposition of the row.

(d) Check your work.
   • Make sure that the diagonal from top left to bottom right contains only zeros.
   • Make sure each row or column includes one each of the twelve pc integers. (No pcs may be duplicated.)

Refer to your matrix to help you complete #7–#11.

7. (a) Beginning with B♭3, notate the pitches of the voice that are sung to the text "Zudringlichkeiten nicht verfluchen." This music begins *immediately* after the voice's first twelve pitches (your answer to #1.)

Note that there are only eleven pitches. Let's find the "missing" pitch!

(b) Write the pc integer beneath each pitch.

(c) What is the name of this row form? (Refer to your matrix.)

(d) Which pc is missing?

(e) Listen again to both voice and B♭ clarinet. Follow your notation above or the row form in the matrix. What happens in the music at the point when you expect to hear the missing pc? Briefly describe the composer's solution to this "missing" pc.

8. (a) Beginning on F4, notate the vocal pitches sung to the words "Was hat Liebesschmerz andern Grund" (the music following your answer to #7) on the staff below.

(b) Write the pc integer beneath each pc.

(c) Compare this music with the beginning of the voice part. Focus on the contour and intervals of each melody. Relying only on your ears and without consulting your matrix, decide how these two row forms are related.

    (1) P

    (2) R

    (3) I

    (4) RI

(d) Consult your matrix to confirm what you heard. Which row form is sung to these words?

9. (a) Beginning with G♭5, notate the final vocal pitches, sung to the words "Als seine Heilung zu suchen, zu suchen?," on the staff below.

Note that there are only eleven pitches. Let's find the missing pitch!

(b) Write the pc integer beneath each pitch.

(c) What is the name of this row form? (Refer to your matrix.)

(d) Which pc is missing?

(e) At the end, listen again to both voice and B♭ clarinet (the lower-sounding clarinet). Follow your notation above or the row form in the matrix. What happens in the music at the point when you expect to hear the missing pc? Briefly describe the composer's solution to this "missing" pc.

10. (a) The E♭ clarinet's first entrance occurs while the singer holds the last syllable of "verfluchen." Beginning on concert pitch A4, notate the first twelve pitches of the E♭ clarinet on the staff below.

(b) Write the pc integer beneath each pitch.

(c) Listen to the beginning of the voice again and compare it with the entrance of the E♭ clarinet. Focus on the contour and intervals of each melody. Relying only on your ears and without consulting your matrix, decide how these two row forms are related.

(1) P

(2) R

(3) I

(4) RI

(d) Consult your matrix to confirm what you heard. Which row form does the E♭ clarinet play?

(e) Transpose the concert pitches above to the pitches that would appear in the E♭ clarinet part. (Tip: Subtract 3 from each integer in the row.)

11. (a) The E♭ clarinet's second row begins immediately after its first statement (simultaneously with the singer's syllable "-schmerz"). Beginning on concert pitch F5, notate the remaining pitches of the E♭ clarinet on the staff below.

Note that there are only eleven pitches. Once again, let's find the missing pc.

(b) Write the pc integer beneath each pitch.

(c) What is the name of this row form? (Refer to your matrix.)

(d) Which pc is missing?

(e) At the end, listen again to both voice and E♭ clarinet (the higher-sounding clarinet). Follow your notation above or the row form in the matrix. What happens in the music at the point when you expect to hear the missing pc? Briefly describe the composer's solution to this "missing" pc.

For each of the melodies below, prepare to do any of the following:

- Conduct and perform the rhythm.
- Sing the melody with pitch names, interval numbers, or pc integers.
- Play it on an instrument.
- Identify pcsets of row segments.
- Transpose the melody to other pitch levels on your instrument.
- Identify the pitch intervals between successive notes.
- Identify row forms.

Strategies for Singing

- Practice singing these melodies by performing the rhythm alone (while conducting), then slowly the pitch alone, then the pitch and rhythm together.
- Sing on interval numbers to focus on intonation (e.g., sing a whole step as "2," a minor third as "3," and so on).
- Once you feel confident of the pitches and intervals, sing in rhythm on "la."
- Modal or pentatonic melodies may be sung on solfège syllables or scale-degree numbers.
- For melodies that exceed your voice range, transfer pitches to octaves that are more easily sung; try to do so at natural breaks in the phrasing.

Melody 1 Alban Berg, Violin Concerto, first movement

The row, P_7, is the first twelve pcs. How do measures 10ff. relate to the row? Consider pcs 1–4 and 5–8 to be ordered segments. How are these two tetrachords related? Consider pcs 9–12 to be another ordered segment. What is the name of this tetrachord, and to which set class does it belong?

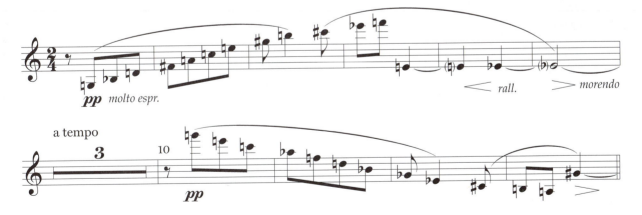

Melody 2 Stravinsky, Four Trios from *Agon*

How does the composer organize his twelve-tone fugue subject?

Melody 3 Arnold Schoenberg, *Variations for Orchestra*, Op. 31

The first twelve distinct pcs are the row. How are the next twelve related to the first?

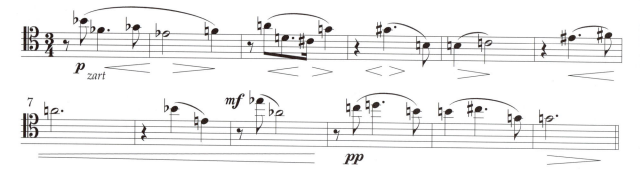

Melody 4 Schoenberg, *Suite for Piano*, Op. 25, Trio

The row, P$_4$, consists of the first twelve pcs in the left hand. Practice performing both parts alone before attempting to put it together. Find all the row forms. How are the others related to P$_4$?

Melody 5   Webern, "In der Fremde" ("In a Foreign Land"), from *Four Songs for Soprano and Orchestra*, Op. 13

Is this melody based on ordered segments?

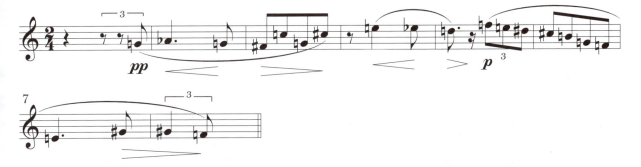

Melody 6   Webern, "Ave Regina Coelorum ("Hail, Queen of Heaven")," Op. 18, No. 3

V. IMPROVISATION

Choose a row from the "Contextual Listening" or "Melodies for Study," or create one of your own. Choose at least two forms of the row to use in an improvisation—a short dance movement—that you will perform on a pitched instrument of your choice. Notate your choices of row form on a transparency or at the board. Select one of the dance rhythms below for the motivic rhythm of your improvisation.

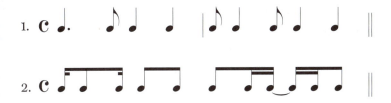

3. $\frac{6}{8}$ [rhythmic notation]

4. $\frac{3}{4}$ [rhythmic notation]

Strategies

- Practice the row forms and the rhythm separately before putting them together.
- Remember, these are pcs, so practice them in every octave available on your instrument.
- Practice expressing the intervals in both conjunct and disjunct lines. Many twelve-tone melodies express each interval in the series as a leap.

Variations

- Create your own dance rhythms.
- Choose row forms that lend themselves to overlaps. See if your classmates can hear where these overlaps occur.
- Create a matrix from your row, and thread your way through one or more forms each of P, I, R, and RI.
- Ask a friend to listen to your improvisation, then play a canon along with you.
- Use the "Contextual Listening" examples and "Melodies for Study" as models for your improvisations.

VI. COMPOSITION

Choose a row from the "Contextual Listening" or "Melodies for Study," or create one of your own. Compose a duet for yourself and a classmate. Consider using techniques we learned in "Contextual Listening" Examples 2–4, and Melodies 2 (Stravinsky), 4 (Schoenberg), and 6 (Webern). In each of these works, the composer expresses the row in relatively simple ways. Their techniques are summarized below.

Strategies for Composing

- Overlap the end of one row form with the beginning of another.
- Choose row forms that permit you to overlap a pc (or pcs) in the middle of two simultaneous expressions of the row.
- Create a melody that is nonretrogradable: that is, a melody in which the pcs occur in the same order whether we perform them forward or backward.
- Compose a canon, making one part a rhythmic augmentation of the other.
- Create a matrix to help you explore the possibilities for your row choices.

Variations

- Include rows of lengths other than twelve pcs.
- Create a piece that is both twelve-tone *and* pitch-centric (that is, a piece that is not functionally tonal but one in which we perceive a "tonic").
- Choose a row based on combinatorial hexachords (hexachords that combine with other versions of themselves to complete the chromatic scale, or aggregate) to ensure that you express the aggregate both melodically and harmonically.
- Choose three instruments, and compose a trio that features combinatorial tetra-chords.
- Serialize other aspects of your composition—e.g., rhythm, dynamics, register, and timbre.

CHAPTER 34 New Ways to Organize Rhythm, Meter, and Duration

Overview

In this chapter, we expand our understanding of polymeter and asymmetrical meters. We also perform and learn to recognize aurally other rhythmic ideas common in music of the last century.

Outline of topics covered

I. KEY CONCEPTS
  Changing Meter
  Polymeter
  More About Asymmetrical Meters
  Hearing asymmetrical meters
  Conducting asymmetrical meters
II. CALL AND RESPONSE

III. CONTEXTUAL LISTENING
IV. MELODIES FOR STUDY
V. IMPROVISATION
  Polymetric Duets
  Ostinato
  Same bar lines, different divisions

VI. COMPOSITION
  Serial Composition
  Percussion Duet
  Ametric Composition

I. KEY CONCEPTS

Changing Meter

In most compositions written before the twentieth century, the music remains in the same meter throughout the piece. Beginning in the late nineteenth century and continuing today, however, composers frequently change meters within the same work, sometimes in every measure. See, for example, Brahms's Variations on a Hungarian Song in Chapter 19's "Melodies for Study" (Melody 2).

Exercise 34.1: Changing Meter

Listen to track 2.25 on your CD, and determine which meters you hear. To help you decide, conduct along with the excerpt.

Meters: _____

At other times, the notated meter signature remains constant but the beat divisions change. Thus, the music might *sound* as though the meter is changing, even if this is not reflected in the notation.

Exercise 34.2: Perceived Changing Meter

Listen to each excerpt below, and determine which single meter signature each might be notated in. If the composer had chosen instead to notate the music with changing meter signatures, how might the rhythm be notated?

1. Track 2.26

Single meter signature: _____

Changing meter signatures: _____

2. Track 2.27

Single meter signature: _____

Changing meter signatures: _____

3. Track 2.28

Single meter signature: _____

Changing meter signatures: _____

Polymeter

Sometimes we perceive two (or more) metric streams simultaneously—a concept called **polymeter**. For example, polymetric music might be notated with separate meter signatures for different parts, or might include extended passages with triplets in simple meter or duplets in compound meter.

Exercise 34.3: Hearing Polymeter

Listen to track 2.29, an excerpt we studied earlier. Focus on the higher and lower parts separately, then on their combined sound.

(a) If we think of each part as being in a different meter, in which meter type(s) might the higher part be notated? _____

(b) In which meter type(s) might the lower part be notated?

_____

More About Asymmetrical Meters

HEARING ASYMMETRICAL METERS

As we learned in Chapter 21, asymmetrical meters have beat units of unequal duration. Often the meters show a 5 or 7 as the top number of their signatures, as in $\frac{5}{4}$ or $\frac{7}{8}$. Sometimes, when the signature's top number is even, the beat units might still be unequal (e.g., $\frac{8}{8}$ might be divided $\frac{3+2+3}{8}$).

> ## Exercise 34.4: Hearing Asymmetrical Meters
>
> Listen to the two excerpts below, and tap each beat. Accent the first beat of each measure as well as the internal beat units. In which meter(s) might each excerpt be notated?
>
> 1. Track 2.30
>
> 2. Track 2.31

CONDUCTING ASYMMETRICAL METERS

When conducting asymmetrical meters, we emphasize the beat unit. When seven is conducted quickly, we use a triple-meter pattern with beats of unequal duration. For example, for $\frac{7}{8}$ in a 3+2+2 pattern, we conduct one long beat for the 3 and a short beat for each of the 2's, as shown below.

3+2+2

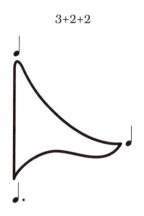

There are many ways to conduct seven slowly to moderately. Sometimes we might combine a quadruple with a triple pattern. At other times we might add an extra beat to a six pattern, as shown below.

4+3

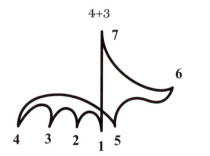

3+4

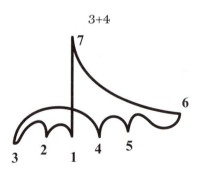

For unequal divisions of eight, we conduct a triple pattern with beats of unequal duration. For example, for $\frac{8}{8}$ in a 3+3+2 pattern, we conduct two long beats for the 3s and one short beat for the 2:

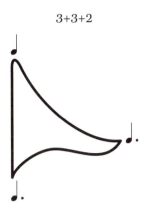

3+3+2

For unequal divisions of nine (such as 2+2+2+3), we typically conduct a quadruple pattern. For a division like 4+3+2, we use a triple-meter pattern with progressively shorter beats.

Practice conducting the patterns until you are comfortable with them. Then listen to the excerpts in Exercise 34.4 again. This time, conduct as you listen.

Exercise 34.5: Performing and Conducting Asymmetrical Meters

The patterns below show both common asymmetrical meters and less common divisions of symmetrical meters. The beat unit is given in the lower staff and the divisions in the upper staff.

Strategies

- Tap the top part in one hand and the bottom part in the other. Emphasize the metric accent and the beat unit. Switch parts and perform again.
- Tap one part and sing the other part on a neutral syllable. Switch parts and perform again.
- Conduct the top part while singing the beat unit on a neutral syllable. Switch parts and perform again.

1. Common patterns based on the quarter note

2. Common patterns based on the eighth note

II. CALL AND RESPONSE

A. Your teacher will perform a rhythmic pattern or patterns, then ask you to perform, write, or identify what you hear.

B. Your teacher will combine a rhythmic pattern or patterns with pitch patterns such as sets or modes. Respond by performing, writing, or identifying what you hear.

Options for performing your response
Maintain the pitch, rhythm, and tempo of the call.

- Tap the rhythm in one hand and the beat unit in the other.
- Conduct (or tap) the beats.
- Sing pitch only (with pc integers or note names).
- Sing rhythm only.
- Sing pitch and rhythm.
- Play on your instrument.

Options for writing your response

- meter signature(s) and/or beat division(s)
- rhythmic notation only
- pc integers
- interval sequence and direction
- pitches
- pc intervals (pci) of the sequence
- note names
- note heads only
- notes and rhythm

III. CONTEXTUAL LISTENING

EXAMPLE 1, TRACK 2.32

Listen to an excerpt from a work for wind instruments by Stravinsky, and complete the exercises below.

1. The excerpt begins with which two melodic pitch intervals?

    (a) m3, M7   (c) M3, M7

    (b) m3, m7   (d) M3, m7

2. Which instruments comprise the ensemble?

    (a) oboe, flute, saxophone, bass clarinet, horn, trumpet, and trombones

    (b) oboes, flutes, clarinet, bassoon, trumpet, and trombone

    (c) flute, clarinet, bassoons, trumpets, and trombones

    (d) flute, clarinets, bass clarinet, trumpets, trombone, and tuba

The excerpt begins with a trumpet theme, which returns several times during the excerpt.

3. Beginning on *do*, write the pitches of the theme's first statement.

4. Beginning on $\hat{1}$, write the scale-degree numbers of the theme's first statement.

5. (a) Beginning on E♭5, notate the pitches of the theme on the staves below. Write the correct clef and key signature (or accidentals).

    (b) Write / and ˅ marks above the pitches of your answer to part (a) to show the accented and unaccented beats in the melody. Place bar lines before each / mark. Assume the quarter note to be the initial beat unit. Count the number of eighth notes between bar lines to determine the meter signature of each measure.

(c) Beginning on E♭5, notate both pitches and rhythm of the first statement of the theme on the staves below. Assume the quarter note to be the initial beat unit. Write the appropriate clef and key signature (or accidentals). Include the meter signature(s) and bar lines. Beam eighth notes to show the beat grouping.

6. How are the second and third statements of the theme related? The third statement

   (a) follows the second in canon;

   (b) is a melodic inversion of the second;

   (c) is a rhythmic augmentation of the second;

   (d) is a rhythmic diminution of the second.

7. Beginning with its fourth statement, the theme is developed in all of the following ways *except* which?

   (a) The opening pitch intervals are larger.

   (b) Only the initial portion is performed.

   (c) It is sequenced down by step.

   (d) It is now in compound meter.

8. The excerpt's final cadence features which of the following items?

   (a) a IV–I progression

   (b) mode mixture (minor tonic)

   (c) an augmented-sixth chord

   (d) a Phrygian resolution

9. The articulation heard throughout the excerpt is

   (a) legato   (c) staccato

   (b) slurs   (d) pizzicato

10. This excerpt is a parody of the music of which earlier period?

    (a) Renaissance   (c) Classical

    (b) Baroque   (d) Romantic

EXAMPLE 2, TRACK 2.33

Listen to a movement from a composition for orchestra by Bartók. Exercises 1–13 focus on the first section of the movement only. This first section lasts until the oboe cadences, right before a new melody begins in the strings.

1. (a) The excerpt begins with a four-note introduction. Beginning on B4, notate this tetrachord on the staff below.

(b) Consider this tetrachord to be unordered pcset A. Play the rotations of set A at the keyboard, and notate them on the staff below. Find the normal order and prime form for set A. To which set class does it belong?

2. In your answer to #1 (a), write order numbers 1–4 above the pitches of set A. Call pitches 1, 2, and 3 set B; pitches 2, 3, and 4 set C; pitches 1, 2, and 4 set D; and pitches 1, 3, and 4 set E. Consider B, C, D, and E to be unordered pcsets. Play the rotations of each set, and notate them on the staves below. What are the normal order, prime form, and Forte number of each set?

Set B: pitches 1, 2, and 3 of set A   Set C: pitches 2, 3, and 4 of set A

Set D: pitches 1, 2, and 4 of set A   Set E: pitches 1, 3, and 4 of set A

Set	Normal order	Prime form	Forte number
B	{ ___ ___ ___ }	[___ ___ ___]	3-___
C	{ ___ ___ ___ }	[___ ___ ___]	3-___
D	{ ___ ___ ___ }	[___ ___ ___]	3-___
E	{ ___ ___ ___ }	[___ ___ ___]	3-___

3. Listen from the beginning until the oboe melody cadences. Briefly describe how the oboe's first pitches relate to the pitches of the introduction.

4. (a) After the four-note introduction, the oboe plays phrase 1. Beginning on E5, notate the oboe's pitches on the staff below. Write the appropriate clef and key signature (or accidentals).

(b) Write / and ˘ marks above the pitches of your answer to part (a) to show the accented and unaccented beats in the melody. Place bar lines before each / mark. Count the number of eighth notes between bar lines to determine the meter signature of each measure.

(c) Assume the smallest value to be the eighth note. Now notate the pitches and rhythm of the oboe's phrase 1 on the staff below. Begin on E5. Write the appropriate clef and key signature (or accidentals). Include the meter signature(s) and bar lines. Beam eighth notes to show the beat grouping.

(d) Which is the pitch center of the oboe melody?

(1) E   (2) F♯   (3) A♯   (4) B

5. Phrase 2 is played by the clarinet. How does phrase 2 compare with phrase 1 (the oboe's music)?

   (a) Phrase 2 is a melodic inversion.

   (b) Phrase 2 begins the same, but ends differently.

   (c) Phrase 2 begins differently, but ends the same.

   (d) Phrase 2 is completely contrasting.

6. (a) Just after the clarinet melody, phrase 3 begins with high pitches in the flute. Starting on D5, notate the flute's pitches on the staff below. Write the appropriate clef and key signature (or accidentals).

   (b) Write / and ˘ marks above the music in part (a) to show the accents in the music. Place bar lines before each / mark. Count the number of eighth notes between bar lines to determine the meter signature of each measure.

   (c) The smallest value is the eighth note. Notate both pitches and rhythm of phrase 3 on the staff below. Beam eighth notes to show the beat grouping. For help, consult your answers to parts (a) and (b).

7. (a) Call the first three distinct pitches of your answer to #6 (a) unordered pcset F. Play the rotations of set F, and notate them on the staff below. What are the normal order, prime form, and Forte number of F?

   (b) How does set F relate to set D?

8. (a) Call the next three distinct pitches of your answer to #6 (a) unordered pcset G. Play the rotations of set G, and notate them on the staff below. What are the normal order, prime form, and Forte number of G?

(b) How does set G relate to set D?

9. (a) Just after the high flute melody, the clarinet returns with a short melody. Beginning on D5, sketch the pitches of the clarinet melody on the staff below.

(b) The clarinet's pitches belong to which traditional pattern?

    (1) major tetrachord

    (2) minor tetrachord

    (3) major pentachord

    (4) minor pentachord

10. (a) The clarinet melody is followed immediately by the music of the horn. Beginning on D4, sketch the pitches of the horn on the staff below.

(b) The horn's pitches belong to which traditional pattern?

    (1) major tetrachord

    (2) minor tetrachord

    (3) major pentachord

    (4) minor pentachord

(c) Add rhythmic notation to your answer to part (a). For help, use the procedure we followed in #6.

11. (a) On the last note of the horn melody, the music slows to a cadential chord. The chord's lowest pitch, C2, is played by the cellos. Sketch the pitches of the cadential chord on the staff below.

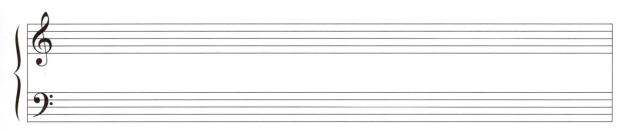

(b) Which of the following represents the pcs contained in the cadential chord?

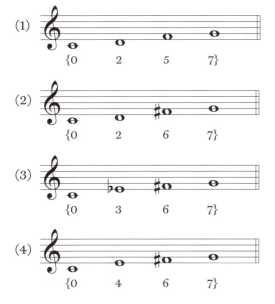

(1) {0   2   5   7}

(2) {0   2   6   7}

(3) {0   3   6   7}

(4) {0   4   6   7}

12. (a) Call the chord of #11 set H. Write order numbers 1–4 above the pcs of set H in your answer to #11 (b).

(b) Call pitches 1, 2, and 3 set J; pitches 2, 3, and 4 set K; pitches 1, 2, and 4 set L; and pitches 1, 3, and 4 set M. Consider J, K, L, and M to be unordered pcsets. Play the rotations of each set, and notate them on the staves below. What are the normal order, prime form, and Forte number of each set?

Set J: pitches 1, 2, and 3 of set H   Set K: pitches 2, 3, and 4 of set H

Set L: pitches 1, 2, and 4 of set H   Set M: pitches 1, 3, and 4 of set H

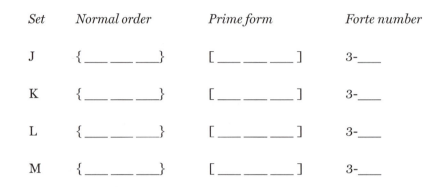

Set	Normal order	Prime form	Forte number
J	{ ___ ___ ___ }	[___ ___ ___]	3-___
K	{ ___ ___ ___ }	[___ ___ ___]	3-___
L	{ ___ ___ ___ }	[___ ___ ___]	3-___
M	{ ___ ___ ___ }	[___ ___ ___]	3-___

(c) Which trichord subsets of the introduction are also found as trichord subsets in this cadential sonority?

13. Just after the horn's cadence, the oboe plays the final melody of the first section. How does the oboe's final melody relate to its first melody?

(a) It is the same melody, but transposed down one octave.

(b) It is a melodic inversion.

(c) It begins the same, but concludes differently.

(d) It begins differently, but concludes the same.

Listen now to the entire movement, and determine its overall form. Use the space below to sketch a diagram.

14. Which is the form of the entire movement?

(a) **A B** (binary)

(b) **A B A** (ternary)

(c) **A B A C B A**

(d) sonata

EXAMPLE 3, TRACK 2.34

Listen to an excerpt from a jazz composition by Dave Brubeck, and complete the exercises below.

1. In which meter signature can the entire excerpt be notated?

   (a) $\frac{5}{8}$

   (b) $\frac{7}{8}$

   (c) $\frac{8}{8}$

   (d) $\frac{9}{8}$

2. Beginning on A4, notate the pitches and rhythm of the first phrase of the melody on the staff below. Use the appropriate clef and key signature (or accidentals). Beam in groups to show the irregular accents of the meter.

3. Beginning on E4, notate the pitches and rhythm of the chromatic line in the lower part of phrase 1 on the staff below. Use the appropriate clef and key signature (or accidentals). Group pitches to show the irregular accents of the meter.

4. Which is the quality of the first chord of the excerpt?

   (a) major

   (b) minor

   (c) MM^7

   (d) mm^7

Phrase 2 is a repetition of phrase 1.

5. In phrase 3, which scale degree is tonicized?

   (a) $\hat{3}$

   (b) $\hat{4}$

   (c) $\hat{5}$

   (d) $\hat{6}$

6. Notate the pitches and rhythm of the melody in phrase 3 on the staff below. Write the appropriate clef and key signature (or accidentals).

Phrase 4 is a repetition of phrase 3.

7. How does phrase 5 relate to the phrases that precede it?

    (a) Phrase 5 is a repetition of phrase 1.

    (b) Phrase 5 is a repetition of phrase 3.

    (c) Phrase 5 is a varied repetition of phrase 3.

    (d) Phrase 5 is a new phrase, not heard before in the composition.

Phrase 6 is a repetition of phrase 5.

8. Which key is tonicized in phrase 7?

    (a) tonic

    (b) dominant

    (c) mediant

    (d) relative minor

9. Notate the pitches and rhythm of the melody in phrase 7 on the staff below. Write the appropriate clef and key signature (or accidentals).

Phrase 8 is a repetition of phrase 7.

10. How is the melody of phrase 9 related to any previous music?

    (a) It is identical to phrase 1.

    (b) It is a transposition of phrase 1 up a third.

    (c) It is identical to phrase 3.

    (d) It is a transposition of phrase 5 down a second.

EXAMPLE 4, TRACK 2.35

Listen to an excerpt from a work for chorus and orchestra by Leonard Bernstein. The excerpt is comprised of eight melodic segments, though we will focus only on the first four. Segments 1–3 contain eight melodic pitches each. Segment 4 contains ten melodic pitches.

1. Which is a correct notation of the rhythm of the first melodic segment?

2. Starting on G5, notate the pitches of the first four segments of the melody on the staves below. (After segment 4, there is a repetition of segment 1.) Write the appropriate clef and accidentals.

3. Which is the form of the first four melodic segments?

   (a) **a a a a**   (c) **a b a b**

   (b) **a a a′ b**   (d) **a b a c**

4. Consider the first half of segment 1 to be an unordered pcset. Call this trichord set A. Play the rotations of set A at the keyboard, or notate them on the staff below. What are the normal order, prime form, and set class for this trichord?

5. Consider the second half of segment 1 to be an unordered pcset. Call this trichord set B. Play the rotations of set B at the keyboard, or notate them on the staff below. What are the normal order, prime form, and set class for this trichord?

6. Consider all the pcs of melodic segment 1 to be an unordered pcset. Call this penta-chord set C. Play the rotations of set C at the keyboard, or notate them on the staff below. What are the normal order, prime form, and set class for this pentachord?

7. Add pc e to set C to create a hexachord. (Pc e is present in the harmony of the first segment.) Call this hexachord set D. Play the rotations of set D at the keyboard, or notate them on the staff below. What are the normal order, prime form, and set class for this pentachord?

8. In traditional terms, set D might be thought of as two same-quality triads a half step apart. Which is the quality of these two triads?

(a) major   (c) augmented

(b) minor   (d) diminished

9. To which traditional scale do the pitches of melodic segments 3 and 4 belong? In segment 4, be sure to include the men's parts as part of the melody.

(a) E Major

(b) C♯ ascending melodic minor

(c) G♯ Aeolian mode

(d) G♯ Lydian mode

10. Consider the pcs of melodic segment 3 to be an unordered pcset. Call this trichord set E. Play the rotations of set E at the keyboard, or notate them on the staff below. What are the normal order, prime form, and set class for this pentachord?

11. Melodic segment 4 is comprised of two traditional pentachords of which quality?

    (a) major

    (b) minor

    (c) harmonic

    (d) Phrygian

12. The pentachords of melodic segment 4 belong to which set class?

    (a) [0 1 3 5 7]

    (b) [0 1 4 5 7]

    (c) [0 2 3 5 7]

    (d) [0 2 4 6 8]

IV. MELODIES FOR STUDY

For each of the melodies below, prepare to do any of the following.

- Conduct and perform the rhythm.
- Sing the melody with note names or pc integers.
- Play it on an instrument.
- Identify pcsets of row segments.
- Transpose the melody to other pitch levels on your instrument.
- Identify the pitch intervals between successive notes.
- Identify row forms.

Strategies for Singing

- Practice singing these melodies by performing the rhythm alone (while conducting), then slowly the pitch alone, then the pitch and rhythm together.
- Sing on interval numbers to focus on intonation (sing a whole step as "2," a minor third as "3," and so on).
- Once you feel confident of the pitches and intervals, sing in rhythm on "la."
- Modal or pentatonic melodies may be sung on solfège syllables or scale-degree numbers.
- For melodies that exceed your voice range, transfer pitches to octaves that are more easily sung; try to do so at natural breaks in the phrasing.

Melody 1 Stravinsky, Theme and Variations, from *Octet for Wind Instruments*
From which scale is this melody derived?

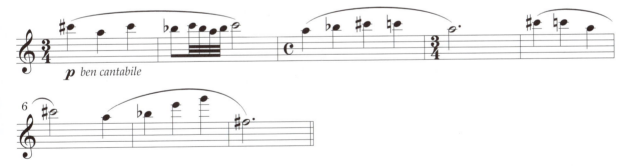

Melody 2 Stravinsky, "Royal March," from *L'histoire du soldat* (*The Soldier's Tale*) (adapted)

Melody 3   Deborah Koenigsberg, String Quartet, third movement (adapted)

Melody 4   Olivier Messiaen, "Danse de la fureur, pour les sept trompettes" ("Dance of Frenzy, for the Seven Trumpets"), from *Quartet for the End of Time*

Melody 5   Rebecca Oswald, *Finding the Murray River*

Melody 6 Luigi Dallapiccola, *Quaderno musicale di Annalibera* (*Musical Notebook of Annalibera*), No. 4

Treat this melody as a duet or as a play-and-sing solo.

V. IMPROVISATION

Polymetric Duets

OSTINATO

It is easy to create a polymetric ostinato. First, select two meters and multiply their beats (the top number in the signature). For example, if we choose $\frac{3}{4}$ and $\frac{4}{4}$, we multiply 3 times 4.

Thus, the ostinato will be twelve *beats* long—four measures of $\frac{3}{4}$ and three measures of $\frac{4}{4}$, heard at the same time.

For the duet, the first performer begins by improvising a four-measure rhythmic ostinato in $\frac{3}{4}$ meter. Once the first ostinato is established, a second performer enters, improvising a three-measure ostinato in $\frac{4}{4}$ as the first performer continues. To make the meters more audible, each person should use a contrasting timbre, choose rhythmic patterns common to the meters, and emphasize the metric accent.

Variations

Try combining other meters as well.

- $\frac{3}{4}$ and $\frac{5}{4}$ (or $\frac{3}{8}$ and $\frac{5}{8}$)
- $\frac{4}{4}$ and $\frac{5}{4}$ (or $\frac{4}{8}$ and $\frac{5}{8}$)
- $\frac{3}{4}$ and $\frac{7}{4}$ (or $\frac{3}{8}$ and $\frac{7}{4}$)

SAME BAR LINES, DIFFERENT DIVISIONS

Sing a familiar simple-triple melody, such as "My Country, 'Tis of Thee." Tap eighth notes in one hand and the beat in the other. Practice simple divisions against the tune (m. 1 below), then compound divisions (m. 2). Finally, alternate simple with compound as shown in the rest of the example below.

For the duet, choose a scale or mode. The first performer sings, improvising a melody in simple-triple meter. After the pulse is established, a second performer accompanies the first, tapping first in simple-triple meter, then in compound-duple meter, and finally in alternating measures of simple and compound meters.

Variations

- Accompany your own improvised melody, tapping as you did for "My Country."
- In the middle of a performance, the second performer listens for the first to change to compound-duple meter. As soon as possible, the second performer changes the accom-

paniment to simple-triple meter. Then when the first changes back to simple triple, the second changes to compound duple. Continue these switches until the conclusion.

- Choose different meter combinations, such as $\frac{4}{4}$ and $\frac{3+2+3}{8}$, or $\frac{9}{8}$ and $\frac{2+2+2+3}{8}$.

VI. COMPOSITION

Serial Composition

Compose a serial work in which each interval class in your series determines the duration. (You may also want to serialize other aspects of the piece, such as dynamics and articulation.) Let the sixteenth note represent the smallest duration. Write for an instrument played by a classmate, and have it performed.

To see how this might be done, look at the series below. The order numbers are shown above the row and the interval classes below.

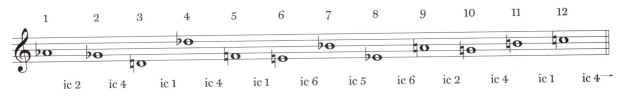

Now we'll use the interval class to determine the duration, dynamics, and articulation. For example, when the interval class between two pcs is 5, we notate the first pitch so that it lasts for five sixteenth notes, and add a f and > to the pitch.

	ic 1	ic 2	ic 3	ic 4	ic 5	ic 6
duration in sixteenth notes	1	2	3	4	5	6
dynamics	pp	p	mp	mf	f	ff
articulation	.	^	gliss.	—	>	tr~

Flute
Whimsical

(Why include ic 3 above? That ic might occur *between* two forms of the row later in the work.)

Percussion Duet

Compose a percussion duet in **A B A** form. In the **A** section, include both mixed and asymmetrical meters. Characterize the middle section by the use of polymeter.

Incorporate some or all of the following ideas:

- The percussion instruments may be classroom objects, such as pencils, books, and desks.
- Plan the length of your individual sections according to the golden mean. The **golden mean** occurs when we divide a composition into two parts in such a way that the ratio of the smaller part (YZ) to the larger (XY) is about the same proportion as the larger part (XY) is to the whole piece (XZ). We can write this proportion YZ:XY~XY:XZ.

```
X                         Y              Z
|-------------------------|--------------|
```

Three adjacent Fibonacci numbers (1, 1, 2, 3, 5, 8, 13, 21, 34, 55, 89, etc.) may be used to approximate this proportion. The farther into the series we go, the better the approximation. For example, if the smaller part (YZ) is 21 measures and the larger part (XY) is 34 measures, the entire composition (XZ) is 55 measures; 21/34 is about the same proportion as 34/55.

One way to apply the proportion shown in the diagram to your **A B A** duet is to plan for the recapitulation of **A** at point Y, or about 62% of the total duration of the piece.

- Create a distinct motive that is a rhythmic palindrome (sounds the same when played backward and forward).

Ametric Composition

Compose an ametric work that you will perform in class. Your composition might feature any or all of the following techniques:

- Feathered beaming:
  gradual acceleration   gradual deceleration

- Timed proportions:

- Graphic notation (this example includes timed proportions, too):

Appendixes

Glossary

1:1 (one-to-one): Counterpoint written so that each note in one voice is paired with a single note in the other voice, using only consonant intervals. Another name for *first-species* counterpoint.

2:1 (two-to-one): Counterpoint written so that one voice has two notes for every single note in the other voice. Permits consonances and passing tones, according to strict rules of voice-leading; in eighteenth-century style, also allows neighbor tones. Another name for *second-species* counterpoint.

3:1 (three-to-one): Counterpoint written so that one voice has three notes for every single note in the other voice. Considered a type of second species according to Fux, but in eighteenth-century practice it is more closely related to third-species counterpoint in its use of dissonance.

4:1 (four-to-one): Counterpoint written so that one voice has four notes for every single note in the other voice; permits consonances, passing tones, and neighboring tones, according to strict rules of voice-leading. Another name for *third-species* counterpoint.

a a b a: The formal design associated with quaternary song form.

A B A: The formal design associated with ternary form.

abrupt modulation: Another term for *direct modulation*.

abstract complement: Two set classes where one representative of each, when combined, make a literal complement. This relationship is shown in the Forte numbers: the numbers before the hyphen sum to 12; the numbers after the hyphen are the same (e.g., 4-Z15, 8-Z15).

accent: Stress given to a note or other musical element that brings it to the listener's attention—by playing louder or softer, using a different timbre or articulation, slightly changing rhythmic durations.

accidental: A musical symbol (sharp, flat, natural, double sharp, or double flat) that appears before a note to raise or lower its pitch chromatically.

added-sixth chord: A triad that contains an extra pitch a major sixth above the bass note.

additive rhythm: An ametric rhythm created when a brief duration (often a sixteenth or smaller) is chosen as a base element, and then several brief durations are added together to form larger durations.

Aeolian mode: An ordered collection with the pattern of whole and half steps corresponding to the diatonic collection starting and ending on A; the same collection as the natural minor scale.

aggregate: A collection of all twelve pitch classes. The term generally refers to the combination of two or more twelve-tone rows so that, together, new twelve-note collections are generated. Aggregates may also appear in non-twelve-tone music.

Alberti bass: A common Classical-period accompaniment formed by arpeggiating triads in repeated patterns, such as root-fifth-third-fifth.

all-combinatorial hexachord: A hexachord capable of all four types of combinatoriality (P-, I-, R-, and RI-combinatoriality).

altered common-chord modulation: A type of modulation whose pivot chord is a chromatic chord in one or both keys (e.g., mixture chord, secondary dominant, secondary leading-tone chord).

altered-fifth chord: A triad or seventh chord that has been colored and intensified by raising or lowering the fifth by a half step.

altered pivot-chord modulation: Another term for *altered common-chord modulation*.

alto: The second-highest voice in four-part SATB writing, usually directly below the soprano.

alto clef: A C-clef positioned on a staff so that the middle line indicates middle C (C4); typically read by violas.

ametric: Music for which no regular meter is perceived; may be notated in nontraditional ways.

anacrusis: Occurs when a melody starts just before the first down beat in a meter; also called an *upbeat*, or pick-up.

anhemitonic pentatonic: A pentatonic scale with no half steps.

antecedent phrase: The first phrase of a period; ends with an inconclusive cadence (usually a half cadence).

anticipation: An embellishing tone whose pitch of resolution arrives "early." An anticipation is unaccented, and almost always a dissonance. It does not resolve by step—rather, it is repeated as a consonance on the next beat, where it "belongs."

applied chord: A dominant-function harmony (V or vii°, with or without the chordal seventh) "applied" to a chord other than tonic. An applied chord typically includes chromatic alterations (relative to the tonic key). Also called a *secondary dominant*.

appoggiatura: A dissonance that occurs on a strong beat and usually resolves down by step. Some theorists restrict this term to an accented dissonance approached by skip or leap; others consider appoggiaturas accented incomplete neighbors (or complete if approached by step).

arpeggiated ⁶₄: A ⁶₄ created when the bass line sounds each note of a triad in turn (root, third, fifth), or alternates between the root and the fifth.

arpeggio, arpeggiated: A chord played one pitch at a time.

articulation: The different ways a note can be attacked and connected to other notes. It might be played very short (*staccato*), held (*tenuto*), or played suddenly and loudly (*sfzorzando*). The notes of a melody may be highly connected (*legato*) or separated.

art song: A song, usually featuring a literary poetic text, written for performance outside the popular- and folk-music traditions.

asymmetrical meter: A compound meter with beat units of unequal duration. These "irregular" beat lengths are typically (though not always) created by five or seven beat divisions, grouped into beat lengths such as 2 + 3 or 2 + 3 + 2.

atonal: Another term for *nontonal*.

augmentation: The process of systematically lengthening the duration of pitches in a musical line. There is usually a consistent proportion in relation to the original melody (e.g., each original duration may be doubled).

augmented interval: An interval one half step larger than a major or perfect interval.

augmented-sixth chord: A chord featuring (♭)$\hat{6}$ in the bass and ♯$\hat{4}$ in an upper voice, creating the interval of an augmented sixth. Such chords usually resolve to V: (♭)$\hat{6}$ and ♯$\hat{4}$ resolve outward by half step to $\hat{5}$.

augmented triad: A triad with major thirds between the root and third and between the third and fifth. The interval between the root and fifth is an augmented fifth.

B♭ instrument: An instrument whose sounding pitch is a whole step lower than the notated pitch. The most common B♭ instruments are the trumpet, clarinet, bass clarinet, and tenor saxophone (the last two sound a whole step plus an octave lower than the notated pitch).

balanced sections: A feature of binary forms in which material from the end of the first section returns at the end of the second section.

bar line: A vertical line that indicates the end of a measure.

Baroque era: The period in Western musical history dating roughly from 1600 until 1750. Some Baroque composers are Johann Sebastian Bach, George Frideric Handel, François Couperin, Antonio Vivaldi, and Henry Purcell. Genres associated with this era are the concerto grosso, oratorio, keyboard suite, and cantata.

basic phrase: A conclusive phrase that consists of an opening tonic area (T), an optional predominant area (PD), a dominant area (D), and tonic closure (T, a cadence on I). Written in contextual analysis as T–PD–D–T, beneath Roman numerals (vertical analysis).

bass: The lowest voice in four-part (SATB) writing. The bass pitch does not always represent the root of a chord.

bass clef: On a staff, the bass clef (also known as the F-clef) rests on the line that represents F3; its two dots surround the F3 line; typically read by bassoons, cellos, basses, and piano left hand.

beat: The primary pulse in musical meter.

beat division: The secondary pulse in musical meter; the first level of faster-moving pulses beneath the primary beat.

bimodality: The simultaneous use of two modes in two different layers of music.

binary form: The formal design of a composition organized into two sections. Usually each section is repeated.

bitonality: The simultaneous use of two keys in two different layers of music.

blue note: One of three possible pitches, derived from the blues scale, that can be altered in popular music for expressive effect: ♭$\hat{3}$, ♯$\hat{4}$ (or ♭$\hat{5}$), and ♭$\hat{7}$.

blues scale: This scale blurs the distinction between major and minor by permitting both $\hat{3}$ and ♭$\hat{3}$ and both $\hat{7}$ and ♭$\hat{7}$. It also allows ♯$\hat{4}$ and $\hat{4}$, and ♭$\hat{5}$ and $\hat{5}$.

borrowed chord: A harmony whose spelling and chord quality are derived from the parallel mode. Most often, chords from the parallel minor mode appear in a major key. Another name for *mixture* chord.

bridge: The contrasting **b** section in an **a a b a** thirty-two-bar song form.

C-clef: A movable clef that may be placed on a staff to identify any one of the five lines as middle C (C4).

C instrument: An instrument whose sounding pitch is the same as the notated pitch. Common C instruments include the piano, flute, oboe, bassoon, trombone, tuba, harp, and most of the string family.

C score: A nontransposed score that shows all the parts in the concert key—i.e., all the pitches in the score are the pitches that the instruments sound. Also known as *concert-pitch* score.

cadence: The end of a phrase, where harmonic, melodic, and rhythmic features articulate a complete musical thought.

cadential extension: A type of extension occurring at the end of a phrase. Typically, the cadence is repeated with little new or elaborative melodic material.

cadential ⁶₄: A ⁶₄ chord that embellishes the V chord. The cadential ⁶₄ is spelled like a second-inversion tonic chord, but it has no tonic function. Instead, it displaces the V chord with simultaneous 6–5 and 4–3 suspension-like motions above the sustained bass note 5̂. Usually occurs on a strong beat.

cadenza: A solo portion at the end of a concerto movement that features rapid passagework and other technical challenges. Can appear in any concerto movement, but is generally found in the first movement after a prominent cadential ⁶₄ harmony in the orchestra, before the beginning of the coda.

cantus firmus: The given melody against which a counterpoint is written.

cardinality: The number of elements in a collection.

center: A pitch or pitch class pervasively heard in a work or section of a work. A center does not imply a functional system of scale degrees in any key or mode (as does traditional functional tonality), but it can establish a sense of hierarchy.

centric: Music that focuses on a pitch or pitch-class center, but not in the sense of a conventional tonal hierarchy.

chaconne: A set of continuous variations in which the entire harmonic texture, not just the bass line, is repeated and varied. While the bass line may remain unchanged for several successive variations, it is usually altered as the chaconne progresses—through rhythmic variation, changes in inversion, or substitute harmonies.

chance: A method of composition or performance that is determined by a random or unpredictable procedure, such as the toss of coins, dice, or the *I-Ching*.

change of bass suspension: A type of suspension in which the bass changes when the suspension resolves; e.g., a 9–8 suspension that becomes a 9–6 because the bass skips up a third.

changing meter: In contemporary pieces, meter that changes from measure to measure.

character variation: A variation intended to reproduce a particular musical style or evoke a certain genre.

chorale: A hymn set for four voices. The voices tend to move together, creating a chordal texture. Often, the melody is given to the soprano.

chord: A group of pitches sounded together. In common-practice harmony, chords are generally built in thirds.

chord members: The pitches that make up a chord. In tonal music, each chord member is described by the interval it forms with the lowest (or bass) pitch of the chord.

chordal skip: A melodic embellishment made by skipping from one chord member to another.

choruses 1 and 2: The outer sections of an **a a b a** quaternary song form. They share the same or similar musical material.

chromatic: Chromatic music includes pitches from outside the diatonic collection. The chromatic collection consists of all twelve pitch classes.

chromatic half step: A semitone spelling in which both pitches have the same letter name (e.g., D and D♯).

chromatic inflection: A method of modulation effected by shifting one pitch by a half step.

chromatic neighbor tone: A nondiatonic half-step neighbor that embellishes a chord tone.

chromatic passing tone: A passing tone that divides a diatonic whole step into two half steps.

chromatic variation: A variation that contrasts with the original theme through increased chromaticism. The chromaticism can embellish the melodic line or elaborate the chord progressions.

chromatic voice exchange: The chromatic alteration of one of the pitches in a voice exchange (e.g., scale-degrees 2̂ and 4̂ in a ii⁽⁷⁾ might exchange places to become ♯4̂ and 2̂ in a V⁷/V).

chromaticized sequence: A diatonic sequence transformed by substituting chromatic harmonies for diatonic ones, or by chromatically embellishing the sequence.

circle of fifths: A circular diagram showing the relationships between keys when sharps or flats are added to the key signature. The sharp keys appear around the right side of the circle, with each key a fifth higher. The flat keys appear around the left side of the circle, with each key a fifth lower.

Classical era: The period in Western music history dating roughly from 1750 until 1830. Some Classical composers are Wolfgang Amadeus Mozart, Franz Joseph Haydn, and Ludwig van Beethoven. Genres most associated with this era are the string quartet, the sonata, the symphony, and opera.

clef: A symbol that appears on the far left of every staff to designate which line or space represents which pitch (in which octave).

closed: Term referring to a melody or formal section that ends with a conclusive cadence on the tonic.

closely related key: Any key whose tonic is a diatonic triad (major or minor) in the original key. The key signatures of closely related keys differ at most by one accidental.

closing theme: A "third theme" that might be found near the end of a sonata-form exposition; part of the second theme group if it shares the same key.

coda: A section of music at the end of a piece, generally following a strong cadence in the tonic. Serves to extend the tonic area and bring the work to a close.

coda/codetta theme: A distinctive, identifiable melody introduced in a coda or codetta.

codetta: A "little coda" at the end of a section or piece.

collection: A group of unordered pitches or pitch classes that serve as a source of musical materials for a work or a section of a work; a large set.

common-chord modulation: Modulation from one key to another by means of a harmony (the pivot chord) that functions diatonically in both keys.

common-dyad modulation: A type of modulation in which two pitches of a chord in the initial key function as a "pivot" between the two keys. Other pitches of this modulating chord may shift up or down a half step, making a chromatic connection.

common practice: The compositional techniques and harmonic language of the Baroque, Classical, and Romantic eras.

common-tone modulation: A type of modulation in which only a single pitch of a chord or melodic line in the initial key functions as a "pivot" between the two keys. Other pitches of this modulating chord may shift up or down a half step, making a chromatic connection.

common-tone theorem: The number in each position of a pcset's ic vector tells two things: (1) the number of times a particular interval class occurs between elements of the set, and (2) the number of common tones that will result when that particular interval class is used to transpose the pcset. The latter principle is called the common-tone theorem.

composite ternary: A formal scheme created by joining smaller, complete forms into an **A B A** form (such as a minuet and trio, or scherzo and trio). The **A** and **B** sections themselves may have their own formal type (such as rounded binary).

compound duple: Any meter with two beats in a measure, with each beat divided into three (e.g., $\frac{6}{8}$ or $\frac{6}{4}$).

compound interval: An interval larger than an octave.

compound melody: A melody created by the interaction of two or three voices, usually separated by register. Often features large leaps.

compound meter: Any meter in which the beat divides into threes and subdivides into sixes. The top number of the meter signature will be 6, 9, or 12 (e.g., $\frac{9}{4}$ or $\frac{6}{8}$).

compound quadruple: Any meter with four beats in a measure, with each beat divided into three (e.g., $\frac{12}{8}$ or $\frac{12}{4}$).

compound triple: Any meter with three beats in a measure, with each beat divided into three (e.g., $\frac{9}{8}$ or $\frac{9}{4}$).

concert pitch: The sounding pitch of an instrument. For transposing instruments, this differs from notated pitch.

concerto: A composition for a solo instrument and orchestra. Concertos often consist of three movements, arranged fast-slow-fast (following a formal pattern similar to the three-movement sonata).

conclusive cadence: A cadence that makes a phrase sound finished and complete. Generally the harmonic progression is V–I, with both soprano and bass ending on scale-degree $\hat{1}$.

conjunct motion: Melodic motion by step.

consequent phrase: The second phrase of a period. The consequent phrase ends with a strong harmonic conclusion, usually an authentic cadence.

consonance, imperfect: The intervals of a third and sixth.

consonance, perfect: The intervals of a unison, fourth, fifth, and octave. The harmonic interval of a fourth is treated as a dissonance in common-practice style.

consonant: A relative term based on acoustic properties of sound and on the norms of compositional practice. A consonant harmonic interval—unison, third, fifth, sixth, or octave—is considered pleasing to hear.

consonant skip: Another term for *chordal skip*.

contextual analysis: A second level of harmonic analysis, showing how passing chords (and other voice-leading chords) function to expand the basic phrase model (T–PD–D–T).

continuo: An instrumental accompaniment that is read from only a given bass line (often with figures). The continuo typically consists of a low bass instrument (cello, bass viol, or bassoon) that plays a single-voice bass line, and an instrument capable of producing chordal harmonies (harpsichord, organ, guitar, or lute). The chordal instrument must realize the bass line harmonically—from figures if given, or following principles of harmonic progression and voice-leading.

continuous: Term referring to a section of a piece that has a tonally open ending and must therefore continue into the following section for tonal completion.

continuous binary: A binary form in which the first large section ends with a cadence that is not in the tonic key. The harmonic motion of the piece must continue into the following section to a conclusion in the tonic key.

continuous variation: A variation form characterized by a continuous flow of musical ideas—as opposed to strong, section-defining cadences—and *Fortspinnung* phrase structure. Continuous variations usually feature a short bass line or harmonic progression that remains constant through repeated variations.

contour motive: A motive that maintains its contour, or musical shape, but changes its intervals; its rhythm may or may not be altered.

contrapuntal: (1) A composition based on the principles of counterpoint. (2) A musical texture in which the interaction of several lines creates harmonies. "Contrapuntal chord" is another name for *linear* or *voice-leading chord*.

contrary fifths or octaves: Motion from one perfect interval to another of the same type, in which the voices move in opposite directions. One of the perfect intervals will be a compound interval.

contrary motion: Contrapuntal, or voice-leading, motion in which two voices move in opposite directions.

contrasting period: A period in which the two phrases do not share the same initial melodic material.

counterpoint: A musical texture that sets two or more lines of music together so that the independent lines together create acceptable harmony; or harmonies set one after another so that the individual voices make good, independent melodic lines.

couplet: Two successive lines of poetic text that rhyme or establish a rhyme scheme.

cross relation: The sudden chromatic alteration of a pitch in one voice part, immediately after the diatonic version has sounded in another voice.

deceptive cadence: The cadence V$^{(7)}$–vi in major, or V$^{(7)}$–VI in minor. Generally, any nontonic resolution from V at a cadence.

deceptive resolution: A midphrase resolution to the submediant from V.

design: In discussions of musical form, the melodic or thematic aspects, as distinct from the harmonic structure.

development: The section of a sonata form devoted to the exploration and variation of motives and themes from the exposition. Generally features sequential and modulatory passages.

developmental coda: A coda having the character and structure of a sonata-form development; sometimes called a "second development."

diatonic: (1) The collection of seven pitch classes that, in some rotation, conforms to the pattern of the whole and half steps of the major scale (a subset of the chromatic collection). (2) Made up of pitches belonging to a given diatonic collection.

diatonic half step: A semitone spelled with different letter names for the two pitches (e.g., D and E♭).

diatonic sequence: A sequence made up of pitches belonging to the diatonic collection. When the sequence pattern is transposed, generic melodic intervals stay the same, but interval qualities change (e.g., major to minor, or perfect to diminished).

diminished interval: An interval one half step smaller than a minor or perfect interval.

diminished scale: Another name for *octatonic scale*, so called because of the fully diminished seventh chords that are subsets of any octatonic scale.

diminished seventh chord: A seventh chord consisting of a diminished triad and a diminished seventh. Sometimes called a *fully diminished seventh chord* to distinguish it from the *half-diminished seventh chord*.

diminished-third chord: A version of the augmented-sixth chord, with (♭)$\hat{6}$ in an upper voice and ♯$\hat{4}$ in the bass, creating the interval of a diminished third.

diminished triad: A triad with minor thirds between the root and third and between the third and fifth. The interval between the root and fifth is a diminished fifth.

diminution: The process of systematically shortening the duration of pitches in a melodic line. There is usually a consistent proportion in relation to the original melody (e.g., all note values may be reduced by a half).

direct fifths or octaves: Similar motion into a perfect interval, permitted only in inner voices or if the soprano moves by step.

direct modulation: Modulation accomplished without the use of a pivot chord or pitch.

disjunct motion: Melodic motion by skip or leap.

displacement: (1) The rhythmic offsetting of a pitch so that it is "held over" like a suspension from one sonority to the next, or "arrives early" before the rest of a harmony. (2) The offsetting of a triadic pitch in a harmony by another pitch, as in a sus chord.

dissonant: A relative term based on acoustic properties of sound and on the norms of compositional practice. A dissonant harmonic interval—second, fourth (in common-practice harmony, as in a 4–3 suspension), tritone, or seventh—is considered unpleasant or jarring to hear.

dodecaphonic: See *twelve-tone*.

dominant: (1) Scale-degree $\hat{5}$. (2) The triad built on $\hat{5}$.

dominant area: One of the harmonic areas in a basic phrase. In a conclusive phrase, the dominant area precedes the final tonic close.

dominant seventh chord: A seventh chord consisting of a major triad and a minor seventh. Occurs diatonically on $\hat{5}$.

dominant substitute: The harmony vii°, vii°⁷, or vii°⁷ (built on the leading tone), which may function as a substitute for the dominant. Because they lack the harmonically strong scale-degree $\hat{5}$, dominant substitutes are weaker in dominant function than V⁽⁷⁾.

Dorian mode: An ordered collection with the pattern of whole and half steps corresponding to the white-key diatonic collection starting and ending on D. Equivalent to a natural minor scale with scale-degree $\hat{6}$ raised by a half step.

dot: Rhythmic notation that adds to a note half again its own value (e.g., a dotted half equals a half note plus a quarter note).

double exposition: A feature of sonata form in some Classical-era concertos, where material in the exposition is heard twice: once played by the orchestra without modulation to the secondary key, and then by the soloist following the standard tonal scheme (and with the orchestra playing an accompanimental role).

double flat: An accidental (♭♭) that lowers a pitch two half steps (or one whole step) below its letter name.

double neighbor: The combination of successive upper and lower neighbors (in either order) around the same pitch.

double passing tones: Passing tones that occur simultaneously in two or more voices, usually creating parallel thirds or sixths.

double sharp: An accidental (✕) that raises a pitch two half steps (or one whole step) above its letter name.

doubling: In four-part writing, a triad pitch represented in two different voices.

downbeat: Beat 1 of a metrical pattern.

duple meter: Meter in which beats group into units of two (e.g., ⁴⁄₄, ²⁄₄, or ⁶⁄₈).

duplet: In compound meters, a division of the beat into two equal parts (borrowed from simple meters) instead of the expected three parts.

dyad: A collection of two distinct pitches or pitch classes.

dynamics: The degree of loudness or softness in playing. Common terms (from soft to loud) are *pianissimo, piano, mezzo piano, mezzo forte, forte,* and *fortissimo.*

E♭ instrument: An instrument whose sounding pitch is a major sixth lower (or minor third higher) than the notated pitch. The most common E♭ instru-

ments are the alto and baritone saxophone and E♭ clarinet.

eighth note: A stemmed black note head with one flag. In duple beat divisions, two eighth notes divide a quarter-note beat; in triple beat divisions, three eighth notes divide a dotted-quarter-note beat.

element: Most commonly, each single pitch class in a set, segment, or collection. The elements of a set or segment may also be dynamics, durations, articulations, or other musical features.

elision: The simultaneous ending of one phrase and beginning of another, articulated by the same pitches.

enharmonic: Different letter names for the same pitch or pitch class (e.g., E♭ and D♯).

enharmonic equivalence: The idea that two or more possible names for a single pitch (e.g., C♯, D♭, B✕) are musically and functionally the same.

enharmonic modulation: A type of modulation in which a chord resolves according to the function of its enharmonic equivalent to establish a new key. Chords that can be spelled (and therefore resolved) enharmonically include fully diminished sevenths, dominant sevenths, and German augmented sixths.

episode: (1) A contrasting section in a rondo; generally less tonally stable than the rondo's refrain. (2) A modulating passage in a fugue.

exposition: In a sonata form, the first large section (often repeated), where the themes and motives for the entire movement are "exposed" for the first time. The typical Classical-era exposition features two primary key areas with a modulatory transition between them.

extension: (1) The lengthening of a motive, melody, or phrase. (2) A pitch added to a triad or seventh chord (e.g., an added sixth, ninth, or eleventh).

falling-fifth chain: Root motion by a series of descending fifths (or ascending fourths), creating a segment (or the entirety) of the chain I–IV–vii°–iii–vi–ii–V–I in major, or i–iv–VII (or vii°)–III–VI–ii°–V–i in minor.

falling-third chain: Root motion by a series of descending thirds, creating a segment (or the entirety) of the chain I–vi–IV–ii–vii°–V–iii–I in major, or i–VI–iv–ii°–vii° (or VII)–V–III–i in minor.

Fibonacci series: An infinite series in which each new member is the sum of the previous two (e.g., 1, 1, 2, 3, 5, 8, 13, etc.). Associated with compositions by Bartók and others, and sometimes used in conjunction with time points.

fifth: (1) The distance spanned by five consecutive letter names. (2) The pitch in a triad that is five scale steps above the root.

fifth species: Counterpoint that combines the patterns of each of the other species. Sometimes known as "free composition."

figuration prelude: A prelude featuring a rhythm based on a consistent arpeggiation scheme. In a sense, the prelude could be notated as a series of chords, with each harmony unfolding according to the arpeggiation pattern.

figured bass: The combination of a bass line and Arabic numbers (figures), indicating chords without notating them fully; the numbers represent some of the intervals to be played above the bass line. Typically found in continuo parts.

first inversion: A triad or seventh chord voiced so that the chordal third is in the bass.

first species: Counterpoint written so that each note in one voice is paired with a single note in the other voice, using only consonant intervals. Also called 1:1 counterpoint.

first theme (group): The tonic-key melody (or melodies) with which a sonata form begins.

five-part rondo: A rondo with the form **A B A C A** or **A B A B′ A**, plus optional coda.

flat: An accidental (♭) that lowers a pitch by one half step.

focal pitch: A pitch or pitch class that is emphasized in a piece through repetition or other means, but does not establish a hierarchy with other pitches in the piece's collection.

Forte number: A set-class-labeling system developed by Allen Forte, in which set classes are ordered by size (or cardinality) and then by ic vector. To each set class, Forte gave a hyphenated number (e.g., 5-35). The number before the hyphen represents the *cardinality* of the pcset, and the number after it represents the pcset's ordinal position on the list; thus, 5-35 is a pcset of five elements that appears thirty-fifth on the list. Each pcset belongs to one of the set classes, and can be identified by its Forte number. (See Appendix 3 in vol. 2.)

Fortspinnung: A feature of Baroque-era works in which a melody is "spun out" in uninterrupted fashion. Continuous motion, uneven phrase lengths, melodic or harmonic sequences, changes of key, and elided phrases are all characteristics of *Fortspinnung* passages.

fourth species: A type of second-species counterpoint in which one voice is rhythmically displaced by ties across the bar. Characterized by its use of suspensions.

fragmentation: The isolation and/or development of a small but recognizable part of a motive.

French augmented-sixth chord (Fr⁶ or Fr$^4_3$): An augmented-sixth chord with $\hat{1}$ and $\hat{2}$ in the upper voices. The distinctive sound of this chord is created by two dissonances above the bass: the augmented sixth and the augmented fourth.

fugue: A composition or part of a composition that features a number of voices (usually three or four) entering one after another in imitation, after which each continues independently but in accordance with the rules of counterpoint.

full score: A score showing each instrumental part in the piece on a separate staff (or staves).

fully diminished seventh chord: A seventh chord consisting of a diminished triad and a diminished seventh. Because its thirds are all minor, it has no audible root; it often appears in enharmonic spellings that indicate different chord members as the root. May be used as a means to modulate to distantly related keys.

fundamental bass: An analytical bass line consisting of the *roots* of a chord progression, as opposed to the sounding bass line.

generic interval: The distance between two pitches as measured by the number of steps between their letter names (e.g., C up to E is a third, D up to C is a seventh).

German augmented-sixth chord (Gr⁶ or Gr$^6_5$): An augmented-sixth chord with $\hat{1}$ and (♭)$\hat{3}$ in the upper voices. This chord, characterized by its perfect fifth above the bass, is an enharmonic respelling of a major-minor seventh chord.

grand staff: Two staves, one in the treble clef and one in the bass clef, connected by a curly brace; typically found in piano music.

graphic notation: The nonstandard symbols used to indicate pitch, duration, articulation, etc., in some nontonal scores.

ground bass: The repeated bass line in a set of continuous variations. It remains constant while the upper voices are varied.

half cadence: An inconclusive cadence on the dominant.

half-diminished seventh chord: A seventh chord consisting of a diminished triad and a minor seventh.

half note: A stemmed white note head; its duration is equivalent to two quarter notes.

half step: The musical space between a pitch and its next-closest pitch on the keyboard.

harmonic ambiguity: Characteristic of highly chromatic passages in late Romantic music. The musical coherence comes not through "strength of progression" (strong root-movement-based chord progressions) but rather through "strength of line": smooth linear connections between chords.

harmonic interval: The span between two notes played simultaneously.

harmonic minor: The natural minor scale with raised scale-degree $\hat{7}$.

harmonic rhythm: The rate at which harmonies change in a piece (e.g., one chord per measure or one chord per beat).

harmonic sequence: A succession of harmonies based on a root-progression chain and with repeated intervallic patterning in an upper voice.

harmony: (1) Another name for a chord. (2) A progression of chords, usually implying common-practice principles of voice-leading.

hemiola: A special type of syncopation in compound meters, in which the normal three-part division of the beat is temporarily regrouped (over two beats) into twos. Also possible in simple-triple meters, using ties across the bar lines.

heptad: A collection of seven distinct pitches or pitch classes.

hexachord: A collection of six distinct pitches or pitch classes.

hexachordal combinatoriality: A compositional technique in which two forms of the same row are paired so that the rows' initial hexachords, when combined, complete an aggregate. Similarly, the rows' second hexachords, when combined, complete an aggregate. There are four kinds of hexachordal combinatoriality, based on the transformational relationships between the row forms: P, I, R, and RI.

hypermeter: A high-level metric grouping that interprets groups of measures as though they were groups of beats within a single measure. Hypermetric analyses may label entire bars of music as metrically strong or weak.

I-combinatoriality: Hexachordal combinatoriality achieved by pairing a row and its appropriate inversion form(s) to create aggregates.

imitation: The contrapuntal "echoing" of a voice in another part.

imperfect authentic cadence: An authentic cadence weakened by (1) placing the I or V harmony in inversion, or (2) ending the soprano on a scale degree other than $\hat{1}$.

imperfect consonance: The intervals of a third and sixth.

incomplete neighbor: A neighbor tone minus either (1) the initial motion from the main pitch to the neighbor, or (2) the returning motion of the neighbor to the main pitch.

inconclusive cadence: A cadence that makes a phrase sound incomplete, as though the music needs to continue further. Generally, either the soprano or the bass ends on a scale degree other than $\hat{1}$.

indeterminate: Some musical element or event in a score that is left to chance (either in performance or during composition).

index number: The value that measures the "distance" between two inversionally related pcsets. If pcsets A and B are inversionally related by the

index number n, then A = $T_n I$ B, and also B = $T_n I$ A. When paired correctly, every pc in one set added to the corresponding pc in the other set will sum uniformly to the index number.

insertion: See *internal expansion*.

integer notation: The system of labeling pcs by number instead of letter name: C = 0, C♯ or D♭ = 1, D = 2, D♯ or E♭ = 3, and so on. We substitute the letters t for 10 (B♭ or A♯) and e for 11 (B).

integral serialism: The extension of serial procedures to musical elements other than pitch. Also called *total serialism*.

internal expansion: The lengthening of a phrase between its beginning and end. Results from immediate repetitions of material, an elongation of one or more harmonies, or the addition of new material within the phrase.

interval: The musical space between two pitches or pitch classes.

interval class (ic): All pitch intervals that can be made from one pair of pitch classes (or transpositions of these pitch classes by the same distance) belong to a single interval class (e.g., M3, m6, or M10). Also called "unordered pitch-class interval."

interval-class vector (ic vector): Six numbers within square brackets, without commas, that describe the interval-class content of a given pcset. For example, the ic vector for the trichord {0 4 6}, [010101], shows that pcs in this trichord can be paired to make one whole step, one major third, and one tritone—no other intervals.

invariance: The duplication of pitch-class groupings in two serial rows or two pcsets; also, anything unchanged after inversion or some other transformation.

inverse: Given a pc or pc interval, the inverse is the corresponding pc or pc interval such that the two sum to 0 (mod12). For example, the inverse of pc 5 is pc 7.

inversion (chordal): A voicing in which a chord member other than the root is the lowest-sounding pitch.

inversion (motivic): A melodic or motivic transformation in which successive generic intervals reverse direction (e.g., an ascending third becomes a descending third).

inversion (pitch): A melodic or motivic transformation in which successive ordered pitch intervals reverse direction (e.g., a +2 becomes a –2).

inversion (pitch class): A transformation in which each pc in a pcset is replaced by its inverse (e.g., the inversion of {0 1 6 7} is {0 e 6 5}). To find the transposed inversion of a pcset, always invert first, then transpose.

inversion (row): The form of a twelve-tone row in which each pc is replaced by its inverse. Abbreviated I_n, where n is the pc integer of the row's first element.

inversionally related intervals (tonal): Two intervals that, when combined, span an octave (e.g., E3-G♯3, a major third, plus G♯3-E4, a minor sixth). When inverted, major intervals become minor (and vice versa), diminished become augmented (and vice versa), and perfect stay perfect. The generic interval numbers of inversionally related intervals sum to 9 (third and sixth, second and seventh, etc.).

Ionian mode: An ordered collection with the pattern of whole and half steps corresponding to the diatonic white-note collection starting and ending on C; the same collection as the major scale.

isorhythm: A repeating series of durations (that may be associated with repeating pitch materials); used in various style periods throughout history, but most prominently in the medieval and twentieth-century periods.

Italian augmented-sixth chord (It^6): An augmented-sixth chord with (doubled) $\hat{1}$ in the upper voices.

key: (1) The key of a tonal piece takes its name from the first scale degree of the major or minor tonality in which that piece is written; this pitch class is the primary scale degree around which all other pitches in the piece relate hierarchically. (2) A lever on an instrument that can be depressed with a finger (like a piano key).

key signature: Located at the beginning of each line of a musical score after the clef, a key signature shows which pitches are to be sharped or flatted consistently throughout the piece or movement. Helps determine the key of the piece.

lead-in: A musical passage that connects the end of one melodic phrase with the beginning of the next.

leading tone: Scale-degree $\hat{7}$ of the major scale and harmonic or ascending-melodic minor scale; a half step below the tonic.

leading-tone chord: Harmonies built on the leading tone: vii°, vii^{ø7}, or vii$^{°7}$.

leap: A melodic interval larger than a fourth (larger than a chordal skip).

ledger line: Extra lines drawn through the stems and/or note heads to designate a pitch when the notation extends above or below a staff.

Lied: German art song of the Romantic era (plural is "Lieder").

linear chord: A "chord" resulting from voice-leading motions. See *voice-leading chord.*

linear-intervallic pattern (LIP): The intervallic framework between outer voices. LIPs underlie all sequences, although sometimes they are hidden behind complicated surface elaborations.

link: Same as *lead-in.*

literal complement: The pcset that, when combined with a given pcset, produces the complete aggregate.

Locrian mode: An ordered collection with the pattern of whole and half steps corresponding to the diatonic white-note collection starting and ending on B. Sounds like a natural minor scale with scale-degrees $\hat{2}$ and $\hat{5}$ lowered by one half step.

Lydian mode: An ordered collection with the pattern of whole and half steps corresponding to the diatonic white-note collection starting and ending on F. Equivalent to a major scale with scale-degree $\hat{4}$ raised by one half step.

major interval: The quality of the intervals second, third, sixth, and seventh from scale-degree $\hat{1}$ in the major scale.

major-minor seventh chord: A seventh chord consisting of a major triad and a minor seventh (abbreviated Mm7). Another name for *dominant seventh chord.*

major pentatonic: A five-note subset of the diatonic collection that features scale-degrees $\hat{1}$, $\hat{2}$, $\hat{3}$, $\hat{5}$, and $\hat{6}$ (*do, re, mi, sol, la*).

major scale: An ordered collection of pitches arranged according to the following pattern of whole and half steps: W-W-H-W-W-W-H.

major seventh chord: A seventh chord consisting of a major triad and a major seventh.

major triad: A triad with a major third between the root and third and a minor third between the third and fifth. The interval between the root and fifth is a perfect fifth. Corresponds to scale-degrees $\hat{1}$, $\hat{3}$, and $\hat{5}$, of a major scale.

measure: A unit of grouped beats; generally, a measure begins and ends with notated bar lines.

mediant: (1) Scale-degree $\hat{3}$. (2) The triad built on $\hat{3}$.

medieval era: The period in Western music history dating roughly from 800 to 1430. Some medieval composers are Hildegard of Bingen, Pérotin, and Guillaume de Machaut. Genres associated with this era are Gregorian chants, motets, chansons, and organum.

melisma: A vocal passage that sets one syllable of text to many notes.

melodic interval: The span between two notes played one after another.

melodic minor: The natural minor scale that includes the raised $\hat{6}$ and $\hat{7}$ as it ascends, but reverts to the natural minor form of $\hat{6}$ and $\hat{7}$ as it descends.

melodic sequence: A motive repeated several times in transpositions (often up or down by step).

melody: A sequence of pitches with a particular rhythm and contour; a tune.

meter: The grouping and divisions of beats in regular, recurring patterns.

meter signature: Located at the beginning of the first line of a musical score, after the clef and key signature, the meter signature indicates the beat unit and grouping of beats in the piece or movement; also called a "time signature."

metric modulation: A means of smoothing what would otherwise be abrupt changes of tempo by introducing subdivisions or group of beats in the first tempo that match durations in the new tempo. The new tempo is recognized in retrospect, much like a modulation by pivot chord.

metric reinterpretation: A disruption in the established regular hypermetric pattern at the cadence. This can occur when a weak measure simultaneously functions as a strong measure in the case of a phrase elision.

metrical accent: The pattern of strong and weak beats based on the "weight" of the downbeat and the "lift" of the upbeat.

Middle Ages: Same as *medieval era*.

middle C: Designated C4 by Acoustical Society of America standards, the C located at the center of the piano keyboard.

minor interval: The quality of the intervals third, sixth, and seventh from scale-degree $\hat{1}$ in the minor scale. A minor second (diatonic half step) is formed between $\hat{7}$ and $\hat{1}$ in a major, harmonic minor, or ascending melodic minor scale.

minor pentatonic: A five-note subset of the diatonic collection that features the minor-key scale-degrees $\hat{1}$, $\hat{3}$, $\hat{4}$, $\hat{5}$, and $\hat{7}$ (*do, me, fa, sol, te*).

minor scale: There are three kinds: The natural minor scale is an ordered collection of pitches arranged according to the pattern of whole and half steps W-H-W-W-H-W-W; it shares the same key signature of its relative major. The harmonic minor scale raises scale-degree $\hat{7}$. The melodic minor raises $\hat{6}$ and $\hat{7}$ ascending, but takes the natural minor form descending.

minor seventh chord: A seventh chord consisting of a minor triad and a minor seventh.

minor triad: A triad with a minor third between the root and third and a major third between the third and fifth. The interval between the root and fifth is a perfect fifth. Corresponds to scale-degrees $\hat{1}$, $\hat{3}$, and $\hat{5}$ of a minor scale.

minuet and trio: The most common type of composite ternary form, generally written in triple meter. Typically the third (dance-like) movement of a Classical-era sonata, string quartet, or symphony.

Mixolydian mode: An ordered collection with the pattern of whole and half steps corresponding to the diatonic white-note collection starting and ending on G. Equivalent to a major scale with scale-degree $\hat{7}$ lowered by one half step.

mixture (or **modal mixture**): (1) Harmonic technique of shifting temporarily from a major key to the parallel minor (or vice versa) in a musical passage. (2) A technique of "mixing" the parallel major and minor modes, used most often in major keys, where the modal scale-degrees $\flat\hat{3}$, $\flat\hat{6}$, and $\flat\hat{7}$ are borrowed from the parallel natural minor.

mixture chord: A chord resulting from the mixing of major and minor parallel keys; also known as a *borrowed chord*.

mobile form: The form of compositions with segments, sections, or movements that may be played in varying orders. While the contents of segments may remain consistent from one performance to another, the overall form of the piece will not.

mod12 arithmetic: An arithmetic that keeps integers in the range 0 to 11. To convert a number greater than 11, divide by 12 and take the remainder. For example, $14 \div 12 = 1$, remainder 2; therefore, 14 mod12 = 2. Used to label pcs in integer notation and perform operations such as transposition or inversion.

modal scale degrees: The scale degrees that differ between major and natural minor scales: $\hat{3}$, $\hat{6}$, and $\hat{7}$.

mode: (1) Rotations of the major (or natural minor) scale (e.g., the Dorian mode is a rotation of the C-Major scale beginning and ending on D). (2) Term used to distinguish between major and minor keys (e.g., a piece in "the minor mode").

mode of limited transposition: Composer Olivier Messiaen's term for pc collections that can be transposed by only a few intervals; other transpositions replicate the original collection. The whole-tone and octatonic collections are examples.

modified strophic: A variation of strophic form. Rather than repeating the melody exactly, the music may be slightly altered from verse to verse.

modulation: A change of key, usually confirmed by a (perfect) authentic cadence.

moment form: The concept that sections of a piece do not have to connect in some logical way or in a predetermined order, but can change abruptly from one style of music to another.

motet: A polyphonic choral work.

motive: The smallest recognizable musical idea. Motives may be characterized by their pitches, contour, and/or rhythm, but rarely contain a cadence. To qualify as a motive, an idea generally has to be repeated (exactly or varied).

musical form: The overall organization of a composition into sections, defined by harmonic structure—change of key, mode, pcset, collection, or row form—as well as by changes in (or a return to) a theme, texture, instrumentation, rhythm, or other feature.

natural minor: The major scale with lowered $\hat{3}$, $\hat{6}$, and $\hat{7}$, arranged according to the pattern of whole and half steps W-H-W-W-H-W-W. Natural minor shares the same key signature as the relative major key.

natural sign: An accidental (♮) that cancels a sharp or flat.

Neapolitan: The major triad built on ♭II; typically occurs in first inversion (Neapolitan sixth), with $\hat{4}$ in the bass and ♭$\hat{2}$ and (♭)$\hat{6}$ in the upper voices. May also appear in root position, with ♭$\hat{2}$ in the bass.

neighbor tone: An embellishment that decorates a melody pitch by moving to a pitch a step above or below it, then returning to the original pitch. Neighbor tones are approached and left by step, in opposite directions.

neighboring $\frac{4}{3}$: A $\frac{4}{3}$ chord arising from neighbor tones in all three of the upper parts (e.g., in the tonic expansion I–ii$\frac{4}{3}$–I).

neighboring $\frac{6}{4}$: A $\frac{6}{4}$ chord that embellishes and prolongs whichever chord it neighbors—whether a tonic, dominant, or predominant chord—and is usually metrically unaccented. It shares its bass note with the harmony it embellishes, while two upper voices move in stepwise upper-neighbor motion above that bass. Sometimes called a "pedal $\frac{6}{4}$."

ninth chord: A triad or seventh chord with a ninth added above the bass.

nonad: A collection of nine distinct pitches or pitch classes.

nonmetric: Another word for *ametric*; having no meter.

nonteleological form: Form in which the music lacks a sense of a goal or direction. Moment form and mobile form are examples.

nontonal: Music that freely employs all twelve pitch classes. The pervasive chromaticism and absence of whole- and half-step scale patterns make a true "tonic" pitch class impossible to discern in nontonal music.

normal order: The order of consecutive pcs in a pcset that (1) spans the smallest interval and (2) places the smallest intervals toward the left.

notated meter: The way in which rhythms are notated in a score. In common-practice music, notated meter and perceived meter are usually the same. In music of the twentieth century and later, they may not be.

note-to-note: Another name for *first species*, or *1:1*, counterpoint.

oblique motion: Contrapuntal, or voice-leading, motion in which one part repeats the same pitch while the other moves by leap, skip, or step.

octad: A collection of eight distinct pitches or pitch classes.

octatonic scale: A scale composed of eight (*octa-*) distinct pcs in alternating whole and half steps.

octave: The distance of eight musical steps.

octave equivalence: The concept that two pitches an octave apart are functionally equivalent.

offbeat: A weak beat or weak portion of a beat.

omnibus: A special chromaticized voice exchange, usually prolonging the dominant. The exchanged pitches form the interval of a tritone, which enables the voice exchange to continue chromatically until the exchanged voices arrive where they began (but up or down an octave). All the resulting chromatic simultaneities are nonfunctional (*voice-leading chords*).

open: A harmonic feature of a phrase or section of a piece in which the end is inconclusive, or in a different key from the beginning.

open score: A score with a staff for every part, unlike a piano score; for example, an SATB choral score on four staves.

orchestration: Music set or composed for a large ensemble.

ostinato: A repeated rhythmic and/or pitch pattern.

overlap: (1) A means of phrase connection in which one phrase ends simultaneously with the beginning of the next. May involve more than one musical layer: while one or more voice parts finish the first phrase, one or more other voice parts simultaneously begin the next. (2) A voice-leading error in which one voice overlaps into the register of an adjacent voice on an adjacent beat.

P-combinatoriality: Hexachordal combinatoriality achieved by pairing a row and its appropriate transposed form(s) to make aggregates.

palindrome: A segment (of pitches, pcs, intervals, and/or rhythms) that reads the same backward and forward.

parallel keys: Keys in different modes that share the same letter name and tonic, such as F Major and F minor.

parallel major: The major key that shares the same tonic as a given minor key. The parallel major raises $\hat{3}$, $\hat{6}$, and $\hat{7}$ of the minor key.

parallel minor: The minor key that shares the same tonic as a given major key. The parallel minor lowers $\hat{3}$, $\hat{6}$, and $\hat{7}$ of the major key.

parallel motion: Contrapuntal, or voice-leading, motion in which both parts move in the same direction by the same generic interval.

parallel period: A period in which the two phrases share the same beginning melodic material.

parody: The compositional borrowing or reshaping of another composer's materials to emphasize particular aspects.

passacaglia: Continuous variations with a repeated bass line. The bass melody (or ground bass) remains constant, while the upper voices are varied.

passing chord: A linear "chord" arising from passing motion.

passing $\frac{4}{2}$: A $\frac{4}{2}$ chord created by passing motion in the bass (e.g., in the progression I–I$\frac{4}{2}$–IV^6).

passing $\frac{6}{4}$: A voice-leading $\frac{6}{4}$ chord, usually connecting root-position and first-inversion chords of the same harmony. We call it "passing" because the $\frac{6}{4}$ harmonizes a bass-line passing tone.

passing tone: A melodic embellishment that fills in the space between chord members by stepwise motion. It is approached by step and left by step in the same direction.

pcset: Abbreviation of "pitch-class set."

pedal point: A note held for several measures while harmonies change above it. Chords above a pedal point do not participate in the harmonic framework.

pentachord: A collection of five distinct pitches or pitch classes.

pentatonic scale: A scale with five pcs. In Western music, the pentatonic scale is a subset of the diatonic collection. The two most common are the minor pentatonic (*do, me, fa, sol, te*) and the major pentatonic (*do, re, mi, sol, la*).

perfect authentic cadence: A strong conclusive cadence in which a root-position V$^{(7)}$ progresses to a root-position I, and the soprano moves from scale-degree $\hat{2}$ or $\hat{7}$ to $\hat{1}$.

perfect consonance: The intervals of a unison, fourth, fifth, and octave. The harmonic interval of a fourth is treated as a dissonance in common-practice style.

period: A musical unit consisting (usually) of two phrases. Generally, the first phrase ends with a weak cadence (typically a half cadence), answered by a more conclusive cadence (usually a PAC) at the end of the second phrase.

phasing: The compositional technique of moving musical patterns in and out of alignment, creating additional sounds and patterns that are not present in the original materials.

phrase: A basic unit of musical thought, similar to a sentence in language, with a beginning, a middle, and an end. In tonal music, a phrase must end with a cadence; in nontonal music, other musical features provide closure.

phrase group: Three or more phrases with tonal and/or thematic design elements that group them together as a unit.

phrase modulation: Modulation accomplished directly, without the use of a pivot chord (e.g., the new phrase simply begins in the new key). Another name for *direct modulation*.

phrase rhythm: The interaction of hypermeter and phrase structure.

phrase structure: The melodic and harmonic characteristics of a phrase or group of phrases, identified by cadence type, harmonic motion, number of measures, and melodic or motivic repetition or contrast.

Phrygian cadence: The half cadence iv^6–V in minor keys, so called because of the half-step descent in the bass.

Phrygian mode: An ordered collection with the pattern of whole and half steps corresponding to the diatonic white-note collection starting and ending on E. Equivalent to a natural minor scale with scale-degree $\hat{2}$ lowered by a half step.

Phrygian II: Another name for the *Neapolitan*.

Picardy third: In a minor key, the raised third of a tonic chord (making the harmony major), typically at an authentic cadence at the end of a piece.

pitch: A tone sounding in a particular octave.

pitch class (pc): Notes an octave (or several octaves) apart that share the same name (e.g., F3, F5, and F2 all belong to pc F). Pitch-class names assume octave and enharmonic equivalence.

pitch-class interval (pci): The interval spanned by two pcs. (1) Ordered pitch-class intervals measure the distance from pc a to b by subtracting (b – a) mod12; the distance can range from 0 to 11. (2) Unordered pitch-class intervals measure the shortest distance between two pcs, either from the first to the second or vice versa; the distance ranges from 0 to 6. "Unordered pitch-class interval" is another name for *interval class*.

pitch interval: The musical space between two pitches, described either with tonal labels (e.g., minor second, augmented sixth, perfect fifth) or by the number of half steps from one pitch to the other. Unordered pitch intervals measure distance; ordered pitch intervals measure distance and direction (shown by preceding the interval number with a + or –).

pitch symmetry: The spacing of pitches at equal distances above and below a central pitch.

pitch-time graph: A graph that plots pitch (the vertical axis) against time (the horizontal axis).

pivot chord: In a common-chord modulation, a harmony that functions diatonically in both the old key and the new key.

pivot-chord modulation: See *common-chord modulation*.

pivot-dyad modulation: See *common-dyad modulation*.

pivot-tone modulation: See *common-tone modulation*.

plagal cadence: The cadence IV–I (iv–i in minor), sometimes called the "Amen cadence." Because the IV–I motion can be viewed as a tonic expansion, and because the plagal cadence often follows an authentic cadence, some use the term "plagal resolution" or "plagal expansion of tonic."

polymeter: Music with two or more different simultaneous metric streams.

polymodality: Music with several modes sounding in different layers of music simultaneously.

polytonality: Music with several keys sounding in different layers of music simultaneously.

postmodernism: A style in which materials originating from different times and styles are combined. The term is borrowed from literary and art criticism.

posttonal music: Music that is not restricted to compositional principles of the common-practice era.

predominant: (1) The triad or seventh chord built on scale-degrees $\hat{2}$, $\hat{4}$, or $\hat{6}$. (2) A category of harmonic function that includes chords that precede the dominant, typically ii and IV (ii° and iv in minor keys), but also the Neapolitan sixth and augmented-sixth chords.

predominant area: A harmonic area in the basic phrase model that precedes the dominant area (T–PD–D–T). Predominant harmonies include ii and IV (ii° and iv in minor keys) plus their inversions and seventh chords. Chromatic predominant harmonies include the Neapolitan sixth and augmented-sixth chords.

primary theme (group): Another name for *first theme (group)*, or first tonal area, in a sonata-form movement.

prime (row): The row in a twelve-tone composition that the analyst considers a starting point, usually the first appearance of the row; labeled P_n, where n is the first pc of the row.

prime form: The representative pcset for a set class, beginning with 0 and enclosed in square brackets. To find the prime form of a set, determine the set's best normal order (which may include finding the normal order for its inversion), and transpose to begin with 0.

prolong: To expand the function of a harmony by means of contrapuntal motion and contrapuntal or linear chords.

pset: Abbreviation of "pitch set."

quadruple meter: Meter in which beats group into units of four (e.g., $\frac{4}{4}$ or $\frac{12}{8}$).

quadruplet: In compound time, a subdivision group borrowed from simple time.

quarter note: A stemmed black note head, equivalent in duration to two eighth notes.

quaternary song form: A song form consisting of four (usually eight-bar) phrases. The first two phrases (chorus 1) begin the same (they may be identical or may differ at the cadence). They are followed by a contrasting section (bridge) and then a return to the opening material (chorus 2), making the overall form **a a b a**. Also known as "thirty-two-bar song form."

quodlibet: A medley, or amalgamated borrowing, of songs; may feature multiple texts, sometimes in different languages.

R-combinatoriality: Hexachordal combinatoriality achieved by pairing a row and its appropriate retrograde form(s) to make aggregates.

raised submediant: Raised scale-degree $\hat{6}$ in melodic minor.

realization: (1) A full musical texture created from a figured (or unfigured) bass. (2) In pieces composed with pcsets or rows, pitch classes in a specific register and rhythm. (3) Performance of a work from a text or graphic score.

rearticulated suspension: A suspension in which the suspended voice sounds again (instead of being held over) at the moment of dissonance.

recapitulation: The final section of a sonata form (or penultimate section, if the movement ends with a coda), in which the music from exposition is heard again, this time with the theme groups usually in the tonic key.

reduction: (1) A score transcribed so that it can be performed by fewer instrumental forces (usually by piano). (2) The underlying harmonic framework and linear counterpoint of a passage of music, revealed after embellishing tones or harmonies have been eliminated.

refrain: (1) The section of a song that recurs with the same music and text. (2) In popular-music verse-refrain form, the second portion of the song; generally in **a a b a**, or quaternary, song form. (3) In rondo form (usually **A B A C A** or **A B A C A B (D) A**), the refrain is the **A** section, which returns with opening thematic material in the tonic key. Another word for *ritornello*.

register: The particular octave in which a pitch sounds.

registral invariance: A compositional technique in which certain pcs are realized as pitches only in one specific register. Also known as "frozen register" and "pitch fixation."

relative keys: Major and minor keys that share the same key signature (e.g., C Major and A minor).

relative major: The major key that shares the same key signature as a given minor key. The relative major is made from the same pitch-class collection as its relative minor, but begins on scale-degree $\hat{3}$ of the minor key.

relative minor: The minor key that shares the same key signature as a given major key. The relative minor is made from the same pitch-class collection as its relative major, but begins on scale-degree $\hat{6}$ of the major key.

Renaissance era: The period in Western music history dating roughly from 1430 until 1600. Some Renaissance composers are Josquin des Prez, Palestrina, Guillaume Dufay, and Carlo Gesualdo. Genres most associated with the era are the mass, madrigal, masque, and instrumental dances.

resolution: The way a harmony or scale step progresses to the next harmony or pitch. The term usually refers to the manner in which a dissonant interval moves to a consonant one.

rest: A duration of silence.

retardation: A rhythmic embellishment where a consonance is held over to the next beat, creating a dissonance with the new harmony. The dissonance is resolved upward by step, creating another consonant interval.

retransition: A musical passage that harmonically prepares for the return of previously heard material. In sonata form, it appears at the end of the development section and prolongs the dominant harmony in preparation for the tonic return of the recapitulation's first theme group. In rondo form, a retransition may appear before any recurrence of the refrain (**A** section).

retrograde: The form of a twelve-tone row in which the pcs are in the reverse order of the prime. Abbreviated R_n, where n refers to the *last* pc of the row, i.e., the first pc of the original, prime row.

retrograde inversion: The form of a twelve-tone row in which the pcs are in the reverse order of the inversion. Abbreviated RI_n, where n refers to the *last* pc of the row, i.e., the first pc of the inverted row.

retrogression: "Backward" progressions that reverse typical common-practice harmonic norms; common in other musical idioms (e.g., V–IV in blues and rock music).

rhyme scheme: The pattern of rhyming in a poetic verse or stanza, generally designated with lowercase alphabet letters. Repeated letters indicate lines that end with rhyming words.

rhythm: The patterns made by the durations of pitch and silence (notes and rests) in a piece.

rhythmic acceleration: The gradual move from long note values to shorter note values in a passage of music; also called a "rhythmic *crescendo*."

rhythmic motive: A motive that maintains its rhythm but changes its contour and interval structure.

RI-combinatoriality: Hexachordal combinatoriality achieved by pairing a row and its appropriate retrograde-inversional form(s) to create aggregates.

ritornello: An instrumental section of a piece that returns. Another word for *refrain*.

Romantic era: The period in Western music history dating roughly from 1830 until 1910. Some Romantic composers are Robert Schumann, Frédéric Chopin, Giuseppe Verdi, and Richard Wagner. Genres most associated with this era are the art song, program symphony, character piece, tone poem, and grand opera.

rondo: A musical form characterized by a repeated section (refrain, or ritornello) alternating with sections that contrast in key, mode, texture, harmonic complexity, thematic content, and/or style (usually **A B A C A** or **A B A C A B** (**D**) **A**). The contrasting sections are called episodes.

root: The lowest pitch of a triad or seventh chord when the chord is spelled in thirds.

root position: A chord voiced so that the root is in the bass.

rounded binary: A binary form in which melodic or motivic features in the initial phrase return at the end of the piece, "rounding out" the formal plan.

row: A specific ordering of all twelve pitch classes.

row elision: One way of connecting rows in a twelve-tone piece: the same pc or pcs are shared at the end of one row and the beginning of the next. Also called "row linkage."

row matrix: A twelve-by-twelve array that displays all possible P, I, R, and RI forms of a row.

SATB: An abbreviation for the four main voice ranges: soprano, alto, tenor, and bass. Also indicates a particular musical style or texture: chorale style.

scale: A collection of pitch classes arranged in a particular order of whole and half steps.

scale degree: A name for each pitch class of the scale, showing its relationship to the tonic pitch (for which the key is named). Scale-degree names may be numbers ($\hat{1}$, $\hat{2}$, $\hat{3}$), words (tonic, supertonic, mediant), or solfège syllables (*do, re, mi*).

scale step: Same as *scale degree*.

scherzo and trio: A composite ternary form in a fast tempo, usually in triple meter. Typically the third movement of a Romantic-era sonata, quartet, or symphony.

second inversion: A triad or seventh chord voiced so that the chordal fifth is in the bass.

second species: Counterpoint written so that one voice has two notes for every single note in the other voice. Permits consonances and passing tones, according to specific rules of voice-leading; eighteenth-century style also allows neighbor tones. Another name for *2:1* counterpoint.

second theme (group): The melody (or melodies) heard at the start of the new key area in a sonata form.

secondary dominant: A dominant-function harmony (V or vii°, with or without the chordal seventh) "applied" to a chord other than tonic (may also refer only to a secondary V chord). A secondary dominant typically includes chromatic alterations (relative to the tonic key). Also called an "applied dominant," or *applied chord*.

secondary leading-tone chord: A leading-tone chord that functions as an applied, or secondary, dominant; usually a fully diminished seventh chord.

secondary set: An agregate formed by combining segments belonging to more than one row form.

section: A large division within a composition, usually set off by a cadence (or other elements denoting closure). May be delineated by repeat signs or a double bar.

sectional: A harmonic feature of tonal forms, in which a section is tonally closed (with an authentic cadence in the tonic key); the section could stand on its own.

sectional binary: A binary form in which the first section ends with a cadence on the tonic. The section is tonally complete and could stand on its own.

sectional variation: A variation form in which each variation is clearly distinguished from the next by a strong conclusive cadence (and often by double bars). Each variation could be played as a complete stand-alone section.

segment: An ordered sequence of pitches or pcs.

sentence: A phrase design with a 1 + 1 + 2 (or 2 + 2 + 4) motivic structure.

sequence: A musical pattern that is restated successively at different pitch levels. See *harmonic sequence* and *melodic sequence*.

sequence pattern: The arrangement of intervals that underlies a sequence.

serial music: Music composed with (ordered) pitch-class segments and ordered transformations of these segments; may also feature ordered durations, dynamics, and articulations.

set: A group of unordered pitches or pitch classes. See *collection*.

set class: The collection of pcsets that contains all possible distinct transpositions of the pcset, as well as all distinct transpositions of its inversion. Pcsets in the same set class also share the same ic vector.

seven-part rondo: A rondo whose form is **A B A C A B (D) A**, plus optional coda.

seventh chord: A chord that can be arranged as a root-position triad with another third stacked on top. This third forms a seventh with the root. There are five types of seventh chords in common-practice tonal music: major seventh, minor seventh, major-minor seventh (dominant seventh), half-diminished seventh, and fully diminished seventh.

sharp: An accidental (♯) that raises a pitch a half step.

short score: A score that shows several parts combined on each staff.

similar motion: Contrapuntal, or voice-leading, motion in which both parts move in the same direction, but not by the same generic interval.

simple binary: A binary form that generally has an ||: **A** :||: **B** :|| or ||: **A** :||: **A´** :|| design.

simple duple: Any meter with two beats in a measure, with each beat divided into two (e.g., $\frac{2}{4}$).

simple meter: Meter in which the beat divides into twos and subdivides into fours. The top number of the meter signature will be 2, 3, or 4 (e.g., $\frac{4}{8}$ or $\frac{3}{2}$).

simple quadruple: Any meter with four beats in a measure, with each beat divided into two (e.g., $\frac{4}{4}$).

simple ternary: A ternary form that is relatively brief (as opposed to composite ternary), with three distinct sections, usually in the form **A B A**. The **B** section generally expresses both a contrasting key and contrasting thematic material.

simple triple: Any meter with three beats in a measure, with each beat divided into two (e.g., $\frac{3}{4}$ or $\frac{3}{8}$).

sixteenth note: A stemmed black note head with two flags. In duple beat divisions, two sixteenths divide an eighth-note beat; in triple beat divisions, three sixteenths divide a dotted-eighth-note beat.

skip: A melodic interval of a third or fourth.

slur: An arc that connects two or more different pitches. Slurs affect articulation but not duration.

solfège, fixed-*do*: A singing system in which a particular syllable is associated with a particular pitch class; e.g., *do* is always C, *re* is always D, etc., no matter what the key.

solfège, movable-*do*: A singing system in which a particular syllable is associated with a particular scale step; e.g., *do* is always $\hat{1}$, *re* is always $\hat{2}$, etc., no matter what the key.

sonata: A multimovement composition for piano or a solo-line instrument (usually with keyboard accompaniment), typically in three or four movements. The first movement is almost always in sonata form.

sonata form: A formal plan with a three-part design (exposition, development, recapitulation) and a two-part harmonic structure (the most common is ||: I–V :||: → I :|| for major keys, with motion to III instead of V in minor keys). Sonata form can be thought of as an expanded continuous rounded binary form.

sonatina: A "little sonata." The first movement of a sonatina is usually a reduced sonata form, with compact first and second themes and a very short development section or no development at all.

song cycle: A group of songs, generally performed as a unit, either set to a single poet's cycle of poetry or set to poems that have been grouped by the composer into a cycle.

soprano: The highest voice in four-part (SATB) writing.

sounding pitch: The pitch that is heard when a performer plays a note on an instrument. For transposing instruments, this differs from notated pitch. Also called *concert pitch*.

spacing: The arrangement of adjacent parts in four-part writing, in which vocal range and the intervals between voices are considered.

species: A particular type of counterpoint, used as a tool for teaching composition. The various species (types) of counterpoint differ by the embellishments permitted and the rhythmic relationship between the voices. See *first species (1:1)*, *second species (2:1)*, *third species (4:1)*, *fourth species*, and *fifth species*.

spelling: The letter names and accidentals of the pitches in a scale, chord, or other musical sonority.

split-third chord: A four-note "triad" with both a major and a minor third above the root.

staff: The five parallel lines on which we write music.

step: The melodic interval of a half or whole step.

step progression: A technique for writing compound melody, in which nonadjacent pitches are connected by an overall stepwise motion.

strain: In marches, the sections corresponding to the **A** and **B** portions of binary (or ternary) forms.

strophe: A stanza, or verse, in a song.

strophic: A song form in which more than one strophe (verse) of text is sung to the same music.

style juxtaposition: A method of composing in which elements strongly associated with one musical style are placed side-by-side with another style without a transition between the two.

stylistic allusion: A musical passage that either literally quotes another composition, or is written in imitation of a previous style, intended to be recognized by the listener as belonging to another time or piece.

subdivision: The third level of pulse in musical meter: beat → division → subdivision.

subdominant: (1) Scale-degree $\hat{4}$. (2) The triad built on $\hat{4}$.

submediant: (1) Scale degree $\hat{6}$. (2) The triad built on $\hat{6}$.

subordinate theme (group): Another name for *second theme (group)*.

subphrase: A melodic and harmonic unit smaller than a phrase. Subphrases complete only a portion of the basic phrase progression and do not conclude with a cadence.

subset: A subgroup of a given set.

substitute chord: A harmony that can stand for another. The most common are vi for I, ii for IV, and vii° for V.

subtonic: (1) Scale-degree $\hat{7}$ of the natural minor scale, so called because it is a whole step below tonic. (2) The triad built on $\hat{7}$ of natural minor.

superset: The larger set from which a subset is derived.

supertonic: (1) Scale-degree $\hat{2}$. (2) The triad built on $\hat{2}$.

sus chord: In popular music, a chord with a fourth above the bass instead of a third. The fourth does not necessarily resolve, as in a typical 4–3 suspension.

suspension: A rhythmic embellishment where a consonance is held over to the next beat, creating a dissonance with the new harmony. The dissonance is resolved downward by step, creating another consonant interval. Suspensions are designated by intervals above the bass; the most common are 7–6, 4–3, and 9–8.

suspension chain: A combined succession of suspensions, sometimes of a single type (e.g., 4–3, 4–3) or alternations of two kinds (e.g., 7–6, 4–3, 7–6 4–3); the resolution of each suspension prepares the next.

symmetrical meter: A meter with equally spaced primary beats within each measure, each beat having the same number of divisions.

symmetrical phrase: A phrase with an even number of measures.

symmetrical set: A set whose pcs can be ordered so that the intervals between adjacent elements are the same when read left to right or right to left. The pentatonic scale, whole-tone scale, octatonic scale, and chromatic collection are all symmetrical sets.

symmetry: Having the same pattern from start to middle as end to middle.

syncopation: Off-beat rhythmic accents created by dots, ties, rests, dynamic markings, or accent marks.

teleological form: Form that gives the listener a sense that the music moves toward a goal; usually associated with common-practice forms.

tempo: How fast or slow music is played. Examples of tempo markings include *adagio* (slow), *andante* (medium speed), and *allegro* (fast).

temporary tonic: The chord to which a secondary dominant or secondary leading-tone harmony is applied; also known as a "tonicized harmony."

tendency tone: A chord member or scale degree whose dissonant relation to the surrounding tones requires a particular resolution in common-practice style (i.e., chordal sevenths resolve down, and leading tones resolve up).

tenor: The second-lowest voice in four-part (SATB) writing. Usually directly above the bass.

tenor clef: A C-clef positioned on a staff so that the fourth line from the bottom indicates middle C (C4); typically read by bassoons, cellos, and tenor trombones in their higher registers.

ternary form: A composition divided into three sections. The outer sections usually consist of the same musical material, while the inner section features contrasting musical qualities (including key), creating an overall **A B A** form. In some song forms, the contrasting section may occur last (**A A B**).

tessitura: The vocal or instrumental range most used by a singer or instrumentalist.

tetrachord: (1) A collection of four distinct pitches or pitch classes. (2) A segment of four consecutive members of a scale.

text notation: A musical score with instructions written in prose or poetry, without any traditional musical notation.

textural variation: A variation written in a texture that contrasts with that of surrounding variations or the original theme. Two possibilities are (1) the simplifying variation, which features only a few voices, resulting in a thin texture; and (2) the contrapuntal variation, which features imitative entries of the voices.

theme and variations: A variation set based on a given theme, in which each variation differs in melody, rhythm, key, mode, length, texture, timbre, character, style, or motive. Theme and variation sets after the Baroque era are usually sectional variations, in which each variation could be considered a brief, stand-alone piece. See also *continuous variation*.

third inversion: A seventh chord voiced so that the chordal seventh is in the bass.

third species: Counterpoint written so that one voice has four notes for every single note in the other voice; allows consonances, passing tones, and neighboring tones, according to strict rules of voice-leading. Another name for *4:1* counterpoint.

thirty-second note: A stemmed black note head with three flags; equal in duration to two sixty-fourth notes.

thirty-two-bar song form: Another term for *quaternary song form*.

through composed: A composition organized so that each section (e.g., each verse in a song) consists of different music, with little or no previous material recurring as the work progresses.

tie: A small arc connecting the note heads of two (or more) identical pitches, adding the durations of the notes together.

timbral variation: A variation that exploits instrumentation and/or sound color different from previous variations.

time-line notation: Music written so that the passing of time is measured out in the number of seconds elapsed between markers.

time points: Locations in a score indicating a musical event; determined by a duration series, a numerical pattern, chance, or a series of proportions.

time signature: Another term for *meter signature*.

tonal music: Music based on the following organizational conventions: (1) melodies built from major and minor scales using scale-degree function, in relation to a tonic scale degree (e.g., $\hat{7}$ resolving to $\hat{1}$); (2) harmonies that relate to each other in functional progressions leading toward a tonic harmony; (3) identifiable embellishing tones (dissonant suspensions, neighbors, passing tones) that resolve (or imply a resolution).

tonal plan: The progression of keys in a composition.

tonic: (1) Scale-degree $\hat{1}$. (2) The triad built on $\hat{1}$.

tonic area: Usually the opening and closing area in a basic phrase (T–PD–D–T).

tonic closure: A conclusive ending that confirms the key of a musical passage, usually accomplished by means of an authentic cadence.

tonic expansion: An extension of tonic function effected by means of contrapuntal motion and voice-leading chords.

tonic substitute: A chord other than tonic (most often the submediant) that fulfills tonic function in the basic phrase model.

tonicization: The result when a chord becomes a temporary tonic by means of a secondary, or applied, dominant. The key of the passage does not really change, and the temporary tonic soon returns to its normal functional role in the primary key.

total serialism: The extension of serial procedures to musical elements other than pitch. Also called *integral serialism*.

transferred resolution: The movement of a tendency tone from one voice part to another prior to resolution.

transition: A musical passage that modulates from one key and establishes another, often by means of sequential treatment. In sonata form, the transition links the first and second theme groups.

transpose: (1) To notate a score for transposing instruments so that pitches will sound correctly in the concert key. (2) To rewrite a section of music at a different pitch level. (3) To add or subtract a constant to pitches or pitch classes in integer notation.

transposed score: A score that shows the pitches as notated in the performers' parts (which may be transposed for certain instruments), rather than the sounding pitches.

transposing instrument: An instrument (e.g., clarinet, saxophone, or horn) whose notated pitches are not the same as the pitches that sound when played.

transposition (row): The form of a twelve-tone row derived by transposing the prime. Abbreviated P_n, where n is the pc integer of the row's first element.

transpositional equivalence: The relationship between two sets such that each one can be transposed into the other.

treble clef: On a staff, the treble clef (also known as G-clef) denotes the line for G4, by means of the end of its curving line; typically read by flutes, clarinets, oboes, horns, sopranos, altos, and piano right hand.

triad: A chord made from two stacked thirds.

triad quality: The description of a triad according to the quality of its stacked thirds and fifth: major, minor, diminished, or augmented.

trichord: A collection of three distinct pitches or pitch classes.

triple meter: Meter in which beats group into units of three (e.g., ¾ or ⅜).

triplet: In simple meters, a division group borrowed from compound meters.

tritone: An interval made up of three whole tones or six semitones: an augmented fourth or diminished fifth. By some definitions, only an augmented fourth is a tritone, since in this spelling the interval spans three whole steps.

tritone axis: Music (in nontonal pieces) that moves from a first pitch center to a second pitch center a tritone away, and then returns; analogous to the tonic-dominant axis in tonal music.

truncate: To cut off a melody or motive before it ends.

twelve-tone: Music with a specific ordering of all twelve pitch classes, called a row. The row is musically realized by means of transformations (transposition, inversion, retrograde, or retrograde inversion) throughout a composition.

unequal fifths: Similar motion from a d5 to P5. Prohibited in strict counterpoint, but allowable in some situations in four-part writing if not placed in the outer voices.

unison: The interval size 1, or the distance from a pitch to itself; interval 0 if measured in semitones.

upbeat: Occurs when a melody starts just before the first strong beat in a meter; named for the upward lift of the conductor's hand. Another word for *anacrusis*.

verse: (1) The section of a song that returns with the same music but different text. (2) In popular song forms, the first section of verse-refrain form; the verse is usually not repeated, and it may be tonally less stable than the refrain.

verse-refrain form: A typical form of popular songs and show tunes: an introductory verse, possibly modulatory, precedes a chorus that is often in quaternary song form (**a a b a**).

vertical analysis: A first level of analysis, assigning a Roman numeral label to each chord and inversion; in contrast to contextual analysis, which interprets function within the basic phrase model.

vocal range: The range of pitches (high and low) that may be sung comfortably by singers of a particular voice type (e.g., alto or tenor).

voice crossing: In four-part writing, one voice written higher than the part above it or lower than the part below it; considered poor voice-leading in common-practice style.

voice exchange: The expansion of a functional area in which two voices exchange chord members (e.g., $\hat{1}$ moves to $\hat{3}$ in the bass, and $\hat{3}$ moves to $\hat{1}$ in the soprano). This skip is often filled in with a passing tone or passing chord.

voice-leading: The combination of melodic lines to create harmonies according to principles of common-practice harmony and counterpoint.

voice-leading chord: A "chord" created by combining embellishing tones in the expansion of a structural harmony. In analysis, we label the individual embellishments rather than the chord, or we label the chord as "voice-leading" (VL) or as a passing or neighboring chord.

whole note: A stemless white note head; equal in duration to two half notes.

whole step: The combination of two adjacent half steps.

whole-tone scale: An ordered collection of pcs arranged so that each scale step lies a whole step away from the next. A whole-tone scale consists of six elements and exists in two distinct forms: pcs {0 2 4 6 8 t} and {1 3 5 7 9 e}.

Ranges of Orchestral Instruments

INSTRUMENT	WRITTEN RANGE	SOUNDING RANGE

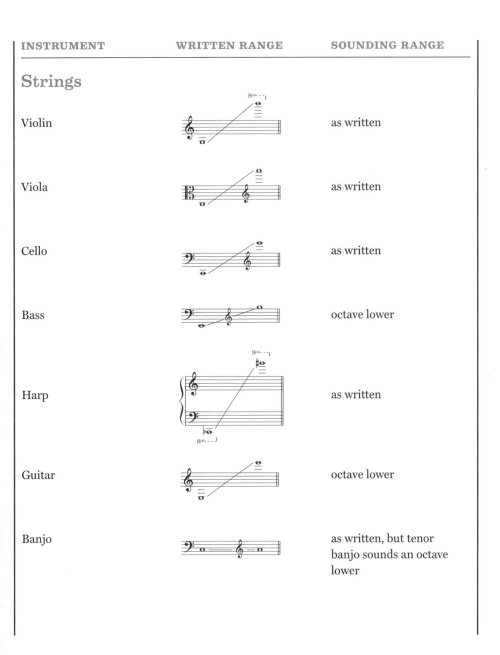

Strings

Violin		as written
Viola		as written
Cello		as written
Bass		octave lower
Harp		as written
Guitar		octave lower
Banjo		as written, but tenor banjo sounds an octave lower

SOURCE: Samuel Adler, *The Study of Orchestration*, 3rd ed. (New York: Norton, 2002)

Woodwinds

Piccolo

octave higher

Flute

as written

Oboe

as written

English horn

perfect fifth lower

All clarinets except bass

B♭: major second lower
A: minor third lower
D: major second higher
E♭: minor third higher
E♭ alto: major sixth lower

Bass clarinet

major ninth lower;
if written in bass clef,
major second lower

Bassoon

as written

Contrabassoon

octave lower

All saxophones

B♭ soprano: major second
lower
E♭ alto: major sixth lower
B♭ tenor: major ninth lower
E♭ baritone: octave plus
major sixth lower
B♭ bass: two octaves plus a
major second lower

Brass

Instrument	Written Range	Sounding Range
Horn (plus pedal notes)		perfect fifth lower
All trumpets except Eb and D bass		C: as written Bb: major second lower D: major second higher Eb: minor third higher Bb cornet: major second lower C bass: octave lower Bb bass: major ninth lower
Eb and D bass trumpets		Eb: major sixth lower D: minor seventh lower
Tenor trombone		as written
Bass trombone		as written
Alto trombone		as written
Tuba		as written
Euphonium		as written; if notated in treble clef, major ninth lower
Baritone		as written; if notated in treble clef, major ninth lower

INSTRUMENT	WRITTEN RANGE	SOUNDING RANGE

Percussion

Timpani — as written

Xylophone — octave higher

Marimba — as written

Vibraphone — as written

Glockenspiel — two octaves higher

Chimes — as written

Keyboard

Piano — as written

Celesta — octave higher

Harpsichord — as written

Organ — as written

Appendix 2 Ranges of Orchestral Instruments

Set-Class Table

NAME	PCS	IC VECTOR	NAME	PCS	IC VECTOR
3-1(12)	0,1,2	210000	9-1	0,1,2,3,4,5,6,7,8	876663
3-2	0,1,3	111000	9-2	0,1,2,3,4,5,6,7,9	777663
3-3	0,1,4	101100	9-3	0,1,2,3,4,5,6,8,9	767763
3-4	0,1,5	100110	9-4	0,1,2,3,4,5,7,8,9	766773
3-5	0,1,5	100011	9-5	0,1,2,3,4,6,7,8,9	766674
3-6(12)	0,2,4	020100	9-6	0,1,2,3,4,5,6,8,t	686763
3-7	0,2,5	011010	9-7	0,1,2,3,4,5,7,8,t	677673
3-8	0,2,6	010101	9-8	0,1,2,3,4,6,7,8,t	676764
3-9(12)	0,2,7	010020	9-9	0,1,2,3,5,6,7,8,t	676683
3-10(12)	0,3,6	002001	9-10	0,1,2,3,4,6,7,9,t	668664
3-11	0,3,7	001110	9-11	0,1,2,3,5,6,7,9,t	667773
3-12(4)	0,4,8	000300	9-12	0,1,2,4,5,6,8,9,t	666963
4-1(12)	0,1,2,3	321000	8-1	0,1,2,3,4,5,6,7	765442
4-2	0,1,2,4	221100	8-2	0,1,2,3,4,5,6,8	665542
4-3(12)	0,1,3,4	212100	8-3	0,1,2,3,4,5,6,9	656542
4-4	0,1,2,5	211110	8-4	0,1,2,3,4,5,7,8	655552
4-5	01,2,6	210111	8-5	0,1,2,3,4,6,7,8	654553
4-6(12)	0,1,2,7	210021	8-6	0,1,2,3,5,6,7,8	654463
4-7(12)	0,1,4,5	201210	8-7	0,1,2,3,4,5,8,9	645652
4-8(12)	0,1,5,6	200121	8-8	0,1,2,3,4,7,8,9	644563
4-9(6)	0,1,6,7	200022	8-9	0,1,2,3,6,7,8,9	644464
4-10(12)	0,2,3,5	122010	8-10	0,2,3,4,5,6,7,9	566452
4-11	0,1,3,5	121110	8-11	0,1,2,3,4,5,7,9	565552
4-12	0,2,3,6	112101	8-12	0,1,3,4,5,6,7,9	556543
4-13	0,1,3,6	112011	8-13	0,1,2,3,4,6,7,9	556453
4-14	0,2,3,7	111120	8-14	0,1,2,4,5,6,7,9	555562
4-Z15	0,1,4,6	111111	8-Z15	0,1,2,3,4,6,8,9	555553
4-16	0,1,5,7	110121	8-16	0,1,2,3,5,7,8,9	554563
4-17(12)	0,3,4,7	102210	8-17	0,1,3,4,5,6,8,9	546652
4-18	0,1,4,7	102111	8-18	0,1,2,3,5,6,8,9	546553
4-19	0,1,4,8	101310	8-19	0,1,2,4,5,6,8,9	545752
4-20(12)	0,1,5,8	101220	8-20	0,1,2,4,5,7,8,9	545662
4-21(12)	0,2,4,6	030201	8-21	0,1,2,3,4,6,8,t	474643
4-22	0,2,4,7	021120	8-22	0,1,2,3,5,6,8,t	465562
4-23(12)	0,2,5,7	021030	8-23	0,1,2,3,5,7,8,t	465472
4-24(12)	0,2,4,8	020301	8-24	0,1,2,4,5,6,8,t	464743

NOTE: Numbers in parentheses show the number of distinct sets in the set class if other than 48.
All brackets are eliminated here for ease of reading.

NAME	PCS	IC VECTOR	NAME	PCS	IC VECTOR
4-25(6)	0,2,6,8	020202	8-25	0,1,2,4,6,7,8,t	464644
4-26(12)	0,3,5,8	012120	8-26	0,1,2,4,5,7,9,t	456562
4-27	0,2,5,8	012111	8-27	0,1,2,4,5,7,8,t	456553
4-28(3)	0,3,6,9	004002	8-28	0,1,3,4,6,7,9,t	448444
4-Z29	0,1,3,7	111111	8-Z29	0,1,2,3,5,6,7,9	555553
5-1(12)	0,1,2,3,4	432100	7-1	0,1,2,3,4,5,6	654321
5-2	0,1,2,3,5	332110	7-2	0,1,2,3,4,5,7	554331
5-3	0,1,2,4,5	322210	7-3	0,1,2,3,4,5,8	544431
5-4	0,1,2,3,6	322111	7-4	0,1,2,3,4,6,7	544332
5-5	0,1,2,3,7	321121	7-5	0,1,2,3,5,6,7	543342
5-6	0,1,2,5,6	311221	7-6	0,1,2,3,4,7,8	533442
5-7	0,1,2,6,7	310132	7-7	0,1,2,3,6,7,8	532353
5-8(12)	0,2,3,4,6	232201	7-8	0,2,3,4,5,6,8	454422
5-9	0,1,2,4,6	231211	7-9	0,1,2,3,4,6,8	453432
5-10	0,1,3,4,6	223111	7-10	0,1,2,3,4,6,9	445332
5-11	0,2,3,4,7	222220	7-11	0,1,3,4,5,6,8	444441
5-Z12(12)	0,1,3,5,6	222121	7-Z12	0,1,2,3,4,7,9	444342
5-13	0,1,2,4,8	221311	7-13	0,1,2,4,5,6,8	443532
5-14	0,1,2,5,7	221131	7-14	0,1,2,3,5,7,8	443352
5-15(12)	0,1,2,6,8	220222	7-15	0,1,2,4,6,7,8	442443
5-16	0,1,3,4,7	213211	7-16	0,1,2,3,5,6,9	435432
5-Z17(12)	0,1,3,4,8	212320	7-Z17	0,1,2,4,5,6,9	434541
5-Z18	0,1,4,5,7	212221	7-Z18	0,1,2,3,5,8,9	434442
5-19	0,1,3,6,7	212122	7-19	0,1,2,3,6,7,9	434343
5-20	0,1,3,7,8	211231	7-20	0,1,2,4,7,8,9	433452
5-21	0,1,4,5,8	202420	7-21	0,1,2,4,5,8,9	424641
5-22(12)	0,1,4,7,8	202321	7-22	0,1,2,5,6,8,9	424542
5-23	0,2,3,5,7	132130	7-23	0,2,3,4,5,7,9	354351
5-24	0,1,3,5,7	131221	7-24	0,1,2,3,5,7,9	353442
5-25	0,2,3,5,8	123121	7-25	0,2,3,4,6,7,9	345342
5-26	0,2,4,5,8	122311	7-26	0,1,3,4,5,7,9	344532
5-27	0,1,3,5,8	122230	7-27	0,1,2,4,5,7,9	344451
5-28	0,2,3,6,8	122212	7-28	0,1,3,5,6,7,9	344433
5-29	0,1,3,6,8	122131	7-29	0,1,2,4,6,7,9	344352
5-30	0,1,4,6,8	121321	7-30	0,1,2,4,6,8,9	343542
5-31	0,1,3,6,9	114112	7-31	0,1,3,4,6,7,9	336333
5-32	0,1,4,6,9	113221	7-32	0,1,3,4,6,8,9	335442
5-33(12)	0,2,4,6,8	040402	7-33	0,1,2,4,6,8,t	262623
5-34(12)	0,2,4,6,9	032221	7-34	0,1,3,4,6,8,t	254442
5-35(12)	0,2,4,7,9	032140	7-35	0,1,3,5,6,8,t	254361
5-Z36	0,1,2,4,7	222121	7-Z36	0,1,2,3,5,6,8	444342
5-Z37(12)	0,3,4,5,8	212320	7-Z37	0,1,3,4,5,7,8	434541
5-Z38	0,1,2,5,8	212221	7-Z38	0,1,2,4,5,7,8	434442
6-1(12)	0,1,2,3,4,5	543210			
6-2	0,1,2,3,4,6	443211			
6-Z3	0,1,2,3,5,6	433221	6-Z36	0,1,2,3,4,7	*
6-Z4(12)	0,1,2,4,5,6	432321	6-Z37(12)	0,1,2,3,4,8	
6-5	0,1,2,3,6,7	422232			
6-Z6(12)	0,1,2,5,6,7	421242	6-Z38(12)	0,1,2,3,7,8	
6-7(6)	0,1,2,6,7,8	420243			
6-8(12)	0,2,3,4,5,7	343230			

*Z-related hexachords share the same ic vector; use vector in the third column

NAME	PCS	IC VECTOR	NAME	PCS	IC VECTOR
6-9	0,1,2,3,5,7	342231			
6-Z10	0,1,3,4,5,7	333321	6-Z39	0,2,3,4,5,8	
6-Z11	0,1,2,4,5,7	333231	6-Z40	0,1,2,3,5,8	
6-Z12	0,1,2,4,6,7	332232	6-Z41	0,1,2,3,6,8	
6-Z13(12)	0,1,3,4,6,7	324222	6-Z42(12)	0,1,2,3,6,9	
6-14	0,1,3,4,5,8	323430			
6-15	0,1,2,4,5,8	323421			
6-16	0,1,4,5,6,8	322431			
6-Z17	0,1,2,4,7,8	322332	6-Z43	0,1,2,5,6,8	
6-18	0,1,2,5,7,8	322242			
6-Z19	0,1,3,4,7,8	313431	6-Z44	0,1,2,5,6,9	
6-20(4)	0,1,4,5,8,9	303630			
6-21	0,2,3,4,6,8	242412			
6-22	0,1,2,4,6,8	241422			
6-Z23(12)	0,2,3,5,6,8	234222	6-Z45(12)	0,2,3,4,6,9	
6-Z24	0,1,3,4,6,8	233331	6-Z46	0,1,2,4,6,9	
6-Z25	0,1,3,5,6,8	233241	6-Z47	0,1,2,4,7,9	
6-Z26(12)	0,1,3,5,7,8	232341	6-Z48(12)	0,1,2,5,7,9	
6-27	0,1,3,4,6,9	225222			
6-Z28(12)	0,1,3,5,6,9	224322	6-Z49(12)	0,1,3,4,7,9	
6-Z29(12)	0,1,3,6,8,9	224232	6-Z50(12)	0,1,4,6,7,9	
6-30(12)	0,1,3,6,7,9	224223			
6-31	0,1,3,5,8,9	223431			
6-32(12)	0,2,4,5,7,9	143250			
6-33	0,2,3,5,7,9	143241			
6-34	0,1,3,5,7,9	142422			
6-35(2)	0,2,4,6,8,t	060603			

SOURCE: Allen Forte, *The Structure of Atonal Music* (New Haven: Yale University Press, 1973) (adapted)

Credits

Index of Music Examples

Arlen, Harold
  "Blues in the Night," 169

Bach, Johann Sebastian
  Agnus Dei, from *Mass in B minor*, 145
  Courante, from Cello Suite No. 1 in G Major, 64
  "Et in Spiritum Sanctum Dominum," from *Mass in B minor*, 66
  Gigue, from Partita No. 3 in C minor, 144
  Kyrie, from *Mass in B minor*, 146
Bartók, Béla
  Two Rumanian Dances, Op. 8a, No. 1, 305
Beethoven, Ludwig van
  Écossaise, WoO 23, 94
  "Lustig, traurig," WoO 54, 94–95
  Piano Sonata in C Major, Op. 53 (*Waldstein*), first movement, 120
  Symphony No. 4 in B-flat Major, Menuetto, 121
Berg, Alban
  Piano Sonata, Op. 1, 306
  Violin Concerto, first movement, 359
Brahms, Johannes
  Intermezzo, Op. 117, No. 1, 119–20
  Piano Sonata No. 1 in C Major, first movement, 120–21
  String Quartet No. 3 in B-flat Major, second movement, 63
  String Sextet No. 1 in B-flat Major, Rondo, 21, 63
  String Sextet No. 2 in G Major first movement, 121
  fourth movement, 262
  Variations on an Original Theme for Piano, Op. 21, No. 1, 205
Burke, Joe
  "Tiptoe Through the Tulips," 261

Clarke, Rebecca
  Sonata for Viola and Piano, first movement, 284–85

Dallapiccola, Luigi
  Quaderno musicale di Annalibera, No. 4, 387
Debussy, Claude
  "Bruyères," from *Preludes*, Book II, 284
  "Général Lavine," from *Preludes*, Book II, 283

Grieg, Edvard
  String Quartet in G minor, Op. 27, third movement, 21–22

Handel, George Frideric
  Suite in D minor, Gigue, 63
Haydn, Franz Joseph
  Piano Sonata No. 45 in E-flat Major, first movement, 231–32
  String Quartet in C Major, Op. 20, No. 2, first movement, 64–65
Hewitt, John Hill
  "All Quiet Along the Potomac To-night," 93–94
Hindemith, Paul
  Concert Music for Strings and Brass, Op. 50, 306

Ives, Charles
  "Premonitions," 305
  "September," 283

Koenigsberg, Deborah
  String Quartet, third movement, 386

Mendelssohn, Felix
  String Quartet in E-flat Major, Op. 12, fourth movement, 22

Messiaen, Olivier
  "Danse de la fureur, pour les sept trompettes," from *Quartet for the End of Time*, 386
Monk, Thelonious
  "Straight, No Chaser," 170
Mozart, Wolfgang Amadeus
  Clarinet Quintet, K. 581, fourth movement, 203–5
  Piano Sonata in A minor, K. 310, first movement, 229–30
  Piano Sonata in F Major, K. 280, second movement, 144
  Piano Sonata in F Major, K. 332, first movement, 145–46
  String Quartet in B-flat Major, K. 458, Menuetto, 94
"My Country, 'Tis of Thee," 261, 388

"On the Eerie Canal" (traditional), 93
Oswald, Rebecca
  Finding the Murray River, 386

Parker, Charlie
  "Billie's Bounce," 169
Perkins, Frank, and Mitchell Parish
  "Stars Fell on Alabama," 261
Purcell, Henry
  "A New Ground," from *Musick's Hand-Maid*, 205
  "Ground in Gamut," from *Musick's Hand-Maid*, 206

Rodgers, Richard
  "Sixteen Going on Seventeen," from *The Sound of Music*, 262

Schoenberg, Arnold
  Das Buch der hängenden Gärten, No. XIV, 306
  Suite for Piano, Op. 25, Trio, 360
  Variations for Orchestra, Op. 31, 360
Schubert, Franz
  "Die Liebe hat gelogen," 143

Scriabin, Alexander
   Five Preludes, Op. 15, No. 1, 23
   Prelude, Op. 59, No. 2, 289–91, 310
   Prelude, Op. 67, No. 2, 289,
      291–92, 310, 312–13
   Prelude, Op. 74, No. 3, 284
Strauss, Richard
   Don Juan, 122
   Don Quixote, 262–63
Stravinsky, Igor
   "Action rituelle des ancêtres," from
      The Rite of Spring, 295–96,
      314
   "Danse infernale de tous les sujets
      de Kastchéi," from *L'oiseau
      de feu,* 285

Four Trios, from *Agon,* 360
"Royal March," from *L'histoire du
   soldat,* 385
Theme and Variations, from *Octet
   for Wind Instruments,* 385

Tailleferre, Germaine
   Sonata in C-sharp minor for
      Violin and Piano, 284
Tchaikovsky, Piotr Ilyich
   String Quartet in F Major, Op. 22,
      Scherzo, 22

Webern, Anton
   "Ave Regina Coelorum," Op. 18,
      No. 3, 361

Cantata, Op. 29, 296–97, 314
"In der Fremde," from *Four Songs
   for Voice and Orchestra,*
   Op. 13, 361
"Nachts," from *Six Songs,* Op. 14,
   293, 313
"Wiese in Park," from *Four Songs
   for Voice and Orchestra,*
   Op. 13, 294, 313

Index of Terms and Concepts

additive *crescendo*, 285–86
Adler, Samuel, *The Study of Orches-
    tration*, 308
Aeolian mode, 269
all-interval tetrachords, 272–73
ametric works, 390
apparent chords, 235
arch forms, 177
arias, in ternary form, 73
art songs, popular songs compared
    with, 150
ascending 5–6 sequences, 238–39
asymmetrical meter. *See* meter
augmented-sixth chords, 128–32,
    206
    chromatic voice exchanges with,
        237
    composing with, 148
    types of, 129–32

bar forms, 151
beat divisions, two against three,
    39–42
binary forms, 71–73
    composing, 95–96, 123–24, 265
    improvising, 94–95
    types of, 74
blue notes, 151
blues, 151–52, 169–70
    chaconne compared with, 176
    composing, 172–73
    improvising, 171
blues scale, 151–52
"borrowed" chords. *See* mixture
    chords
"bracket" notation, 30, 237
bridge (in song), 151

cadence(s)
    authentic, 71
    sections and, 71
cadential ⁶₄ chord
    chromaticized, 236–37
    composing with, 148
chaconne, 176–77
changing meter, 364–65

chorus, 151
chromatic embellishment, 3
chromatic mediant chords, 101–2
chromatic sequences, 237–39
chromatic voice exchanges, 236–37
chromaticism, 234–65
closely related keys
    defined, 29–30
    modulation to, 29–39
closing theme (CL), 209, 224–25
coda, 177, 210
codetta, 122, 207
"colon" notation, 30, 237
combinatorial hexachords, 363
common chords. *See* pivot chords
common-tone diminished seventh
    chord, 235
common-tone embellishing chords,
    234–36
common-tone German augmented-
    sixth chord, 235
common tones, 30
composite binary forms, 74
composite ternary forms, 74
    improvising, 95
composition
    ametric work, 390
    with asymmetrical meters, 26
    blues piece, 172–73
    instrumental duet, 265
    keyboard-style works with Roman
        numerals and figured bass,
        26–27, 69, 96
    keyboard trio, 124
    parallel period with Neapolitan
        sixths, 148
    parallel period with phrase
        expansion, 26
    percussion duet, 389–90
    popular song, 172–73
    ragtime piece, 264–65
    rounded binary melody, 95–96,
        123–24
    sectional variations, 207
    serial music, 362–63, 389–90
    with set classes, 333

short work with contemporary
    elements, 286–87
short work with sets, 307–8
simple ternary melody, 96
sonata-form movement, 232–33
three-phrase melody of modula-
    tory period and phrase
    expansion, 68
concertos, composite ternary form in,
    73
conducting
    asymmetrical meters, 6, 366–68
    duple meter, 120
continuous variations, 176–77
    improvising, 206–7

deceptive resolution, 237–38
dependent transition, 209
development (in sonata form), 210,
    216–17, 225–26
diatonic modes, 268–69
diminished scale, 271. *See also*
    octatonic scales
diminished seventh chord, 271
Dorian mode, 269
Durchführung, 210

exposition, 209–10
extensions, chord, 152–53

falling-fifth progression, 42–43
    chromatic, 237
falling-third progression, chromatic,
    237–38
Fibonacci numbers, 390
figural variations, 175, 178, 245
figured bass, composition with,
    26–27, 69, 96
first theme group (F), 209, 213–14,
    219–21
form(s)
    binary, 71–73
    hierarchy of, 70–71
    one-part, 71
    sonata, 208–10
    ternary, 73–74

Forte numbers, 310–15, 339
French sixth chord, 129–32

German sixth chord, 129–32
golden mean, 390
ground bass, 176–77, 205–6

"hook," 151, 154

improvisation
    accompanied melodic, 66–68
    additive *crescendo* and subtractive
        diminuendo, 285–86
    blues, 171
    consequent phrases with phrase
        expansions, 25
    melodic, 24–25, 146–47
    modulatory periods, 68
    with octatonic scales and subsets,
        332–33
    polymetric duets, 387–89
    popular song, 172
    ragtime melody, 263–64
    rounded binary form, 94–95
    serial music, 361–62
    sonata-form movement, 232
    variations, 203–7
    waltz, 122–23
    whole-tone to pentatonic sets,
        306–7
independent transition, 209
index number, 292
integer notation, 274
interludes, 175
interval class (ic), 272–73, 293
interval-class vectors (ic vectors),
        293–97, 324, 327
inversion (I), 335–37, 344–63
Italian sixth chord, 129–32

jazz rhythms, 154, 163

lead sheets, 171
Lydian mode, 269

major-minor seventh chords, exten-
        sions to, 153
marches, composite binary form in,
        74
melodic embellishments
    identifying, 81
    in jazz, 171
meter
    ametric, 390
    asymmetrical, 6–7, 366–68
    changing, 364–65
    hearing, 6
    performing rhythm patterns, 6–7
    polymeter, 365
Mixolydian mode, 269

mixture chords, 99–101
    chromatic voice exchanges with,
        237
    composing with, 124
    in popular songs, 173
modal mixture, 99–101
    chromatic voice exchanges with,
        237
modes. *See* diatonic modes
modulation
    to closely related keys, 29–39
    hearing, 33–39
    methods for, 30
    notating, 30–31
    performing, 31–33
    tonicization compared with, 29
modulatory period(s), 31
    creating, 42–43
    improvising, 68
movable zero, 311

Neapolitan sixth chord, 125–28
    composing with, 148
    identifying, 132
normal order, 290

octatonic scales, 270–74, 285–86,
        332–33
octatonic tetrachords, 271
ostinato, polymetric, 387–89

pandiatonicism, 284
passacaglia, 176–77
passing ⁶₄ chord, 148
pentatonic scales, 269–70, 285–86,
        306–7
phrase expansions, 10, 25, 162
Phrygian cadence, 128
Phrygian mode, 269
Phrygian sixth chord. *See* Neapolitan
        sixth chord
pitch-class intervals (pci), 336–37,
        344–63
pitch-class set (pcset), 288
pitch set, 288
pivot chords, 30, 31
    chromatic pitch and, 37
plagal resolution, 124
polymeter, 39, 365, 387–89
popular songs
    art songs compared with, 150
    composing, 172–73
    form of, 151
    harmonies, 152–53
    improvising, 172
prime form (P), 309, 334–37, 339,
        344–63

quaternary forms (quatrains), 71,
        151

rags
    composing, 264–65
    composite binary form in, 74
    improvising, 263–64
Read, Gardner, *Music Notation: A
        Manual of Modern Practice*,
        308
recapitulation, 210, 217–18, 227
    in arias, 73
refrain, 151
retransition (r), 175, 210, 226–27
retrograde (R), 336–37, 344–63
retrograde inversion (RI), 336–37,
        344–63
rhythms, jazz, 154, 163
riffs, 155, 163–64, 171
Roman-numeral progressions,
        composition with, 26–27,
        69, 96
rondo, 177–78
    creating, 203–5
rounded binary forms, 71
    composing, 95–96, 123–24
    hearing, 74
    improvising, 94–95
    sonata form and, 208
row, 334–37. *See also* twelve-tone
        rows
row matrix, 345–46, 350, 354–55,
        362–63

scale(s)
    blues, 151–52
    octatonic, 270–74, 285–86,
        332–33
    pentatonic, 269–70, 285–86,
        306–7
    whole-tone, 273–74, 285–86,
        306–7
scale degrees, tonicizing, 2–5
second theme group (S), 209, 214–16,
        222–23
secondary dominant, tonicization
        and, 3–5
sectional variations, 174–76
    composing, 207
sections (formal), 71
segments, hearing pitch relationships
        between, 334–37
sequences, chromatic, 237–39
serialism, 334–63
set analysis, 288–308, 320–29,
        373–78, 381–83
set class (SC), 309–15, 320, 327,
        373
sets
    identifying, 288–89
    inversionally related, 312–15
    inverting, 291–92
    transposing, 289–91
    transpositionally related, 309–12

seventh chords, extensions to, 152–53
simple binary forms, 71
simple ternary forms, 74
    composing, 96
"slash" notation, 30, 237
sonata, 207
    composite ternary form in, 73
sonata-form movements, 208–33
    composing, 232–33
    form, 208–10
    improvising, 232
submediant chords, 101–2
subtractive *diminuendo*, 285–86
symphonies, composite ternary form in, 73

ternary forms, 73–74
    composing, 96
    composite, 74
    improvising, 95
tetrachord(s)
    all-interval, 272–73
    octatonic, 271
    set-classes of, 316–17
text painting, 153–54, 157, 162, 165–67, 173
tonicization
    modulation compared with, 29
    of scale degrees other than V, 2–5
transition (t), 209, 214, 221–22, 223–24
transitions (in variations), 175

triads, extensions to, 152
trichord(s), 293–95, 320, 328, 331–32
    set-classes of, 315–16
tritone, 272
"turnaround," 173
twelve-tone rows, 334–63

variations, 174–77
    improvising, 203–7
verse, 151
voice exchanges, chromatic, 236–37

waltzes, improvising, 122–23
whole-tone scale, 273–74, 285–86, 306–7
wind ensembles, 264